An Ordinary Man

An Extraordinary Life

A sole survivor
With true grit

George Edison Nicholau

© 2013, George Edison Nicholau

ISBN: 978-0-9913062-0-6

Library of Congress Control Number: 2013922492

Forward

This is the story of a young boy whose Greek heritage, family values and upbringing through the Great Depression, shaped him into an overachiever, collegiate athlete, All-American family man, and entrepreneur living the authentic American Dream through mishaps and hard learned lessons enabling him to live a happy, useful, Christian life.

The story begins with George, a now 95 year old grandfather in his life's recollection, as he flashes back to the many humorous, poignant, rewarding, tragic, and compassionate stories that comprise the life of George- a life worth living.

Acknowledgements

The publishing of my memoir was an exercise of enjoyment and gladness. Throughout it's multi-year composition I was reliving my youth, and revisiting priceless moments in my ORDINARY life's EXTRAORDINARY journey!

I wish to give due credit to Anne-Marie Waldsmith for the long hours spent reviewing my literary effort and for her editing expertise. Her input made a great difference and is much appreciated.

I also thank my incredibly talented grand-daughter Elizabeth Adams Forbes for gracing the pages of my memoirs with sketches of a sampling of the shoes in my closet. I am amazed at her God-given talent.

Special kudos to daughter Edie for her invaluable talent and time in the editing of the final edition. And to daughter Dorre for her initial, most valuable literary contribution.

And of course, to each of my daughters, Dessi, Dorre, Jamie, Terre, Jorgi, and Edie, for without their contributions, there would be no warrant for the memoir.

To all of my extended family for their patience and pertinent contributions.

I especially thank, with all my heart and devotion, my resilient, understanding bride of 64 years, Gaye.

Lastly, due to my golfing hiatus, while engrossed in my memoirs, I extend my apologies and condolences to my golfing, money-vulture cronies, for depriving them of their assured weekly pocket-money income.

Table of Contents

PART ONE

The Columbia Café
The Nickel Prodigy
The Gift of Humility and Empathy
Newspaper Escapades
That's Peachy!
A Loyalty Lesson
The Den of Iniquity
The Opium Den
Andy's Bakery
Homonym
Se Agapo
Puppy Love
The Entrepreneurial Spirit
To Be Or Not To Be (Hint: I'm still here)
Fun With Harry Hooper/The Payless Years
Nicholau Enology
Mom and Pop, B.G. (Before George)
Despina Katsanos Nicholau
Greek Pathos

PART TWO

The Virtuoso
High School Shenanigans
For The Love Of The Game
Welcome to Cal!
Living The Dream
Epsilon Phi Sigma
Near Misses And Other Antics
A Sucker Is Born
The Prankster
The Courting Days
Football & Pharmacy; Time to Walk The Walk Off The Field
REALITY: Make Smart Choices in Your Lifespan
Anchors Aweigh!
The Bell Tolls For Me
Oh, Karithia!
Farewell To Arms
Living Room Gridiron

PART THREE

Nicholau Construction Co.
Christmases Past
EXTRAordinary Miracles on 25th Street
Where There Is A Need, There Is A Means
Last But Not Least
The Games We Played And The Home It Made
Oh, What Mothers Must Endure
Discipline Is Never Easy
SafeSave Pharmacy Is Born (And Edie, too)
CHRISTOS ANESTI!
Misadventures in Golf
From Golf Shoes To Loafers
Eminent Domain
The Realities of Parenting
Chris Delegans, Enter Stage Right
Joe Namath?
What's In A Name
Only Because You're Jewish
A By Your Leave…
Denny Boom
We Lose Our Jorgi
Education
A Weak Moment of Braggadocio
PGA West, a.k.a. Paradise
Epilogue and Epigraph: A Tale of Two Hearts

Dedication

With deep love this memoir is dedicated to my God-loving Mother and Socrates Father, whose love and wisdom has sustained me throughout my adventurous years. And to my late brothers Nicholas, Alexander, and sister Athena whose memories continue to motivate and inspire me to live my life in a manner that would honor their short-lived earthbound lives.

To my angelic wife Gaye for without her unselfish, deep love, tolerance, and bottomless support of my every whim and adventure, there would be no *extraordinary* material for a memoir.

To my beautiful, lovable daughters Dessi, Dorre, Jamie, Terre, Jorgi and Edie, their understanding husbands, and my grandchildren. I respectfully thank them all for letting me lean on them these past 15 creative, exhilarating, reminiscing years.

AN ORDINARY MAN
AN EXTRAORDINARY LIFE

A *sole* survivor with true grit

PART ONE

The Columbia Cafe

Congratulations! Your reward for browsing the introductory pages of this saga earns you a humbled personal invitation into my bedroom closet for the "sole" purpose (pun intended) to gaze upon thirty-nine pairs of shoes, ranging from tennies to Gucci's, to genuine alligator oxfords.

Thirty-nine pairs of shoes is not exceptional. However nine of the pairs are newsworthy. Seven of them are Keith Highlanders

1939-1942 wing tipped oxford vintage! Two pairs are Foot Joys, all white, plain toe style dress shoes. Although the Highlanders have enjoyed cyclical styling throughout the past fifty-five years, I cannot recall the last time I wore them. Oh yes, they are in excellent "concours" condition- 8 ½ D, my perennial size. The white Foot Joys, to my recollection, have yet to make a fashion comeback.

Why haven't I discarded or worn any of them during these past decades? That is what much of this narrative is all about. Possibly before I finish it, I may find the answer. Or better yet, you'll find it for me. Let's see.

For starters, as a 9 year old, I had no inkling as to the degree the caliber of one's shoes could impact one's overall persona. Heck, during the depression, in the summer vacation months, I went barefoot more often than shod. And when shod, a JCPenny $2.99 special on tennies served the purpose well.

Go back with me to the year of our Lord 1929, the year of the infamous stock market crash that triggered the onset of the Great Depression. Being the "baby" sibling of a surviving single parent of four children; two older brothers and a sister, (my father having passed into Heaven in April 9, 1928) I was privileged- I use the word advisedly-to inherit my two older brother's hand me downs; and was glad to get them. My sister, God rest her soul, being the love of my parent's life, a year older at ten years of age, was not so encumbered.

Wait! I'm getting ahead of my story. It was not always that way. When my father immigrated to America from his native country, Greece, he first settled in Savannah, Georgia with acquaintances he knew from the old country. Offering his services for a stipend to any and all opportunities that availed themselves, he methodically worked his way west. There, in 1906, in the HUB city of Marysville, he founded the Columbia Café. Why Marysville? Because its' climate reminded my dad of his native land, and the modesty of the people made an indelible impression on him.

Historical Marysville
Luisa Garzon Leger, Artist

Soon, the lucrative Columbia Café, a family enterprise, became the centerfold of the community. It was not an ordinary eatery. It enjoyed an enviable Northern California reputation of excellence in food preparation. At that time, Marysville was the third largest city in California, known as "The gateway city of the northern mines." Dignitaries and legislators from the State Capitol in Sacramento joined Marysville local professionals and blue-collar people alike, to enjoy succulent ethnic cuisine of the old country, along with contemporary choices of steak, fresh fish, and fowl dishes served to perfection. The wine offerings were second to none. It was a common practice for game hunters to bring their seasonal prey to the Columbia Café for personal preparation.

The Columbia Café, the largest restaurant North of Sacramento, was accommodated with two entrance addresses, 217 and 219 D Street. A spectacular elongated window display refrigerated with ice cubes separated the two address entrances to the restaurant, featuring the fresh catch of the day artistically placed on ice, along with various cuts of meat and poultry. It encouraged the clientele to invite a waiter to the display and point to the entrée of their choice. From the inside of the display the waiter would remove the choice to the kitchen, where it would be trademark prepared and served.

Featured in the dining room of our home is one of the priceless mementos from the Columbia Café. The circular perimeter of the colored metal tray has the following scripture inscribed in bold gold letters:

Two Best Places To Eat
Home and the Columbia Cafe

<p style="text-align:center">Truth in advertisement at it's best</p>

The 217 D Street entrance encouraged blue-collar fast food service for breakfast, lunch, and dinner, to accommodate the work schedules of the clientele. The 219 D Street entrance catered primarily to evening diners with their families, dates, state dignitaries, and professionals from the area. Of course, the blue-collar families and workers were welcome and indeed encouraged to avail themselves of the perquisite booths. And they frequently did so.

How does all this tie in with my shoe fetish? Patience and you shall see.

I mentioned the assets and glamour of the Columbia Café during the roaring twenties, as I believe it has a direct bearing on the shoe subject. From abundance to poverty in a relatively short period in time can play havoc on an impressive nine year olds' psyche. I am guessing that is why I cannot discard those signature shoes. Subconsciously, if not consciously, I am constantly preparing for that inevitable rainy day. That, regardless of my current success I may be enjoying. Silly I know. Not warranted, I know. Yet inescapable for me to ignore! Or escape.

It was in my sophomore year of high school when I first became conscious of my shoes. So much so, that I would designate them to the focal point of my wardrobe. Goodbye tattered tennies, hello leather, winged-tipped, oxford, soled shoes. Puberty does play an intricate part in one's persona.

Back to the Columbia Café, and the perceived impact it played in my shoe dilemma. I mentioned the restaurant was started in 1906. Banner years followed leading into the early twenties and continued on free rolling into the boisterous

Downtown D Street at the turn of the century
Marysville, California
Luisa Garzon Leger, Artist

mid-twenties. And as the business climate flourished so did my Dad. He rode the crest to it's fullest. He was constantly improving the service, and investing in upgraded facilities for the restaurant.

Suddenly, with subtle inconsequential warning, as happened to countless others, the economic bubble burst, delivering the infamous Great Depression of 1929. During the embryo years approaching the Wall Street crash, the Columbia Café endured two years, from late 1927 through 1928, of devastating monetary losses. During those years, my father, like countless others, thinking it was an aberration of the economy, kept a status quo operation until the inevitable happened: BANKRUPTCY!

In those days there was no Chapter 11 legislation to alleviate the bankruptcy. The door of a business deeply in debt was authoritatively padlocked with a glaring bulletin posted explaining why. My father took his adversity very personally. A past pillar of the community, he hung his head low, and literally worried himself sick. His self-esteem plummeted to the point where he became marginally dysfunctional. During the thriving years of the business, my father saw to it that money was set aside for a possible rainy day. In those days a welfare program was a family's responsibility, not a government liability. The money saved over the past years weighed heavy on my father's mind. He constantly was dwelling on the fact he owed money to creditors who faithfully trusted him throughout his business career. Now, due to the sudden about-face in the economy, his word and honor were compromised. He knew what he had to do. And you will see how through this adversity I became the recipient of the greatest heritage a son could ever hope for from a father.

My father constantly harped to his three sons and daughter from the time we were old enough to understand, "<u>Never do anything whatsoever that would compromise the integrity of the family name</u>".

True to his edict, during this crisis, at great expense and compromise to his family's social status, he deterred not one iota from acting in the most honorable way to protect the integrity of the Nicholau name. Accordingly, he approached my mother with the following proposal. He related as far as the law was concerned, all business assets, fiscal inventory, and fixtures were under government control to be liquidated, and the funds realized would be pro rata distributed to his creditors. However, the total assets would not cover the outstanding warrants, and those that trusted him would be financially hurt to the extent that some of them could be pushed over the brink of financial solvency. He emphasized that the family name and honor were at stake, and that was his primary concern. The honor of the Nicholau name was the main heritage he aspired to will to his children. Thus, he asked my mother if she would be willing to forgo the bulk of the many years of savings to cover the difference between the monetary return of the bankrupt procedure and the remaining outstanding balance of debt due his creditors. He emphasized there was no legal obligation for her to concede. And yet, there was no hesitation on my mother's part but to do exactly that which he proposed. Accordingly, in the final analysis, all outstanding debt of the bankruptcy was covered dollar for dollar!

The Nicholau name remained untainted. By his standards money was expendable, while honor was non-negotiable.

The Nickel Prodigy

Earlier I promised to clarify my statement "how through adversity I became the recipient of the greatest heritage a son could receive from a father". I can best do this by sharing with you one of the most vivid incidents that reflect my father's raw expression of heartfelt love and devotion towards his children.

On special occasions, rather than the usual expression of gifts of material nature, for a special treat, my father would gather his family about him, and talk to us about the importance of honor and education. He would do this in such an enjoyable way, that we would look forward to his "Rap sessions". A priceless gift. One could sense the glowing pride that welled in his eyes for his children as he talked to us. He always ended a session with expressions of aspiration for our future. His incessant dream was that one of his sons become a doctor, one a military officer, and one an educator. For his daughter he wished for her to be a well-educated person. Within a short generation all of the above have come to pass, and far exceed, albeit through his two surviving children and many grandchildren.

From my father's unfathomable love, I will now narrate an unforgettable happening in my life.

It was an early Sunday afternoon in February of 1928, just two months before Dad's demise, when I shamefully embarrassed my father. His mind was constantly preoccupied with bankruptcy, compounded by the Great Depression, yet he would try to forget his worries by playing checkers with his very close friend, Bill Callas, aka "Wood Chopper". I was three months into my ninth birthday. At that time we lived in a dwelling above a saloon in the commercial part of town. The city's major theater, The National Theater was located cattycorner from our house located on 2nd and E Street. The price of admission for youngsters was a nickel; five cents. In the past, many were the times I would ask my dad for a nickel to go to the matinee movies, and was seldom denied, even in our current financial state. There was a catch, however, that compromised my desire for the theater. It was this: I knew after the movie I was expected to sit down and relate the story to my father. In those days, the plot invariably featured a white- hat hero who always came through in the end. I was therefore challenged to relate to my father the moral of the plot. His contention was that a movie must impart a moral to justify its' production. (Boy, have things changed.) As a wise nine year old, I soon became privy to weighing the entertainment value of a movie against the obligatory assignment that went with the package. More often than not, I would take the assignment gladly, for that meant I could lose myself in the theatrics of the big screen. Oh boy, did I love that!

On this particular afternoon my father's focus was intent on his checkers game as I patted him on his thigh, and at the same time repeatedly asked him for a nickel to go to the show. Without looking away from his checker board he instinctively moved his right hand from his brow, continuing his concentration on the game, as he had done many times in the past, while simultaneously reaching into his pocket seeking the nickel to give to me.

    Suddenly, without warning, he uncharacteristically pulled his hand from his pocket, and exclaimed in a harsh native tone, "Fevya apo etho! Kathe mera thelis na pas sto theatro!"
Translated, "Get away from here! You are always wanting to go to the movies!" (I used the Greek phonetics, for when Dad chose to communicate in his native tongue, you knew he was irritably probed. In this case, exacerbated by the 'absent' nickel.) Obviously startled, I was disappointed and must have drastically shown it, for his good friend, Wood Chopper, reached into his pocket, tossed me a dime, and remarked, "Afto to pethi na pa i sto theatro." Translated, "Let the boy go to the show". At that moment, my father swept the checkers off the board onto the floor. Got up from the kitchen table and left the room.

    And that is when I first realized how much my father loved me. As down and out as he was, he would not deny me the price of a movie~even if it meant parting with his last nickel. The nickel he didn't have. As young as I was, I realized being caught off guard not having a nickel so depressed him, and so frustrated him, that to avoid his embarrassment he admonished me for "always wanting to go to the movies". His emotion was exacerbated when his friend, meaning well, tossed me that dime. To this day tears well in my eyes whenever I recall that moment. My respect and love for my father was born not out of material gifts, but for that which was true heartedly intended to be given. OH! the powerful message of a nickel when you don't have one. I constantly challenge myself to pass on his legacy of love, honor, and education to my children. Even, at times in idiosyncratic ways. I will always be grateful to the prodigy nickel incident in my life. It embodies the greatest definition of love between father and family members! God bless you Dad for your true, insatiable love.

Nick, Al, Dad, Athena and Me, 1920

The Gift of Humility and Empathy

Personally volunteered charity during the depression did not have an odious connotation it seemingly has evolved into today. More fortunate neighbors had empathy for the less fortunate, and helped out in meaningful ways. Those of us in need of a charitable gesture were grateful and sincerely appreciative towards the abettor.

During my grammar school days, I was the recipient of charitable gestures by an optometrist, Dr. Brown, and a dentist, Dr. Hall. Both provided goodwill pro bono assistance. Through their efforts, I received corrective eyeglasses and much needed dental repair. Upon reflection, I credit their concern for my well being as a positive contribution to my present enjoyment of good health.

And now, for passing on the baton of empathy. My parents upbringing which emphasized love and respect for my fellow man, together with the optometrist's and dentist's benevolence, ingrained in me an empathetic attitude towards those whom we perceive to be in need of assistance of some kind.

Let me share with you an incident that has been permanently ingrained in my mind since the day it occurred. I relate this, not as an example of a good Samaritan, for I assure you it would pale in comparison to the many compassionate acts people have performed over the course of their lifetime. I do, however, relate it to impress upon you 'what goes around comes around'. The year to the best of my recollection was 1931-1932. It was during that time of the Great Depression when the exodus of Oklahomans to the Golden State of California took place. This influx of "Oakies", as they were referred to, was exacerbated by the Dust Bowl catastrophe of that era that engulfed the state of Oklahoma. They lost all of their rich productive land due to the eternal dry spell accompanied by violent unrelenting windstorms that literally converted their valuable productive soil into sand dunes. With no irrigation capabilities, they had no alternative for survival but to salvage whatever life-saving comforts they could load onto their "jalopy" cars, forgo their land, and head west to California. John Steinbeck famously chronicled their journey and tribulations in his novel <u>The Grapes of Wrath</u>.

A proud people, they would volunteer for farm work, no matter how demeaning, or how hard it would be, just to earn enough money to enable them to move on to the next harvesting job. They would follow the fruit-harvesting season and camp in many instances in their jalopy, or campgrounds if affordable, or wherever they found isolated land. Through selling my newspapers on my bicycle, pedaling several miles to the various camping grounds surrounding Marysville during the harvest season, I had come to respect the "Oakies" as honest, hard working, family oriented countrymen.

One particular summer day I was biking across the D Street bridge (now rerouted and named the E Street bridge) heading for one of the campsites south of Marysville. About a quarter mile off the bridge, I stopped at a gas station to get a drink of water. While there I noticed a family of five; husband, wife, and three small children, one of them a toddler. The wife and the three children were seated in their jalopy, loaded to the hilt on it's sides, back, and on top with all of their salvageable worldly possessions. Due to my proximity I could not help but hear the husband pleading emotionally with the gas station attendant to trust him with a couple of gallons of gasoline, so that he could look for a place to bed down for the night. He promised (and I noticed him crossing his heart) to pay the attendant the next day, as he was certain he would find work in the peach harvest area. The attendant replied, "I only work here and have no authority to trust anyone".

    As I listened to the husband pleading, tears welled into my eyes. Up to that moment I always pictured myself as a street-smart, tough kid. My hand without thinking, reminiscent of my Dad, reached into my pocket pulling out my newspaper change of 40 cents. I gave the money to the attendant and told him to give that much worth of gas to the man. Gas at that time was 9 cents a gallon!! The husband grabbed me with both hands by my shoulders tearfully saying over and over again, "God Bless you son". "God Bless you son". I did not know how to respond for fear I would start crying. So, I hurried to my bike, and I saw the husband talking to his wife. Before I could pedal away, both husband and wife looked back towards me with the most sad, yet endearing, appreciative and grateful look I had ever experienced before, or since.

    I do believe the Good Lord heard him, and granted his request, because God, to this day, continually bestows blessings upon my family and me.

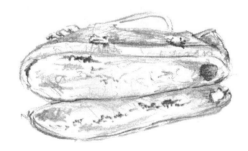

Newspaper Escapades

As a second grader, encroaching upon my 7th birthday, I started my career as a street selling newspaper boy. How I miraculously survived the previous 6 years of my youth's impetuosity, is one of the best kept secrets of my memoirs. Frankly, I have no clue as to how I managed it. Fasten your "mind belt". You are in for some entertainment provided by my formative puberty years. Upon recall it seems surreal. There were moments during my grade school years where absentmindedly my mind would wander in the classroom, and I would reflex out of the blue, and shout loud and clear, "MARYSVILLE APPEAL DEMOCRAT PAPER!!! READ ALL ABOUT IT!!!" The disruption as you can imagine, was startling and embarrassing to me. This would mostly occur the school day following an extra edition such as election results, high interest boxing matches, or tragic national news events—the Lindberg kidnap story, for example. The Jack Dempsey vs Tunney world's heavy weight boxing match warranted an extra edition. I mention the Lindberg and Dempsey vs. Tunney news so that you may get an inkling as to the time period of which I write. Radio broadcasting in the late twenties and early thirties was a novelty. Television was but a twinkle in some inventors' eye. These extra newspaper editions were the lone, timely source of detailed information on current happenings of interest. Even at the age of 7 years, I would stay out in the late hours, until I sold at least 40 "EXTRA, EXTRA, READ ALL ABOUT IT" papers, which was exceptional in the depression years. After covering the downtown area, I would get on my bike and hit the neighborhoods yelling "MARYSVILLE APPEAL DEMOCRAT PAPER, EXTRA, EXTRA, READ ALL ABOUT IT". Forty sales would net me $1.00. Again, to put that in perspective, one dollar would buy over 9 gallons of gasoline in those days. (Upon review of this writing, on 4-11-2008, gasoline is selling for over 4 dollars a gallon. I just threw this in for the hell of it.)

I recall as a tough little barefoot paper boy, I would earn five cents betting other kids I could stand on the midsummer hot railroad tracks which ran in front of the Democrat Daily Newspaper office longer than they could. We would do this among other eccentric dares, while waiting for our quota of papers for the day. On the rail bet, I would win every time. No contest. Of course, because the bottoms of my feet were calloused from going barefoot I enjoyed a distinct advantage over my adversaries. Finally, I had no takers among my usual cronies, and resorted to betting the would-be paper customers who commented on my bare feet, that if I stood on the railroad tracks that ran through Marysville's main street, D Street, for a given length of time, would they buy a paper? Whether from curiosity or for amusement, there would be some takers. Depending on the temperature and the length of time agreed upon, I did not always win that bet. But most of the men, seeing my agony, to soothe their conscience, bought a paper anyway. What is not clear in my mind to this day is whether I went barefoot by choice or necessity. Truth be known, it was for both reasons.

Here I am, far left; a street-smart, tough kid

Moving on with my newspaper escapades, of which there are several, I recall the day I went into the saloon to sell my papers. As usual I would approach each person in the bar, asking if they would buy a paper. Now and then I would get a positive response. This particular day, there was a man sitting on a bar stool, well into his cups. I went to him and asked him if he would buy a paper from me. He looked at me and said, "Boy, how many papers do you have?" I told him, "I have 10, why?" "Give them to me", and he placed 50 cents on the bar. WOW! Did I hit the jackpot. I gave him the papers, pocketed the 50 cents—a fortune—and turned to leave the place. The bartender caught my eye when I looked back as I was approaching the exit door and gave me a wink, while motioning with his finger to come back. This, as a street-smart kid, I understood meant later. After what I considered an eternity—five minutes, give or take a few—I snuck back into the bar, and at the door end of the bar were my 10 papers…to be sold again. I picked them up and left the premises with euphoria while fondling my pocketed 50 cents tip!!

Not always was my bar venture newspaper experience a plus. On another occasion, I approached an intoxicated man, sitting on a barstool, and he grabbed me by my hair and started to lift me up. I rose onto the tip of my toes before he let go. The bartender scolded him, and the customer tipped me with a quarter—twenty-five cents. I was ecstatic! Ouched, but still ecstatic.

Hey! Here is a by-your-side newspaper venture I share with you just for the hell of it: my first and only time I was behind bars when found guilty of a misdemeanor. While selling my papers one day, I was pedaling along on my bike on the sidewalk yelling, "APPEAL DEMOCRAT", when I became distracted by a potential customer across the street. At that moment I ran into a man on the sidewalk with my bike and thus, I was charged not only for riding my bike on the sidewalk, but for literally running into the Chief of Police, Mr. La Fortune. Mr. La Fortune grabbed my bike and said, "boy, you come with me!" I was jailed. Yes I mean jailed! He took me to the police station and put me into a cell. He never said another word. He just left me there. I started to cry, and about an hour later I was released after I promised not to ride on the sidewalks again. I learned my lesson, and to this day, I fear the "gendarmes". I am willing to bet, that I am the only newspaper boy to criminally introduce himself to the Chief of Police.

On that note come to think of it, as a newspaper boy, I also believe I was the first paperboy to open "charge accounts" for some of my customers. This came about as I wanted to be the first newsboy available to the known paper buyers at the various business establishments. By rushing there on my bike as soon as we received our newspapers from the Appeal Democrat office, I would drop off a paper at the customers' establishment without waiting for my nickels, and rush onto the next store and do the same until I covered all known established customers, total of 6. Then later in the day, I would go back and collect my nickels. This innovative, risky method allowed me to beat my competition to most, if not all of the first come customers. I took pride in knowing I was the most successful newspaper boy during my long tenure dating from the second grade through my freshman year in high school. Of course, being number one took some sacrifices and dedicated effort. But my psyche gave me no choice in the matter. Unlike my classmates (during my grade school years through freshman year) who enjoyed after school comradeship and team sport participation, I would head directly from school to the Appeal Democrat office to pick up my allotted papers for the day.

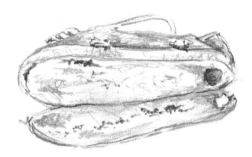

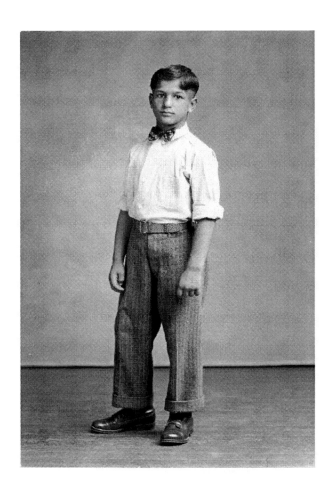

My First Lifetime Investment

Three times a year in the months of April, August, and December, I would seek my gifted New York Life Insurance Company Flat-Iron, 8 Inch tall, triangular bank, with it's guarded combination lock on it's bottom. It was a mini model replica of the New York Life Insurance Co. building situated in New York. (A picture of the bank is below) When filled to it's capacity with nickels, dimes, quarters, half dollars and even a few dollar coins accumulated from my paper selling ventures, it was taken from it's hidden place in the "fovritos skotinos" i.e.; from the "scary dark room" in our house, and placed on the hard surfaced kitchen table. There, a grand opening ritual took place in a celebratory mood.

    I would patiently manipulate and maneuver the combination, until by chance the silver coins would spill out from their four-month incarceration onto the top of the kitchens' hard vinyl table. The ensuing reverberation of the coins' tumbling, framed a welcome jingling, ear-pleasing symphony. The penny-wise 'opera' was a most welcomed tune. So profitable a melody, I booked it's performance every three months for four more years~ the extent of my newspaper days.
    To see all of that loose change collected in one place on the kitchen table during the heart of the Great Depression was mind-boggling!
    Above I stated "guarded" combination, due to the fact that there were, on rare-occasions, the need for this ten year old lad to stealthily raid the personal Nicholau Reserve Bank for a self

determined emergency. With that confessed undocumented bank withdrawal, I will move on with my personal bank novelette.

When the treasured loose coins were secured in their appropriate coin wrappers, the total would amount to $50.00, give or take a dollar or two! A year's earning would factor into a $150.00 savings from my newspaper enterprise!! The fifty-dollar increment wrapped coins were transferred to the Deker Jewitt Bank, which sadly, during the Great Depression went belly up. In their final settlement, however, I did receive a good percentage of my savings which came in handy during my college years.

The genesis of this saga was born in 1929 during my 10th year on this planet. At that time, Mr. Arthur Hutchinson, an employee of the New York Life Insurance company, and a man of Greek decent, was sitting at our kitchen table selling the merits of The New York Life Insurance policy, speaking in Greek, to the widowed mother about her four children. His point being, it was a good saving policy while at the same time a salvation, should a disaster occur. He emphasized the younger the insured candidate, the more forgiving the yearly premium. That point, and the safety of having a savings account feature within the insurance policy, was the convincing factor for the policy purchase. (In another part of my memoir I am very sad to report, the policy did factor into a much needed, timely, key benefit)

The timing of the New York Life Insurance Co. representative's visit to our home, at the end of April 1929, was uncanny. I had actually just emptied my savings bank with the money spread on the table when he arrived!! During his visit, he was impressed with my savings and used my age as an example of how affordable it was for me, a ten year old client, to own an insurance policy, while at the same time, the policy would act as a savings enterprise investment. He suggested at my young age a $50 yearly fee would qualify me for a $3,000.00 life insurance policy. Mother agreed to the policy and I paid on the spot with the exposed coins on the table!! Leaving me a balance of $1.35 to seed my next savings. He insisted he would take the loose coins as is, and place them in a currency bag to be mailed in for the initial payment. This was done, ergo, the birth of the Iron Bank Story.

For your perusal I am enclosing a photo of a copy of the letter addressed to me by Mr. Kingsley, President of the New York Life Insurance Company, dated May 21, 1929.

NEW YORK LIFE INSURANCE COMPANY
51 MADISON AVENUE, MADISON SQUARE
NEW YORK, N.Y.

KINGSLEY
PRESIDENT

May 21, 1929.

George Ed. Nicholaou,
Marysville, California.

Dear George:-

Our Mr. Arthur Hutchinson, Director of the Pacific Branch Office, has recited the circumstances under which you have applied for a $3,000 policy in this Company, paying the premium from nickels and dimes that you had earned by selling newspapers, and he has sent on the bag in which you had accumulated this money.

Mr. Hutchinson has also sent on your photograph, and tells me that your two brothers, Nicholas and Alexander, each have $3,000 with the Company, and that you have a sister who expects to take out a policy later.

I write not only to commend your industry in saving your money as you did, but your wisdom in investing your money in this way. Follow up this line of economy, hard work and careful investment, and you will some day become a rich man.

Very truly yours,

That's Peachy!

Being an innovative entrepreneur, I hit upon a way I could supplement my newspaper income during peach harvesting season by selling peaches at the Marysville Train Depot to travelers passing through from eastern states to their California destination. I learned the train-stop schedules and during peach harvesting season, I waited for potential customers with a #10 size grocery bag full of peaches. My asking price was 25 cents a bag. I could only handle 4 bags in the carrying basket attached to my bike.

**My brothers Al and Nick
In front of the Marysville Train Depot**

Now the fun part of the story. Earlier in the day, before I would pick up my newspapers, I would go to our grocery store and get 4 paper bags. On my bike, I would ride over the (then D Street Bridge) now the E Street Bridge, and on for another 2 miles to the peach orchards in the area south of Marysville. Before the time of harvest, the peaches were beautiful looking, but not quite ready to be picked. I would nevertheless choose and pick the most appealing looking peaches filling my four grocery bags to the brim. From there, back into Marysville I would pedal, getting to the designated Depot on time to sell my peaches.

The "entrepreneur" newspaper boy had one more chore to complete before displaying his merchandise for sale. Because the early peaches weren't juicy-ripe, I would take two peaches from each bag and gently rotate and tap them on the sidewalk so that when I displayed one in my hand as I walked and ran alongside the passenger compartments on the train shouting, "Peaches, fresh peaches 25 cents a bag!", the juice from the decoy peach would be trickling down my wrist. Now bear in mind this was during the summer months of June and July where the temperature would at times be pushing the 100 degree mark, and the only air conditioning on the train, in those days, was an open window. Can you imagine how appealing a juicy, cool-looking, ripe peach would be under those conditions? Well it took me less than 5 minutes to sell my 4 bags of peaches. It was first come first serve. And another 15 seconds to clear out of the area before the victims discovered the innocent deception. Considering the time and planning and effort I put into the peach transaction, I rationally soothed my conscience. After all, even a "not-so-ripe" peach under the circumstances is better than none; I would think.

Turns out I was wrong. It occurred several days into my escalating successful retail peach venture. This particular day it wasn't so hot that the windows of the passenger train were open. Therefore, for the first time I climbed the steps into the train during it's stop and went through my selling spiel. Of course I displayed the ripe peach and sold all 4 bags in the first car I entered. Now my escape plan took a fraction longer than I anticipated for I had to make change for the last customer. No sooner did I get off the train, when a passenger's window flew open, and a "Don Larsen-like" fast (peach) ball came flying at me. One reached its' mark and the bruise it left on my thigh made me grateful for the near missiles that sailed by. Thank God I survived, and thank God in the following week the peaches really were ripe. No need for deception or preplanned escape routes. What a difference a week makes during peach harvesting season!

Yet another peach train episode needs to be told. When in possession of ripe July peaches, I had no reason for an escape plan. In this scenario I would always enter the passenger compartments and sell my 4 bags of juicy peaches, and then gloat over my customer's thanks for the privilege of buying true, fresh peaches from me. This one time, it took longer than usual to sell my last bag of peaches. Well wouldn't you know it, I was so preoccupied in selling that last bag that I did not realize the train was pulling out of the station. Panicking, I ran to the still-opened passenger car door, and I jumped as far as I could, away from the moving train, to avoid any chance of tumbling backwards towards the track. The jump was so successful, I cleared not only the adjoining railroad track parallel to the ongoing track, but even cleared the top of the levee that both tracks ran on, landing on the downhill side rolling to the bottom about 10 feet down from the moving train. Bruised, yes! Happy and elated, yes! The alternative was to stay put for thirty miles north of Marysville into Oroville, the next train stop. Now take into account, at that time, I would have been an 11 year old newspaper stowaway, peach-venturing boy, getting off the train in Oroville, wondering how to get home from there at 5:30pm. I nursed my bruises, got on my bike, and thanked God I survived the day. And was still in my hometown.

A Loyalty Lesson

I was a veteran newspaper boy of three years, and around 10 years old when I heard of a promotion in the area being sponsored by the Sacramento Bee newspaper. If a boy could sign up three new subscriptions for the Bee, he would earn a Timex wristwatch. Boy did that news excite me. Immediately I started to comb all of the residential homes in Marysville with the total commitment that I would not quit until I wore that Timex wristwatch on my wrist. Three days of dedicated goal-oriented miles of door ringing, up one side of the street and down the other, in the residential districts of Marysville, I finally hit the jackpot with my third subscription for the Sacramento Bee. I was rewarded my Timex as promised, and wore it on my left wrist as promised, and bragged to all my peers by showing off my pride and joy watch.

Two days later, as I went to the desk of the Appeal Democrat office to pick up my twenty papers for the day, Mr. Logan, the manager of the Appeal Democrat, asked me what time it was. I proudly looked at my wrist watch and replied,

"Two fifty eight, Mr. Logan"

"That's right. Where did you get that wrist watch?" he inquired.

I excitedly exclaimed, "From the Sacramento Bee for signing up three subscriptions for the paper." I was down right proud I earned it...and didn't steal it.

"Well, George, you won't be needed here anymore", he retorted, as he removed the Appeal Democrat papers from my hands.

"Maybe you should see if you can sell the Sacramento Bee papers from now on."

My reaction was a 180 degree turnabout; from elation to the depths of depression. I started to cry and asked, "What did I do wrong?" He just walked away from the counter.

As I had mentioned before, the newspaper office was just across the street from my home, so I went crying home to find my mother. She was with a close friend, Mr. James Bravos. (Who, as it would turn out 21 years later, became my father in law) He and my mother were with two other men, and in the process of making wine for personal use. The Greek culture always served wine with their noon and evening meals. Mr. Bravos stopped what he was doing, grabbed me by the arm and literally dragged me from my back yard "winery" across the street, and into the Appeal Democrat office. There he demanded to speak to the sales manager, Mr.

Logan. I can still see Mr. Bravos, dressed in overalls stained with purple grape juice addressing Mr. Logan in a scolding tone demanding to know why a young boy, who did nothing dishonest to earn a wrist watch, and who daily met his twenty paper quota for the Appeal Democrat, was fired.

To paraphrase Mr. Bravos' message, "This boy's loyalty to the Appeal Democrat over three years was never questioned, and in his mind thought it wasn't wrong to grasp the opportunity to *earn* a wrist watch."

"Fire this boy," he continued, "who is solely financially dependent on his newspaper change, and I promise you that you will have more than three Sacramento Bee subscriptions to worry about! It will be more like a hundred Appeal Democrat cancellations. Shame on you! Now give this boy his 20 papers and be done with it!!!"

Mr. Logan complied. And as proud as I was of my Timex, I never wore my Sacramento Bee wristwatch while selling the Appeal Democrat paper. Mr. Logan, to his credit, had a point. One can't serve two masters at the same time. A subtle message in loyalty was belatedly ingrained through my innocent pursuit of a wristwatch. Thank you Mr. Logan for a lesson well learned, and for giving me a second chance…albeit because of Mr. Bravos' intercession.

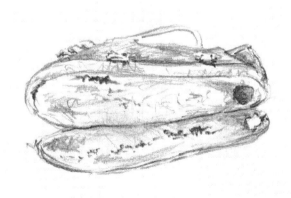

**James Bravos
Coming to my rescue at age 10
And later, becoming my Father in law**

The Den of Iniquity

Now I will share with you some risqué adventures involving my Call House newspaper customers. The Call House entrepreneurs employed an innovative security system to meet their fail-safe needs. Keep in mind, I was under 11 years of age during my exposure, and I use the word exposure advisedly. Unlike today's sex omniscient youths, I was still wet behind the ears. Accordingly, much of what I saw of Call Houses, other than knowing they were a camouflaged rooming house, had no meaningful bearing on my puberty development of the birds and the bees.

All the Calling Houses had one thing in common. They all had narrow steep stairs ascending to a reception room located on the second floor of a building. The ground floor of the building was occupied with various vocations, that putting it charitably, did not impose a conflict of interest with the adventures on the second floor of the establishment.

It didn't take me but a few times in navigating the stairs to discover one of the steps was stealthily wired to activate a buzzer alerting the Madame of the House to the intrusion of either a potential customer, delivery man, or that an arm of the law was ascending the staircase. The alerted Madame's decorum would instinctively be compatible with the intent of the ascender. Now add one more classified intruder, a promiscuous, bright eyed, devilish, loveable, young, newspaper boy whom the Madame hesitantly accepted as a friend of the "court".

The girls on the other hand, took an instant liking to their brash paperboy and presto, before I knew it, I accumulated among them, five new customers in the three separate Call Houses I "worked". They trusted me explicitly. Even to the point where I would, on mischievous occasions, skip the buzzer-step and surprise them while they were lounging about in their skimpy "business" attire. At times, depending on previous close calls with the gendarmes, I would scare them out of their wits~but never (darn it) out of their "attire" as they suspected an unscheduled raid. After a superficial scolding, they would hug me and buy a paper. When it comes to grading my most loyal customers, they were breastfully~ I mean boastfully~ the best.

While reminiscing on my newspaper days, I find although it was a time-disciplined adventure, it was also a fulfilling experience. At the outset of my newspaper selling days, I mentioned how I would stay out to sell my papers until all twenty were sold. Let me indulge upon you just how committed I was to daily accomplish that feat and still be able to participate in high school seasonal sports from 3pm to 5pm, at the expense of my normal business hours, throughout my freshman year. Having started as a newspaper boy in 1925 at the age of 7, I had accumulated some very loyal customers over the years who sanctioned my sports participation and would wait for me to buy their paper later in the day. Thus, during my freshman high school year of sport participation, I retained my number one status throughout my paper selling years. This, even though my competitors were on the street with their papers from 3:20 in the afternoon!

The Opium Den

I, being a mischievous and adventurous personality, entertained no inhibitions as you will see, when it came to meeting my self-imposed daily quota of newspaper sales. In fact, the more daring and exciting the challenge, the more it appealed to me. Specifically, in the pursuit of selling my papers, none of my competitors could muster the courage to knock on the one-way mirrored door in the shady part of town seeking admission into a secured ill-lit narrow hallway, at the end of which would be a second one-way mirrored security door for positive friendly identification by a designated security henchman. If the intruder along the 15ft passageway was identified "friendly", the door would be unlocked from within. That was the sophisticated state of the art security procedure in the thirties for the I.F.F. (Identification: Friend or Foe) This was the routine of the overt-covert Marysville opium-permeated, illegal card and keno gambling establishments of the late 20s and 30s. A plethora of bars and saloons used similar one-way mirror entrances during the prohibition. These measures were discarded for the bars only after the repeal of the prohibition law of 1932.

Because a few of my established newspaper card-playing customers frequented the place, I was classified 'friendly' at the tender age of 8, and was admitted into the opium den. In that environment I would invariably make two to three sales, while at the same time get an eyeful of the zombie effect opium had on those smoking the opium-spiked Turkish water pipes. Their gurgling sound blended with the permeated dope aroma in the room. Please do not read racism into my observations when I noticed only Asians participating in the ritual. I must comment that there was no criminal element from their act. It seemed as though it was a cultural thing and they enjoyed their habit as we do our morning coffee. No doubt it was an ethnic characteristic they brought with them from their native country, China. (I often wonder if my light-headed utopian feeling I experienced was from selling 2 to 3 papers, or from the deep breaths I took in the process. I'm kidding. I'm kidding.)

I must volunteer the fixed 'stony' gazed look in their eyes did register an indelible impression upon me that convinced me to never engage in mind altering experiences. That exposure has served me in good stead during my formative high school and college years. For that, I am ever grateful.

As a nine year old kid, I was immune to fear. Outwardly, yes. Inwardly, not so. Assumptions, assumptions, oh how they compromise one's life. I just recalled out of the blue, many were the nights I was awakened, and trembled in my bed at the young age of 9.

Because of the financial hardship endured since my father's demise, Mother rented out my bedroom, which faced the lighted E Street, and moved me to a converted 'bedroom' situated off of our kitchen, far away from my former accustomed street-lit bedroom. My new room now faced north into the darkened 2nd Street Northern Electric Passenger Depot, where hobos congregated during the night.

At first I considered it a sign of manhood, for it signaled to me I now earned a big brother status. My two older brothers slept in a room next to mine. But here is where the situation takes on a new life. I was now in a dark room all by myself. I started hearing the inevitable night noises I never noticed before. I would hear creaking noises throughout the night that go with the territory of a changing climate in an aged building.

I would conquer my fears by pulling my blankets up over my head and lie motionless, hiding from the culprit source. So far so good. But there were isolated nights after two a.m. when all the bars in the neighborhood were forced to close for the night. The alcoholics and winos would then gather at the depot seeking shelter. Many were the nights one of the winos would fall bruising his head or bloodying his face, crying for help. Others would become belligerent among themselves over a bottle of wine, or a 'can-heat highball', severely pushing each other. Intermittently there were yells for help. On these occasions I would be scared to death trembling under the covers. I was too embarrassed to go running to Mommy, or my two older brothers. It didn't seem to bother them at all. Would they think me a scaredy-cat little brother? That, I would avert at all cost. Daylight was my ally and I would welcome it by coming out from under my covers and actually fall into a deep sleep until awakened by my brothers who were totally unaware of my traumatized fearful behavior.

The side effects of the can-heat brand of alcohol (generic name for STERNO) were a detriment to the hobo's health. It blinded many of them. Yet they could not afford whisky for their alcoholic syndrome. It was can-heat now or the bends later. Some recognized the poison of can-heat but ignored the perils of over indulging in cheap wine substitute. In either case it was a wake up call for a nine year old boy of what not to do when he grew into manhood.

Andy's Bakery

On the lighter side, I developed a poaching technique born from a sweet tooth fetish I nursed while on the job selling newspapers. My premeditated sweet tooth supplier, on any given day, would be targeted among one of the following three 'philanthropists'; my Uncle Charles Breakfast and Lunch Counter Nook, Mr. Tom Cohiles' Lunch and Coffee Shop, or Andy's Bakery, which specialized in sesame ringed bread (kouloura), doughnuts, cookies, pies, and cakes. Guess which one of the three earned most of my plotting? That's right~ the Bakery.

Now for my M.O. First off you must remember all of this is taking place in the heart of the Great Depression. Each business establishment was operating with a jaundiced budget, and had to economize discerningly in order to make a living. So, considering the economic circumstances, a 'freebie', no matter how minute, could register a negative effect on the bottom line of a business establishment. This fact was of course not a concern to a poor, youthful paperboy. My high percentage success rate for the sweet tooth mission went like this. Before going into action, I would case the 'joint' (I use that phrase affectionately) that I planned to con for that particular day. For the bakery, I would try to time my plot when Mr. Efstratis's son, Ted, a close friend of mine, would be helping at the counter of the bakery. I would approach Mr. Efstratis to see if he wanted to buy a paper. I knew he didn't— because I'd never sold him one. Yet my game plan had to be played out to the hilt. I would put on my Oscar award-winning, St.

Bernard droopy-eyed look, and complement it with a longing stare at the cookie or doughnut of choice. Ted would then invariably look towards his father for a plus or negative sign as the charade was being acted out. Most times, Mr. Efstratis would grunt an OK, and march back to the oven room of the bakery, not wanting to witness the loss. Ted, would then hand me my prize and I would be on my way.

At Uncle Charles lunch counter I would make my move when my older cousin, Nick, was tending the shop. Without hesitation he would respond to my wanting look and offer me a piece of pie, which I gladly devoured. Cousin Nick was a third brother to me. I hope he too, being an only child of my Aunt and Uncle, considered me as his brother. P.S. Uncle Charles was aware of the charade, yet made no mention of it. I knew he approved.

At Mr. Tom Cohiles' counter, depending upon the day's business, he would pacify my longing with a piece of pie. He was a very kind, hard-working man, tending to the customers all by himself to support his wife, 2 daughters, and son. As a rule, I would be rewarded with a treat at his day's end if there was a pie or part of one still available before closing shop for the day.

**My cousin, who was like a brother to me
Nick Charlie Nicholau**

Homonym

In the year 1929, my tenth year, I recall an incident in which, unwittingly, I was the brunt of a humiliating experience. At that age, I would attend all the local Marysville Giants Valley League baseball practices as a self-volunteered bat boy. The players took a liking to me, as I did to them. I was a favorite "go-for kid". This particular night the incident went like this. The Giants were having an infield and outfield practice when Wiz Pappas, the manager, called all his players to his side and ordered them to play a three-inning practice game. Hank Wolf, the Giant first string catcher, called for me, and when I got by his side he said, "George, go to my locker and bring me my cup." I enthusiastically replied, "Yes sir Mr. Wolf", and off I went to his locker. Sure enough, I found a paper cup on the shelf of his locker and hastened back to the catcher. Upon my presentation of the cup to Mr. Wolf, the nearby players all started to laugh. Hank Wolf just took the cup from my hand and said, "Thanks." One of the older kids there laughingly explained to me my faux pas. With my embarrassed red face I joined him in laughter. The paper "cup" was definitely not the proper armor for the occasion!

Se Agapo

Lest my memoirs gives one the impression of an irresponsible, freelance, reprobate kid during my devilish newspaper adventures, now is a good time to put that image to rest. I can best accomplish this by giving you further insight into my father's parental guidance. His axiom as mentioned earlier, "Do nothing to embarrass or compromise the integrity of the family name," was chiseled in stone. Falter on this truism and you will pay the consequences. Obviously upon reflection, as I write my memoirs, I confess I have somewhat, innocently compromised Dad's edict from time to time, but never aborted it or denigrated it.

At the tender age of 8 years old during my newspaper career, I committed an act that triggered the capital penalty of Dad's good character edict. The punishment rendered was metered in such a way, it left an indelible impression for life in my mind.

Now, the detailed facts of my miscreant act. The time of day was around 6 p.m. on a day in July. My two brothers, Nick and Al, along with their two friends Gus and Harry Karnegas, decided to get on their bicycles and head for the Woolworths's soda fountain, located on D Street, for a milkshake. The store was three blocks from our home and I begged them to let me tag along. I knew I could jog and keep up with them because of the traffic congestion. My brother Al said, "OK, I'll get you an ice cream cone". And off we went. As we approached the Woolworth's store located as mentioned on D Street, the proprietor happened to be taking a break. He was standing on the sidewalk in front of Woolworth's when my brothers and their friends placed their bikes next to the gutter of the sidewalk, as was the custom in those days. At that moment as I jogged next to the bikes the proprietor saw me, and at once shouted, "Get that boy....he's going to steal one of your bikes! He has been stealing marbles from me for days and I have yet to catch him in the act!!" It so happened I had a close call earlier that very day, and when I heard him shout, 'Get that boy!' I was gone running, not jogging, back home.

Forget the ice cream treat. I forfeited. It was inconsequential compared to the penalty I was about to pay. My brothers, upon returning home, couldn't tell my father soon enough what transpired at Woolworths. They told my father about my marble escapades. That evening after dinner, my dad asked me to come forth. Trembling, knowing why I was being paged, I stood before him. The following dialogue was in Greek. I mention that because when Dad disciplined us kids in his native tongue, we knew we were in for a world of hurt. In this instance, the operative word is hurt, with a capital H.

Briefly, here is how the 'interview' went. By translating it from Greek to English it will undoubtedly lose some of it's intensity, but the final message will come across loud and clear.

"George, your brothers tell me you have a lot of marbles. Is that true?"

"Yes, papa"

"George," always George, I guess for emphasis, "How did you get the marbles?"

"My friends gave them to me."

"George, why did your friends want to give you marbles?"

"Because they wanted me to play games of marbles with them."

"George, did all of the other boys have their own marbles?"

(Boy am I ever getting in deep with my evasive, untruthful answers)

"Yes", and this was my first truthful response.

"George, I will ask you again, where did you get the marbles? Your brothers tell me that you got them from another source."

"Papa, I did get some marbles from the Woolworth's store. I found them on the floor and picked them up"

"George, you picked them up from the floor. George again, did you offer to give them to a clerk, or did you think because you picked them up from the floor, you found them, and therefore you could keep them? Did you let the clerk know you were keeping some marbles you found on the floor?"

"No papa"

"George, now that you told me where you got the marbles, explain to me how you took them. I don't believe you picked them up from the floor. So, George, how did you get the marbles?"

"I took them"

"Again George, how did you get the marbles?"

"Papa, I took them"

43

"No you didn't George. One last time, and don't tell me you took them. George, how did you get the marbles?"

Now crying, I sobbed, "Papa, I stole them!"

"Again, George, how did you get the marbles?"

With my body jerking, I again sobbingly cried, "I stole them papa!"

"Yes, you stole them. Now I am going to punish you first for stealing, but secondly, and more importantly, for lying about it."

Dad's capital punishment was delivered with a special branch from one of our garden fig trees. He was a master in maximizing the effectiveness of meeting pain with a branch switch without causing bodily harm. Dad did not use a switch often. Most of his discipline was delivered with a philosophical lecture on right vs. wrong, and honor vs. dishonor. To be truthful, I would rather receive a sting or two on my buttocks from the switch than a philosophical lecture. A discipline lecture from Dad left its telltale mark on your brain for days on end. To this day, I thank God it did just that.

Now I emphasize that in my dad's mind, my current transgression was so egregious it merited capital punishment with a capital P, *and* a lecture with a capital L. Therefore I received both the switch and the lecture for my marble/lying debacle. The encore switch routine was painfully effective. The lecture was denigrating, but delivered with so much love it left a lifelong mark.

Continuing on, after due process for that day's punishment I got the message and assumed that would be the end of it. Wrong again! The first thing I was ordered to do, was to go to the manager of the Woolworths store the very next day and confess to him, " I stole marbles from your store." Then, I was to return all of the marbles to him with the promise, "I will never steal again", and I had to ask for his forgiveness. This I did and his forgiveness I received. Gad, that was a hard thing for me to do. Funny thing though, right after I confessed and returned the marbles, I felt relieved from a deep burden and was actually proud of myself. I did a lifetime of growing up in that instance.

Now having received the manager's forgiveness, I thought I was in the clear. Not so. I was still in deep water with my dad, but I didn't know it. That night after dinner, dad again asked that I stay at the table. When the rest of the family departed he asked,

"George, how did you get the marbles?"

"I stole them papa"

"Yes, you stole them." And zing went the switch against my upper arm.

"Ouch!"

"George, will you ever do that again?"

"No papa." Zing went the switch again to my upper arm.

"Ouch!"

"See that you don't"

"I won't do that again papa"

Day #3 Post Confession:

"George, will you ever steal again?"

"No papa"

"Good. Now I am proud to be your father. Always be truthful and do nothing to tarnish the family's name, and you will be respected by all. George, you know I love you. Se agapo." Hearing that from Dad after my deserved capital punishment motivated me to regain his trust and faith in me. Love is a powerful incentive for righteousness.

Incident closed. Lifelong lesson learned.

At this writing it has been over 80 years since my lesson about honor, and I continue to love and thank Papa for his parental genius. He instilled in me the ultimate reward of truthfulness, honor and love. I am doing my utmost to pass that message onto his grandchildren, great grandchildren, and great-great grandchildren. From his heavenly vantage point I am confident they are a blessing to him as they are to their parents and grandparents. After all, his grandkids are the greatest!

Nick, me, Dad, Athena, Mom, and Al, 1923

Puppy Love

Fast forward from the marble escapade. I am now a grown man of 15 years. A freshman at Marysville Union High School. As a freshman, I am showing positive signs of stardom in the three major sports of football, baseball, and basketball, with football as the primetime of the three. With that background, I was noticed~ at least in my mind, by the fairer sex in my class. For the first time, during my puberty state, I fell into the throws of puppy love. Which, of course, at the time I relegated to be the real thing.

I will document my puppy love experience to highlight how being an insecure young boy, living on "the wrong side of the tracks", played out on my self-esteem in the social arena. Please mentally slip into my 1933 tattered tennies and place yourself in my home, located on the second story of a saloon!! With that background, envision the aspirations of a young whippersnapper fantasizing being in love with the most popular, affluent, beautiful, attractive girl in all of Marysville High School. She was always dressed like a model, accessorized with noticeably stylish shoes that further embarrassed me with my faithful tennies, whose soles were detached from the upper canvas, making them flip-flop with every step I took.

With that picture in your mind and abetted with the economic social disparity in my mind, I will proceed to the crux of the high school puppy love expose. In the beginning I would avoid any direct confrontation with Peggy Steele, daughter of well-to-do parents, for fear it would jeopardize my juvenile fantasies. Hey, at that age there is no such thing as puppy love, no, it's the real thing! Right?

I recall an incident during my newspaper selling days. One day, while selling my daily-allotted papers, I bellowed out, "EXTRA, EXTRA, READ ALL ABOUT IT!! DEMPSY-TUNEY WORLD CHAMPIONSHIP FIGHT!!!", when I accidentally bumped right into Peggy who just walked out of Bradley's Department Store, the nicest clothing store in Marysville. I was so embarrassed, due to my accoutrements, and shocked, due to almost knocking her over, I just kept on walking….hoping for a customer to bail me out…without even acknowledging the collision. I could not exit the scene fast enough! A faux pas, no doubt, due to the economic disparity that existed between us. Peggy, to her credit, did say, "Hi George!".

Imagine, at this writing, in my geriatric nineties, I still recall that moment in my life while now enjoying the amenities of a prosperous life. What I have learned in the interim, but did not know in my youth, is in reality, there is no basic separation between the have and have-nots if you believe in yourself. In most cases the challenge to live a happy, useful, and productive life rests with the individual. Economic barriers are just one of the inevitable speed bumps along life's journey. The final control of one's destiny rests within oneself.

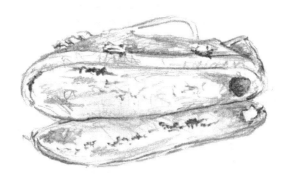

The Entrepreneurial Spirit

Having a strong work ethic ingrained in me by my father and mother, and seeing the effects of prosperity when working toward a worthy goal in America, there was a period in my life during my high school freshman year when I held four jobs at one time. It occurred in 1933 during the Great Depression. During the summer months I was to report to Jim Poole's jewelry store, at that time located on the first floor of the Hart Building on the corner of 4th

and E Street in Marysville. My hours were from 12:00 to 1:30pm while Mr. Poole would take his lunch break and rest in the back of the store. I was to answer the phone and watch over the store for security reasons, and if a customer came in I was to alert Mr. Poole. Many were the times when I arrived for work, he would have just received a shipment of diamonds that would be spread out on his workbench to be sorted according to karat weight and clarity. The confidence and trust Mr. Poole had in this 14 year old newspaper boy was worth twice the 50 cents a day he would give me at the end of my Monday through Saturday schedule.

From the jewelry store job I would head to the Marysville Appeal Democrat office at 3:00pm to get my twenty papers to earn another 50 cents that day.

The third job of the <u>day</u>, arguably a misnomer, because it was a night job, was to report at 8:00pm as a night watchman at the garage across the street from my home. I was to allow big rig trucks in and out of the locked garage during the night to accommodate their individual schedules. (I slept on a couch in the office and responded to a bell activated at various times by the truck drivers.) I lucked into the job when I tried to sell Mr. De Long, the garage owner, a newspaper while he was seated at the Columbia Bar located beneath my home. By coincidence that day, he put an ad in the paper for the position. As he bought a paper he asked me if I was interested in earning $3.00 a day working for him. "THREE DOLLARS A DAY? REALLY?", I enthused. He said, "Check with your mother and let me know tomorrow…yes or no." Because the garage was just across the street from our home, and he was familiar with our family, he volunteered, "I know I can trust you to be dependable." Wow. Talk about hitting the jackpot. Come to think about it, I was quite an entrepreneur during the summer of 1933, earning $5.00 a day! My enterprises consisted of: 50 cents from Mr. Poole, 50 cents from selling papers, $1.00 from my peach "business", and lastly $3.00 as a night watchman. There was no doubt in my mind that there was and is Someone up there looking after me, and I know Who that was and is. Thank you, God.

To Be Or Not To Be
(I'll give you a hint…I'm still here….)

My mind now wanders to an incident during my high school years, which is pertinent to my longevity of life and is worth revealing. This adventure took place at 11pm on a Wednesday evening. The place was at the Marysville Community Swimming Pool, located at the time, on the corner of 9th and B Street, adjacent to the jewel landmark of the city of Marysville; Ellis Lake. The pool was open to the public in the summer months from 11am to 9pm. The pool access was free from 11 to 3pm. After 3pm to closing time, it was 25 cents. It was not uncommon for two of my buddies and I to cap off an evening of merry making by sneaking into the closed swimming pool after hours by climbing a chain linked fence. After which we would discard our clothes and skinny dip for a cool swim. My, it was refreshing. Especially so, because the price was right. The fact we were "pooling" one over (pun intended) on the eyes of the city authorities lent added spice to the occasion. My accomplices were Gavin Mandry, who later became Mayor of Marysville, and Lex Doust, who later became the owner of the Chevrolet dealership in Marysville. As I was the accomplished high-diver of our group, I would head directly to the 10 foot high diving board, springing at the end of the board until I reached an approximate 4 feet above the 10 foot board, where I would execute a jack knife, one and a half summersault, clearing the edge of the board by 6 inches, and quietly knife into the water below. A show off, possibly. A thrill-seeker, certainly.

On this particular dark, moonless Wednesday night, unbeknownst to me, the pool was drained for clean up maintenance. Being pitch dark, I started doing my pre-dive exercise at the end of the 10 foot high diving board when Mandry shouted, **"George! There's no water in the pool!!!"** The shock was traumatic. It took me a couple of decelerating springing efforts before I became stable at the end of the board. My knees were so weak they couldn't support me and I found myself kneeling and hanging on in a prone position for dear life at the end of the board. It literally took me 5 minutes of crawling from the end of the board back to the ladder leading me down to the pool's deck. When I finally reached the ladder it took me another couple of minutes to pick myself up to a standing position in order to descend from the board. Each step was methodically researched before descending to the next. A stark difference from my previous cavalier showing off, ascending two ladder rungs at a time. I was literally flirting with a state of shock. I was still trembling after climbing back over the fence to freedom from the swimming pool. I was a 17 year old high school student at that happening. I am enjoying my 93rd year of life while proof reading this draft of my memoir. That is what I referred to earlier with the 'longevity of life' comment.

That life-threatening ordeal triggered my memory back to another life threatening experience. You may recall, I would display a decoyed ripe peach alongside the open windows of the passenger train to sell my merchandise. On very rare occasions when the peaches were truly ripe, I would still have a bag left after covering all the passenger cars on one side of the train. To save time and energy, rather than run to the front or rear of the long train to get to the other side, I would get right behind the front train wheels of the particular car I was near. I figured, if the train would start to move while I was under it, I would have time to scamper out the other side before the rear wheels of that car would reach the point from which I started. It made sense to me that this was a logical time saving effort that allowed me to get to the other side of the passenger cars. This I did several times without incident. "To be or not to be"~ the invulnerability of youth's mentality!

On this particular day the conductor happened to spot me readying myself to cross under the train, and yelled at me, "GET BACK! NOW!" As I did so, he held me by my arm and said, "Son, you stay right here beside me until the train pulls out from the station." Having hold on my arm with authority, I had no choice in the matter. "Now," he continued, "I want you to stare at the back of the wheels where you were about to cross to the other side." He continued to hold onto me to assure himself that I would obey his order. I stood fast, and within 3 minutes, though it seemed like an eternity, the train started to leave the station. Before the train could move forward, the airbrakes on all of the cars had to be released. Because of the incline of the station's railroad tracks, coupled with the characteristic behavior of these airbrakes, all cars suddenly reflexed backwards due to gravitational force, approximately 3 to 4 feet. Had I started to go under the train at the same time the train released the airbrakes to leave the station, I would have been history. The conductor saw my shock, let go of my arm, and said, "Kid, you have been living on borrowed time. Now behave yourself and enjoy your life." I was speechless but emphatically convinced. That conductor's paternal concern over a wayward newspaper boy left an indelible impression on me.

Fun With Harry Hooper
The Payless Years

Two life threatening close calls recorded in sequence, although happening 6 to 7 years apart (the train episode when I was 10 and the diving incident when I was about 17) is two too many for me. Moving on to some more pleasant and less harrowing memories, I've arrived at my Payless Drugstore antics. Starting my sophomore year in high school I was successful in getting a job at the new Payless Drugstore opening in Marysville. Goodbye newspaper boy, hello drugstore stock boy. Harry Hooper, a cofounder of the chain with Mr. Calloway, was a sports enthusiast and had been following my high school sports career, which worked in my favor when I interviewed for the opening stock boy job. (Note of interest, The Payless Drugstore of which I write was the precursor to the Payless chain stores one is familiar with today. At that time, Mr. Calloway and Mr. Hooper were the founders and sole proprietors of the Payless name. Later they sold the name rights to the present mammoth chain of Payless Drug Stores.) Now back to my story. During the football season, my hours at the store on weekdays were after practice from 5:30 to 10pm. The exception would be Friday game nights. On Saturdays I worked from 9am to 10pm. On Sundays I worked 10am to noon, and 3pm to 9pm. After football season I would report to work at 3:30 on school days.

I gave up basketball and baseball when I started my job. I was paid 25 cents an hour, which netted me an average of $11 to $12 a week! Sure did beat the $3 per week I made selling newspapers my freshman year. Also during the year, I had promoted myself from just a stock boy into a clerk position. The clerk position, besides a token raise to 35 cents an hour, had a monetary fringe benefit attached to it. I said I promoted myself. Let me explain. The store's popularity, being the first and only discount drugstore in the community at that time, exploded like a wheat fire in a windstorm. When customers were waiting to be served, I would just jump in and help them. I was familiar with the stock arrangement and the pricing of the merchandise, so it just didn't feel right to be putting stock away when people were waiting in line. Right? Ergo, a new classification: stock-clerk boy. Now, besides a 10 cents raise, I was introduced to PM (an acronym for Profitable Merchandise) incentives. Its format follows. I can best explain it using "Ipana" toothpaste, a trademark product during that era. Ipana is only one of the many trademark items in the store that I could have picked.

    Mr. Hooper would contract with drug manufacturers who would produce a generic toothpaste under their store name with a similar formula of the expired patented rights to Ipana. Emphasis, 'similar' to the trademark named product. In it's generic form the product was priced at an appreciable savings to the customer over the trade name product, and yet produced a higher net profit for the store. Thus, PM became a big-ticket item in the bottom line profit of the business. Also, there were on occasion for competitive reasons, special promotional campaigns of trademark merchandise offered by some companies as an incentive to the retailer to sell a set dollar figure of the item and thus receive a rebate from the parent company. On those occasions the promotion item would qualify the clerk to earn rewards, as they too made a higher positive net for the retailer. In the back of the merchandise area of the drug store, each clerk would have his or her PM sheet posted on a bulletin board. Via the honor system, when a clerk would sell a posted PM item, he or she would put a mark after that listed item.

Your next paycheck would include the PM money you earned during that pay period.

Having made a short story long, I will now state why I did so. I was the top PM clerk in the store during all of my years of association with Mr. Hooper's Payless Drug Store! What really pleased me was the knowledge that I was not abusing the PM system, as regular customers would ask for me or wait for me to serve their needs. On popular trademark items I would study the formula and match it with the Payless generic formula. If I found the similarity was such as not to affect the purposeful integrity of the product, I would share that information with the customer and point out the savings over the trademark item. The choice was then left to the customer. However, when a generic choice was made, I would tell the customer to please return the item to me if not satisfied, for full credit towards the trademark product. Rarely was the product returned, and many a time the repeat customer would ask for the generic item. They trusted my recommendation and that is a wonderful reward in itself. At the end of the month my paycheck would include as much as $10 by way of nickels and dimes earned by PM merchandise. An impressive bonanza at the time.

While working at the store, I became interested in the pharmaceutical aspect of the business. I was able to read the doctor's handwriting on the prescriptions, understand the pharmaceutical Latin abbreviated direction code for the prescription, while learning each drug's therapeutic effect. I found it all to be very informative, challenging, and exciting. And therein lies the genesis of my future pharmacy degree and career.

Now get this! And believe it for it is the glaring truth. On a take-off of my competitive newspaper charge account entrepreneurship, I conjured the following modification to enhance my sales volume. In the interest of time, and for a self-serving cause, when customers crowded the store while shopping for bargains, I would adlib a quickie customer service procedure. It was this:

Having beforehand anticipated an added influx of customers due to a sale, I would remove $5.00 in small change from the cash register and pocket it, i.e. pennies, nickels, dimes, quarters, fifty cents and three one dollar bills. When making a sale I would put the customer's money directly into my pocket. Then make the necessary change, if needed, and immediately move on to the next available customer. Thus avoiding having to go back to the cash register after each sale to complete the transaction.

This method allowed me to serve more customers as a time convenience to them, and, to quickly move on to another awaiting customer. This innovation increased my PM sales, which added dollars into my month's paycheck.

When it quieted down I would go to the cash register and ring up one total sale to cover all of the sales I made, and put all of the money from my pocket into the cash register. The cash register always reconciled at day's end.

One day, while the store was crowded with customers, Mr. Hooper also joined us from his office to help out. When he observed my transactions he was shocked! During a break he took me into his office and questioned me in a money-laundering tone, "What's with your money-pocketing??" I, unaware of his ulterior motive, enthused "In this way I can serve more customers as a convenience to them, and as an opportunity to sell more PM items." Hearing that, in a surprised sympathetic tone, "George, that is not an acceptable way to serve the customers. Each sale must be rung up and a receipt given to the customer. That procedure serves two purposes. One, for the customer's record, and two, for inventory control for the store. No more pocket transactions, ok?" "Yes, Mr. Hooper", I uttered.

Upon proof reading the above on this day, I am positively amazed at what I just documented. As stated above, it is the glaring truth!

Lesson learned. There is no substitute for on-the-job training to best learn the "how-to" formula for success, especially for an innocent high school sophomore competing in the adult world.

Not all of my Payless Drugstore experiences were of a serious nature. You may recall, I started my drugstore story several paragraphs back with the phrase "drugstore antics". Here is why. In the late thirties, I can't remember the exact year, Northern California experienced a major earthquake with the epicenter near Oroville. There was a genuine concern regarding the effect the quake had on the integrity of the Oroville dam, which was engineered to regulate flow of water throughout the lower northern valley. That fear was played up in the local papers. The community was genuinely apprehensive about ensuing danger and failure of the dam, which fed the Feather and Yuba Rivers. Well, a week after that scary event, I pulled a stunt at the pharmacy that, at the time I thought was hilarious. But in hindsight, it wasn't.

It was 9:30pm, a half hour before closing. The retail part of the store had merchandise displayed on both sides of the entrance door, with the center space of the store accommodating three elongated gondolas heavily stocked with sundry merchandise. Over each of the gondolas were three light fixtures that hung from the 15-foot ceiling on linked chains. There was a display of beach balls, among other things on one of the gondolas. At that hour, Doc was in the back of the store working on some prescriptions as I was attending the front of the store. (The head employed pharmacist, who went by the name of Doc, was a small man in his mid sixties, 5'6", bald, plump in stature, with dark rimmed glasses. He would relieve shifts for Mr. Hooper.) It was very quiet and I got bored and hit upon a prank that I knew would get Doc's attention. I got a beach ball and directed it at the light fixtures hanging on the chain from the ceiling over the gondolas, hitting them and causing them to swing back and forth. When I had all three of the light fixtures in motion, I went to the toothpaste display on the side of the store, knowing they were unbreakable, and started to shake them from their display onto the floor, all the while shouting, "Doc, Doc, Quick! Earthquake!"

Doc rushed from the back of the prescription area seeing the chandeliers swinging and merchandize falling to the floor (as caused by my back hand) and my body swaying while facing him. He grabbed the counter for balance and froze there speechless with his fearful wide eyes fixed staring into space with his lower jaw dropped in awe. Seeing him so frightened I recanted and started laughing while cluing him in on the prank. The next thing I knew he came after me with a vengeance, and I was out the door and down the street hearing him holler, "You're fired, you're fired!"

Pharmacists, and especially relief pharmacists, were a scarcity, and Doc's message was: "Either George is fired, or I quit!" You be the judge as to which of the options was more pragmatic to Mr. Hooper. Being a resilient 16 year old kid at the time, I reported to work the next day as though nothing had happened the night before. Wrong. Something did happen the night before and my job was in jeopardy. It was Doc's call. Mr. Hooper left it up to me to do whatever it took to convince Doc that I was not only sorry, but that I would never, ever do anything like that again. This I did convincingly and Doc forgave me. I was back on the job as Doc's henceforth little Fauntleroy helper.

One other caper I must share with you was carried out on Mr. Hooper himself. You see, most every evening around 9:45, 15 minutes before closing time, Mr. Hooper would come forth from his office in the back of the store and say, "George, before you close this evening see that you display this…do that….dust this….mop that…clean out the display windows….." always something. That something would usually take me 15 to 20 minutes *past* closing time, depending on the number of customers that needed to be served in the interim. This particular evening I had a game plan on hold, should he approach me with his usual last chores. On one of the side displays we had a string of thirty alarm clocks we were promoting in our next newspaper ad. At thirty minutes before 10pm, while Mr. Hooper was preoccupied in his office, I started to wind each clock, and set the alarm for 10pm sharp. The ticking sound throughout the store resembled a cricket's paradise. True enough, as was customary, Mr. Hooper did have last minute orders for me and then escaped back to his office. Evidently due to my alarm setting, or the clock's inefficiency, no matter the cause, some of the alarms started ringing prematurely! Panicking, I rushed to the display to stop the early culprits, but so many of the thirty clocks were misbehaving, I did not know which ones to attend to. I reasoned, 'the hell with it', the cacophonic message ("it's time to go home!") would not only be loud, but long! Mr. Hooper came forward wanting to know, "What's going ON out here!?"

I fabricated a lie, "Mr. Hooper, in as much as we are running a special on our alarm clocks, I wanted to be sure they were functioning properly."

"Good thing, George. How are you coming on your closing chores?"

"I'm gaining on it Mr. Hooper."

When I had finished my chores some of the clocks were still misbehaving or merely responding to my errant time-setting. "George", Mr. Hooper said, "I suggest you find something to do until the last clock responds to your settings. Then you can report to me if we have any malfunctioning clocks." When concocting schemes to make a point, be prepared to pay the price when they backfire.

"Of course Mr. Hooper," I responded, "It is comforting to know that they are all functioning properly."

Guess who got the best of that prank? Oh well, live and learn, as the saying goes.

With that said, I am still grateful to Mr. Hooper for the overall training I received under his tutelage. (Oh, yes, all of the clocks stopped ringing by the time I left at 10:20 that evening.) I hope!!

Nicholau Enology

You know what? Another impressive switcheroo. This is as good a time as any to invite you into my youthful memories of the Nicholau enology factory. It took place during the prohibition era previously referred to in this memoir. The luxury of a ¾ acre yard in the city's lower end, our home lent itself ideally to the annual stealth production of four fifty-gallon barrels of wine. The key equipment and the overall process was already in place, as my dad had ventured into the olive oil manufacturing business in the early years of the twentieth century. Much of the olive oil manufacturing equipment proved ideal for our wine 'factory'.

In the homemade wine making process there comes a time after the first crushing of the grapes, when it is necessary to further crush them to extract the last drop of juice from the stems and pulp ("chipura") of the grape vine. I believe you will be amused to read how it was accomplished in the Nicholau Enology Factory.

After the crushing of the grapes, within the 5 foot diameter by 4 foot deep water vat, I am told to take off my shoes and socks, wash my feet, climb a ladder, with a baseball bat in hand, and jump onto the crushed grape pulp. From that position I stomp with my bare feet while plunging my bat over and over onto the previously gear-crushed grapes, extracting the last ounce of clear juice in the process. This is a productive, tedious, and exhausting conditioning exercise. Yet it was one I always looked forward to. At the time, I acted like a juvenile playing in the mud without getting spanked. On second thought I often wondered if the hazardous occupational air quality environment had something to do with my looking forward to the "stomping at the grapes" date. I must admit after stints of my post stomping chore I felt liberated and light headed.

Let me remind you that this wine making for personal use was taking place during the prohibition! A family was restricted to one barrel at the most, if that. However, with a large family of our cultural background, complimented by a multitude of visitors, the four barrels barely survived their primary mission at the Nicholau resort.

Now that we filled the barrels, where and how do we stow them away? (I'm assuming the legal time for prosecuting the "crime" has elapsed.)

This is how.

With brute manpower, a twelve by ten foot rectangular hole six feet deep was dug out in the most secluded section of our three quarter acre backyard. The excavation was then covered with railroad ties over which was placed yards of the newfound dug up dirt. It was camouflaged to look as though the area was untouched. Presto, a natural air-conditioned wine cellar! By Dad's rule of thumb a barrel of wine was not to be tapped before a minimum of four years aging in the barrel to a maximum of seven years. The aging process was a critical part of the finished product. This wine, it is important to understand, was a cultural element primarily for family use and also for Greek community celebrations of holidays, i.e. Easter, birthdays, and name day gatherings at our home, of which we had many. I emphasize it was not a commercial product.

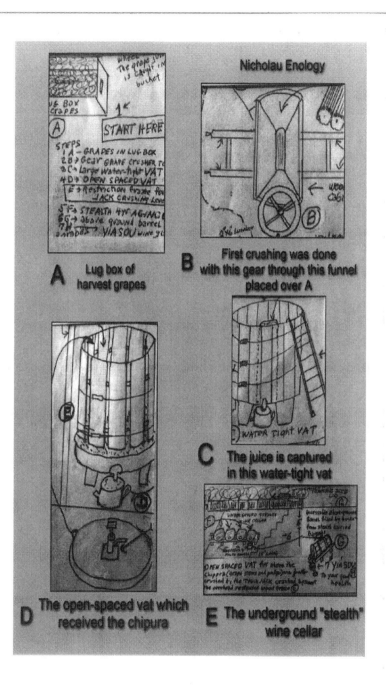

Mom and Pop B.G.
(Before George)

While I am reminiscing, let me share some points of interest about my dad, Edison Nicholau. The narrative that follows is part of my heritage and makes me proud to be part of his lineage.

In 1912 war was declared between the Turks and the Greeks due to the Turks invasion onto Greek soil. At that time my father was well established in Marysville, California, successfully enjoying his Columbia Café enterprise. Upon reading of the conflict, he told his brother, my Uncle Charles whom he incorporated in the restaurant venture, that he was going back to Greece to fight for his native country. He made it clear to all aware of his plans that he would do no less for his adopted country, America, if it was at war. As a matter of fact, it was his wish that one of his sons would become an officer in the U.S.A. military force. (This did become a reality when during WWII, I served with a rank of Lt.jg on a minesweeper.)

In the Greek army he was ranked a corporal. During battle he was wounded by a bullet passing up through his army cap, glancing off the top of his forehead, leaving a serious wound inches above the hairline of his right eye. Rendered unconscious, his fellow soldiers rescued him by pulling him back from the front line of battle. His wound was of such a serious nature he was granted rehab leave. During his rehab, armistice between the two countries was negotiated, ending the war. I am in possession of his bullet holed, blood stained soldier's hat, and a large framed picture of Dad in uniform with his head bandaged.

**The hat my dad wore when he got shot
while fighting for his native country, Greece, 1912**

Dad spent his rehab leave at his village of birth, Alagonia, located in the mountains approximately 20 miles east of Kalamata, Greece. While there he met his wife to be, Despina Kastanos, the only child of Alexander and Athena Kastanos.

In the village it is a Greek custom that one contemplating marriage MUST adhere to a pre-courtship tradition before any chaperoned dating is permitted. The customary procedure calls for the potential groom, or the bride, to inform his or her father that he or she is interested in a particular person. The parents then, between themselves, negotiate the "prica", or dowry of the marriage. For example, when a potential bride informs her parent of an interest in someone, that parent would engage a third party to approach the father of the potential groom to see if he wished to be involved. If so, the third party person would proceed to mediate a dowry from the father of the girl to the potential groom. The binding "prica" is agreed upon between both sets of parents and then the couple is allowed to court under the supervision of a chaperone. As convoluted as the process appears, it is hard to fault when looking at the nonexistent divorce rate between the arranged marriages of that era.

Even more convoluted is the marriage ceremony. I wonder if it has changed since 1935, when I had the opportunity to be a guest of a wedding ceremony while our family was visiting the village.

All of the bride's guests are invited to her house on the wedding day. All of the groom's guests are invited to his house on the wedding day. At each home the celebration is in full swing. There is a lamb (or lambs) on a spit being turned by hand by several volunteer guests at each household until it's ready to be devoured. Notice I said 'devoured' not served. For each guest saunters over to the spit area when so inclined and a fresh carving of lamb is cut and given to the guest. Greek retsina wine is free flowing. All the while Greek music is being played on the mandolin or on the bouzouki while guests join in song and traditional Greek folkdances. It is a festive sight to behold. Now, mind you, this is going on simultaneously, and separately, at the bride and groom's respective houses. Depending on the set time of the wedding ceremony all of the bride's guests leave the house with the bride in tow and march from her home singing and celebrating throughout the village main square to the groom's house. There the celebration continues with all guests mixing together. At a reasonable time before the wedding ceremony, all the guests of the bride and groom now march together to the village church for the wedding ritual. After the wedding ceremony the newlyweds lead the guests back through the village square in a celebratory mood to the bride's home where the celebration continues in full force. After a seemingly appropriate time, the bride and groom leave the celebrations while the party continues on into the wee hours of the following morning, with guests eventually dispersing in the afternoon.

In my father's case he forsook the dowry formality. He personally approached Despina's father to ask for permission to court her. He emphasized to the father that he wished no dowry, but he brought to fore that soon after the vows he and his bride, if it was meant to be, would be traveling back to America where he had his restaurant business awaiting him. A cavalier approach in that era, to put it mildly. A day after my father's visit with Mr. Kastanos, permission for his daughter's hand in marriage was given. The typical ceremony then took place, and the rest is history. Years later, my mother confided in me how she longed to be Dad's bride when he was convalescing in the "horio" (village), and had communicated her wish to her parents before Dad approached her father.

Wedding portrait of my parents
Despo Kastanos & Edison Nicholau

All mothers are glorified by their children. And children more so by their mothers. And that is as it should be. So beware of my prejudice as I brag about the virtues of my mother. I do believe, however, you'll agree with me, she was a most courageous woman.

    Being an only child, she inherited all of the chores of the household. It was not uncommon to see her in the middle of the village main street, trudging along with a heavy bundle of kindling wood strapped across her upper back gathered from their "boxe". (small plot of land) Or you might see her carrying a large bucket of water balanced on her head. There were no plumbing conveniences, no electricity, nor was there gas supplied to the house. There were no customary conveniences that we take for granted. The water was carried from the village community water well. Hygiene plumbing consisted of an adjacent outhouse. Candlelight substituted for electricity. Window openings were sheltered with homemade drapes and wooden shutters. Glass panes and screens in the village homes were unheard of as late as 1935! All cooking was done in the house fireplace. Another chore for my mother was to help her parents look after the two donkeys they possessed. As essential as an automobile is to the American family, so is the donkey to the village family. Where are the donkeys housed? In the dual donkey garage beneath the main drafted floor of the house. You learned to adjust to their braying and restlessness, as well as their characteristic odor. If we looked after our cars with the same passion the villagers looked after their animals we would never need to trade them in.

    This reminds me of an incident during a family trip to Greece in which I became a key player as I accompanied my 90+ year old grandmother on one of her routine log gathering chores to feed the hungry fireplaces for warmth and cooking tasks.

    It was late afternoon when my grandmother decided to go with one of her donkeys to her "boxe", (an acre or two of land which she inherited) located a half-mile down the mountain trail from the house. As her fifteen year old grandson, I wanted to tag along. My grandmother led the way on foot and insisted that I ride the donkey, as she was unable to. When we reached her plot of land there were several large tree branches laying about which were the primary target for her mission. Together we would choose rather large in diameter, discarded branches for the fireplace to load onto the donkey. There was an art to loading the timber so that it would balance on the donkey's back. Grandma, satisfied that the donkey's load was maxed out, started back up the mountainside heading for home. So far so good.

But wait, along the way, Grandma spotted a discarded large branch of wide girth lying alongside our path. She immediately stopped in her tracks and started to lift the log to place it on the donkey's back. Seeing her intent, I joined her in placing the log on the donkey. The donkey violently rejected the extra load by braying and trying to dislodge it. The moment my grandmother noticed this, she immediately, with my help, removed the log from the donkey. Of course I thought that was the end of that, and that we would discard the 'prize' then and there. Not so fast. Grandma picked it up from one end to drag it, as heavy and cumbersome as it was, with the full intent by hook or by crook to get the timber to the house, even if it meant stopping many times along the way. Imagine a 90 year old, five foot two, grandmother of slight build and frame, hassling a piece of lumber that challenged the endurance of her petite body, up the mountain trail, bound and determined to get it home! I emphatically insisted that I carry the branch. But she kept arguing, "No, no, no! It's too heavy for you!" Not too heavy for a fragile 90 year old grandmother, but too heavy for an athletic 15 year old grandson? Go Figure!

With grandma's fortitude and goal-oriented discipline, one begins to appreciate and fully respect the hardship and sacrifices my devoted ancestors endured, that we may enjoy the fruits of their labor.

I only knew Grandma Athena 3 to 4 months of her 90 plus years, and yet she instilled in me a lifetime of love and willpower that has held me in good stead in my pursuit to live a happy, useful life. From this memory I have discovered the genesis of my 'doing' philosophy, which I will dwell upon later. I hope she is as proud of my epiphany as I am of its source.

Oh yes, a rarity, after due process, i.e. fanatic insistence, I did convince her to let me carry the unexpected fortune to her house. In so doing, it taxed me to such an extent, with many much needed stops for rest, that I wondered how she could have prevailed. That she would have prevailed, I did not doubt. But how, remains a mystery.

Back to my mother's childhood days in the village. Her formal schooling consisted of a second grade grammar school level. Educating daughters in the village at that time was not a high priority, rather, having an obsequious well-mannered daughter, was. Mother was a free spirited child. She did her duties, but also exhibited "tomboy" qualities. She showed no disrespect to her elders, still her zest for life did, on occasion, push the envelope of femininity. Suffice it to say the villager's love for the spirited Despina was second only to that of her proud parents Athena and Alex Kastanos.

Mother arrived in America early 1914 at the age of 19-20 years as the bride of an eminently successful entrepreneur in the community, Edison Nicholau. But finding herself in a foreign country complete with a foreign language and culture was overwhelming. To add to her despair she was expecting her first child, my oldest brother Nicholas, in the month of September 1914. Basking in the Greek culture, my father met his parental responsibilities when he rented a house for his wife and soon to be family, and made arrangements for the household monetary needs. My mother, God bless her, from that nucleus was expected to create a happy home. That is, do the necessary daily chores, go shopping for groceries and other essential household needs that a Hellenic husband expects. Now bear in mind, at that time Mother did not even know how to pronounce a meaningful English word let alone speak a sentence. Not to worry. Father and Mother's love for one another progressively overcame their dilemma. Dad arranged for a Greek employee of the restaurant, who spoke English, to go with my mother for her household shopping needs. Mother, on her own, by astute listening and with the guide of a Greek to English book, soon mastered English words to communicate enough to get by on her own, no longer needing assistance to get her through her daily obligations in America. And that is only the beginning.

Despo Kastanos Nicholau, My Mother

A year to the month, that is September 1915, my other brother Alexander was born. With limited space at the current living quarters located on the corner of 3rd and G Street in Marysville, Dad rented a more spacious home for his family; the one I referred to earlier, located on 2nd and E Street, over a bar in the lower business district of Marysville. It was conveniently located 2 blocks from the Columbia Café, making it handy for Dad to walk to and from work, as he could not drive a vehicle. Also, the location favored my mother when shopping for groceries and other needed household staples, as the stores were also in walking proximity. It was at this address my sister was born in 1917, and I was born in 1918.

My mother quickly acclimated to the community lifestyle by getting acquainted with several established Greek families in the area. One who befriended her was Lula Vallas, 9 years her junior, the single child of George and Aglaia Vallas. Ironically, Lula ended up being my mother in law 34 years later. What a small world in which we live. Lula attended the local convent school located on 7th Street and occasionally tutored my mother in the

English language. Although Mother was limited to two years of formal education in her native tongue, she displayed exceptional affinity for the English language. She was so proud to be in America, she made a pledge to herself that one day she would become an American citizen. In 1930, give or take a year, she successfully passed her citizenship test to bring her fondest American dream to fruition. By this time she was a 36 year old widow and the mother of four.

Let me put this into perspective. Envision a 36 year young widow with three sons and a daughter living over a bar in a rented home during the depths of the Great Depression, and you may begin to grasp the severity of her plight. She was a woman of strong character, who devoted her full attention and energy to the welfare of her children.

First off, she took in boarders. She would average 5 to 6 hours a day in her ¾ acre backyard planting, nursing, harvesting vegetables, and caring for her 2 fig trees, an orange tree and a lemon tree. Her yard commitment produced the main source of our daily vegetable diet. She also raised rabbits for another food source. She picked and canned peaches during the peach-harvesting season. She made her own jelly and jam, picked and cured several types of olives. She made yogurt and feta cheese from goat's milk. Of course you are already aware of her involvement in wine manufacturing, which saved her from having to buy table wine to go with her boarding meals. By doing all of the above, she was able to feed and clothe her family. (Governmental programs were not available at that point in time.)

But let us not stop there. This unique pioneer woman went a couple of steps further in her innovative self-supporting efforts. She learned to drive an automobile. She passed the drivers license test two years after the death of her husband. Necessity was the motivation for her automobile venture. None of her contemporary Greek women friends could drive a car and she wasn't about to ask their husbands for needed transportation. She knew a close elderly friend of her late husband, Louis Gianopoulos, who had a ranch and an old Oldsmobile touring automobile. She enquired if he would teach her how to drive a car at the ranch where there would be no traffic to contend with. He gladly consented to do so. Anytime Mr. Giannopoulos had to come into town for supplies he was welcomed at our dinner table, unannounced.

Mother never cooked a meal just for her family and known boarders. She always prepared enough food for unexpected company; company I facetiously add, appeared often enough to question the 'unexpected' classification. But that was the way it was with Mother. Her reputation as a great cook preceded her. The spontaneous guests were always welcomed. There were no set measurements or time requirements involved in her cooking. Ask her for a recipe and here is what you'd get: Three pinches of table salt, check for taste, heat water until the count of five with your finger in the pot, etc….just keep tasting for final product.

Mother, a pioneer woman of her time

Now that we have Mother's boarding house entrepreneurship documented let me add a mind-boggling edition to her list of uniqueness. It was not uncommon for hunting friends to share their game successes with Mother, knowing they would be invited to the table when she would cook the eligible birds of the particular hunting season; dove, quail, pheasant, ducks and geese. Also, cottontail rabbits during any part of the year. All of us kids, and Mom, developed a great appetite for the wild game birds and were disappointed when we encountered an unreasonable time lapse between game meals.

A dear family friend, Sam Theros

Sam Theros, and elderly countryman and a very close and trusted friend of my father and mother, who owned the bar over which we lived, was an excellent shot with the twelve gage shot gun. He could not drive a car. Accordingly, Mother would chauffer him on hunting days along with my two older brothers whom he had taught to shoot a shotgun. Mother became the official taxi for the three ardent hunters. Well, many were the times Mother would be sitting in, or waiting by, the parked car while the hunters cased a field for their prey, when an in-season bird, quail or dove, would escape from the hunters toward the car. Mother became frustrated seeing them fly by so close to her. Sure enough, before you knew it, she learned to shoot a shotgun and became good enough to shoot birds on the wing that flew within her range!! Another crutch eliminated from her dependency list. I want to impress those of you who should read my memoirs that the description of my mother is not only valid but unembellished.

In 1958 my mother passed over into heaven. Dessi then 8 years old, Dorre 7, Jamie 5, and even Terre at 3 years of age, I am certain, recall rare moments of bliss each of them shared with their "Yiayia". (Grandmother) Not yet born, Jorgi and Edie's recollections are garnered from stories they heard over the years about their grandmother, Despo.

Greek Pathos

I share this period of my life that you may have a more in-depth mental picture of my mother.

What I am about to write will be a difficult, but a worthy task. Thanks to my sister Athena, our family has a copy of a diary she kept, with chronicled entries of the pathos. The Greek Tragedy that I now reveal is documented as I remember it to be, 72 years ago.

The year was 1935 when my mother took a gargantuan step in her life to see to it that her children could experience first hand the environment of her youth, and in so doing, meet their grandmother, Athena, a widow, in her early 90's. The setting was Alagonia, Greece, a mountain village outside of Kalamata. My grandmother's exact date of birth was not known. My maternal grandfather, Alexander, was fatally knifed years earlier by a fellow villager at the village "cafenio" (coffee shop). It was the favorite hangout of the elderly in the "horio" (village) where card games were always in session. He was a witness to a game of cards when the participants got into a knock-down, drag-out fight. Grandfather Alexander, knowing both combatants, intervened to separate them when he was fatally wounded by a knife thrust under his heart by one of the antagonists. This event took place in the early 1930's. After that incident Mother made every effort to persuade her mother to come to America to live with us. Her efforts were to no avail. Grandma Athena, at that age, did not want to leave the lifetime village of her home.

So, in the summer of June 1935, after the schools were out for the summer, Mother gathered her 4 children into her Desoto touring automobile, and had a friend drive us to Roseville, a 40 mile jaunt, where we boarded a train headed for New York. In New York we booked a passage on the largest ocean liner in the world at that time, the Italian ship Rex. From New York it took over a week with a day stopover in Naples, Italy, before docking at Pireas, the port for Athens, Greece. After a couple of days in Athens, we boarded a train to take us to Kalamata. Of interest, when the train from Athens to Kalamata would encounter steep mountain terrain it would trudge along so slowly that my brothers and I would get off the train and trot or walk along side it for stretching exercise. That is how slowly the trains maneuvered the mountainous terrain in 1935!

**Me, Mother, Alexander, Athena and Nick
Around 1930**

While traveling from Kalamata to the 'horio' of Alagonia, a paved roadway, (and I use the word 'paved' advisedly) was only available half of the way. When the 'paved' roadway came to an end, we got off of the bus and onto donkeys for another one and one half hour adventure up and through mountainous terrain before reaching our final destination-- Alagonia—a pseudonym for "the end of civilization". Upon arriving at my mother's birthplace, she nonchalantly reached behind a wooden entrance gate of the premises to retrieve a key hidden from unwelcome transients. It must have been the villages best kept secret. For it had valiantly served its purpose for 21 years since Mom left the horio for America.

My Yiayia's home in Greece
Notice the "garage" below for the coveted donkey

The house, an American acronym for cabin, even in 1935, had no electricity. Light was supplied by candles and wick lanterns. No running water. Water had to be retrieved from the community village well. It featured a wood-burning stove, no glass windows, just openings covered with curtains and wooden shutters for privacy and protection from inclement weather. With one or two exceptions, that was the culture of the village homes.

There we were, a mother with a 17 year old daughter and 3 sons ranging in age from 15 years (myself, the youngest) to 20 years (Alexander), to 21 years, (Nicholas, the oldest). The whole family bedded down in a one-bedroom home (cabin) with none of the amenities we were accustomed to. All of this was accepted in good faith and with a complete understanding among the family.

The trip to date was exciting with interesting happenings along the way. However, here is where the story takes on a new life of tragic proportions. The third day at the village Mother came down with a high fever. It was frightening. A doctor from Kalamata was called upon to check her, and he diagnosed her with typhoid fever! He volunteered there was a mini epidemic at that time in Kalamata. The only medicine he prescribed—there were no antibiotics, penicillin or sulfa drugs available at that time—was a daily vitamin B injection as a nutritional supplement for the infected digestive tract, and damp towels on her forehead to relieve the high fever. Normally aspirin, being available at that time, would have been the ideal drug to reduce fever, but aspirin exacerbated the internal bleeding common in typhoid infection.

Nick, Athena, Me and Al in Greece, 1935

The disease is very contagious, being primarily transmitted from the unsanitary outhouse environment by flies. There were no sewer-engineered facilities in the village. Each household had its own "out house" over which the flies continually hovered, and bed netting was the sole relief from the flies. The nature of the disease consisted of up to 30 days of fever before relief was in sight. Typhoid attacks the digestive tract causing hemorrhages that can, due to the loss of blood, lead to death. When finally fever free, if you survived, you could expect another 30 days of rehabilitation before being strong enough to continue on in life. In Mother's case the fever was so sever that she hallucinated and didn't recognize any of us or where she was. With forced fluids and the vitamin B shots as her only nutrition, she lost 40 pounds at the end of her 30-day fever term.

However, on day 14, in the deepest throws of her illness, while still hallucinating, my oldest brother Nick came down with typhoid fever also. He likewise, due to a 105*-106* fever, hallucinated, but was very belligerent in his hallucinated state. He would not let the doctor near him with that long, dull needle for his vitamin B shots. He went from 180 pounds to 134 pounds at the end of his typhoid siege.

My brother, Nick

To further aggravate the situation, a week later, 21 days into Mother's fight for survival, my sister Athena came down with a high fever. At this point, brother Alexander said, "That's IT! I'm going to Kalamata and from there to Athens to make earlier arrangements for our return trip to America!" At that point I was still asymptomatic.

During brother Al's absence, Mother slowly regained her strength and would go to Nick's bed and place a damp towel on his forehead, before stumbling over to Athena's cot and do the same for her. I was still healthy and helped all I could with the chores around the house. The villagers avoided our house for fear of contracting typhoid. Little did they know that flies were the major culprits. Several inhabitants of the village did come down with the disease, but not with the severity with which it hit our family.

In the interim, the return ticket mission seemingly accomplished, brother Al was now on his way back from Athens to Kalamata when he, too, came down with a high fever. Upon reaching our Aunt Olga's house in Kalamata, the doctor advised him to rest there.

I painfully remember on September 21st, 1935, my sister Athena, at the age of 17, fell victim to the disease and passed over into heaven. My mother, my brother Nick and I were devastated. The thought of burying her only daughter, our only sister, in a simple wooden box, as was the custom in the village, so far away from our happy lives and home in America, was an unbelievable happening. Athena had just turned 17, graduated from Marysville High School, and was in the embryo of her womanhood years. I have no doubt that Mother only survived the ordeal solely due to her devotion and love of her surviving sons.

My beloved sister Athena, before her passing in 1935

Within days of Athena's death news arrived in the village that Al had a high fever with typhoid and was bedded at Aunt Olga's house in Kalamata. With brother Nick fever-free and fast regaining his strength, Mother's plan after Athena's traumatic burial, was to go immediately to Kalamata. But wouldn't you know it, I then came down with typhoid fever. Nevertheless, because my temperature was manageable, 102* just two days into my diagnosis, I was put on a donkey, and we left for Kalamata. While leaving the village behind was no problem, leaving Athena buried there was an insurmountable problem with no pragmatic alternative solution.

Upon arriving in Kalamata I was immediately placed into a hospital. With all that had transpired one would think things could not get any worse. Things could and they did. When each of us boys was born in America, my father innocently shared all of the birth certificate information with his father in Greece. My grandfather, in a proud braggadocio way, registered us in the village, too. Unbeknownst to us, we were in fact dual registered citizens of Greece and America! As such, in Greece we were eligible for military conscription at the age of 21. Brother Nick just turned 21 on September 22, 1935 during his rehabilitation. Sure enough, a letter to the village in his name was forwarded to Aunt Olga's home in Kalamata. He was to report for duty in the Greek Army within a week! Through complicated machinations and bribes, he was smuggled out of Greece and onto a ship, *traveling alone*, headed for America, thus successfully escaping service in the Greek Army.

Back in Kalamata, I would emphatically inquire how my brother Al was doing during my Mother's daily visits in the hospital. My mother would reply, "He is doing fine. You get well." That was comforting to hear. Until one day the nurse visited me right after Mother left the room for a moment and said, "Please do not keep asking your mother how your brother is doing, He passed over into Heaven several days ago." September 30th, 1935; eight days after my sister Athena succumbed to typhoid. The nurse further volunteered that after each visit with me, Mom would break down completely and was frightened that I, too, would not make it.

That did it! I got out of bed that very day, dressed myself, and when Mother came, I was up and about and said, "Mom, let's go home."

She had already buried Al up in the village beside Athena.

**My beloved brother Al
Before passing into heaven in 1935**

As hard as this tragedy was on our family, I cannot fathom the pain that my grandmother Athena endured at the loss of her granddaughter and her grandson, all the while witnessing the devastating grief of her only child, Despo.

It is at this time I wish to share with you my memory of Gabriel~ an unbelievable ally. He was born and reared through his junior year in the horio, Alagonia. He spent one year in Kalamata and from there, enrolled at Athens University where he earned a degree in teaching. Gabriel was indispensable during this staggering episode that befell us while in Greece. He met my sister Athena when we first arrived in Kalamata, and they hit it off really well. When Athena died, he was absolutely devastated. He was in love with Athena and I believe my sister loved him.

Gabriel took care of all the details for my brother Al's burial beside my sister's grave in the village of Alagonia. He also managed all of the travel arrangements necessary to get Mother and me passage from Pireas onto the Italian liner Conte de Savoiya, which my brother Al had arranged back to New York before he fell ill and passed over into heaven.

I did not realize that Gabriel and my sister were in love during our 1935 trip to Greece. It was not until 60 years later, when my brother Nick was going through an old trunk of keepsakes in his garage in Lincoln, California. It was at that time Nick found Athena's diary, which up until then, we did not know existed. You see, my sister Athena kept a timeline of all happenings in her personal diary from the day we departed from Marysville for Greece, beginning Saturday, June 8th, 1935, through September 4th, 1935. On September 5th, when she fell ill, the pages in the diary went blank through September 20th. She passed away on September 21st. On September 21st the writings continued, only not in Athena's hand. Gabriel assumed the insurmountable task of finishing Athena's diary after she died. The handwriting in the diary changes abruptly and as it does, the heartache is palpable. Quoting from his writings, "God knows how I am able to state these things when firey tears roll down and blur my vision onto my cheeks, and great sobs up-heave my chest." He goes on, "She would stay with me all afternoon teasing and joking......""But how was I so blind to love......"

The diary~ in Gabriel's hand~ relived the tragic pathos leading to Athena's demise from Sept. 5 through Sept. 20 and continued describing Al's death, until Mother and I departed for America. I am including excerpts from Athena's Diary as written by Gabriel, so that from his heartbreaking account of the Greek Tragedy, which happened to me and my family, you may better understand this devastating period in 1935.

Athena's Diary

**As recounted by Gabriel Panagopoulo
1935**

The blank page and leaves before me conceal one of the world's greatest silent dramas played in this far-off corner of Alagonia and Kalamata, Greece.

Our heart is near breaking from sorrow, and grief rends us incapable of even thinking of how this tragedy occurred. God knows how I am able to state these things when fiery tears roll down and burn my cheeks, and great sobs upheave my chest.

I will use this part of the diary to state things that happened while the blank pages passed. It is rather a terrible play of fate against human beings. Unluckiness and fatality reached the most miserable extent dealing incredible blows and rendering our hearts unhealingly wounded.

My father first informed us of the arrival of a family of his great friend and relative Edison Nicholau consisting of a mother, a daughter, and three boys. After a few days I met the boys at a shop of an uncle of theirs. We had a keen time for I had a lot of time to see a person from America and to speak English with them.

Afterwards I met their sister Athena, and believe me I sure did like her. Meanwhile her Mother had fallen sick and I was not able to see her.

The days rolled on with a stillness that penetrated the heart. More than once did I propose to the boys to go up and see our beautiful mountains. But always a sad shaking of the head referring to Mother's condition, was the answer. Only once did I succeed when we had the boys and the girl up for the whole day. We had dinner together and passed a delightful afternoon with some music by my family orchestra. After dinner we went and sat in a bed rigged up between two trees. A cool breeze came from below while the trees murmured a song of happiness and content.

Nick, Al, and George and my brothers started a stone throwing contest besides matching their wits with jokes and teases. I climbed up on the bed and Athena came up after me. We had a delightful little chat with an eyeful of the scenery. Our conversation slipped lightly from subject to subject. Time literally flew. Her general bearing impressed me greatly. She seemed to have exactly what I admire in women. Besides beauty she had good manners, smiling complexion, good nature, and humorous talking. Her auburn luxuriant hair crowned majestically the noble features of her regal head.

Later we went down to the chief part of the village where the Nicholau dwelling was. Their Mother's illness was serious. Owing to Mother's illness, the children were usually out in coffee shops. After playing some cards, we went to recline and rest a while. Al joked a little but worry got the best of him.

About the end of July Mother was on the way of recovery. At the end of the month I went up to see their Mother and to my surprise found everybody ill. Nick and Al were in bed. Athena and George seemed lighter, but they too were weak. The next day Nick was the same and the others improved. Doc said that Nick had typhoid fever and the others had too much fig eating.

Mother could only stagger when she got up after Nick. She was dizzy too and not able to think well on account of the accursed illness. This happened in the first days of August. Al looked worried more and more after the new blow but he tried his best to look after the property. His Grandmother's brother and he starting selling property here in auctions. This proved a trying affair for Mother because everybody wanted to have the estates without paying anything for them. The auction being turmoil, finally all the relatives stopped coming to the house, and Mother and children, sick or not, were left by themselves.

This tragedy now reaches it's full height. The family all alone in a strange part of the world and nearly all things missing even the necessities. The rest of the children suffering from bad food, worse sleep, and worry. The Mother hardly being able to stand, herself. You should see the kids bodies black and blue with insect bites that would keep them awake at night. They scratched themselves so much that the irritated skin produced large sores which would often bleed.

Politics had a finger in the modern Greek plague. The Greek relatives favored one of the two doctors here; the worst and least experienced. He would come in, touch nothing, say nothing, and do nothing. He was afraid of catching the disease. The only thing he would do is give a hypodermic without touching the patient's skin, and then wash his hands thoroughly, and then order someone to open the door for him. The other doctor was much more skilled but the Greek relatives did not want him. Once he came and there was a riot between the relatives. Nick hated the doctor and did not hold back his feelings on a too direct way either. Why, even when he gave a hypo, his needles would bend and tear the skin. Thus passed all of August.

Nothing else happened again this month except when I tried to take Athena for a picnic twice. She could not come because the poor girl was so busy with Nick's illness. Only when I went down every afternoon, we would go into an adjoining room while Mother tended to Nick and we would have a delightful chat on different subjects. She would stay all afternoon with me, teasing and joking and lying on the couch besides. Ah, how was I so blind? It was love. My thoughts wander back to that beautiful past, and my heart aches and yearns for the return of that superb and too good to be real dream. I never heard a complaint from her ever smiling, beautiful little mouth. Her patience was inexhaustible.

By the end of the month Nick showed steady signs of recovery but still things were difficult because there wasn't the proper food to give him. Besides that he had delirium from weakness and Nick was completely out of his head. He had to be guarded every hour and moment because he would all of the sudden jump out of bed and wreck himself on the floor. Hence, new sleepless nights for Al and Athena. When Nick's condition was better, however, Al made a trip to Athens in order to fix tickets and renew their papers that had expired, for their return passage home.

The next day, Thursday, I came down as usual, to find my Athena in bed. That day was the first day of the blank pages of her diary. And I, who am now with great chagrin, filling in, and who was a complete stranger when the family first started from Marysville, California. I brought a young army doctor friend of mine to see Nick. He assured us that Nick would be O.K., but when he looked at Athena, he told us she had typhoid. That was a shock to poor Mother and to me. Now you can imagine Mother's position. Nick was still out of his head, and Athena in bed. Little George was left to her. Al was in Athens. No relatives because all were not satisfied with the property dealing. A bum doctor. No house, no bed, or any other furniture, nothing but sickness. Lastly, milk was not to be found so I was obliged to bring some down every morning.

Athena's fever climbed abruptly. This made her quiet, though she was always very patient. Her captivating smile and her sweet but fainter than usual voice held me a prisoner at her bedside as

I'm now of her memory. One could hardly think that fate was so generous to me only to show me how cruel it could change. I was told she called for me when I was absent. It is so dreadful.

Meanwhile the days rolled on and we expected she would take Nick and her Mother's course. Nick was still out of his head. Georgie was obliged to stay always indoors, and especially to keep the flies away. I was the only one to substitute him and thus give him a little rest. I could sit at her bedside forever. She would see me and always give me that bewitching smile and whisper me something wonderful. That was heavenly harmony.

The doctor would come and shove the hypodermic needle. The needle would bend and curve. Her limbs showed great black spots of the hypo and pained her very much. The doctor never took the cigarette from his mouth, even when it burned him. He was so afraid to take disease by contamination. A beast and not a doctor.

Her Mother would always worry. More than once did she express her fear of death. Sentiment and her great love to her offspring had the same effect when Nick was ill too. A terrified, grief-stricken Mother would beg assistance of anyone entering. She literally did not know what to do. Few entered and still fewer would assist.

Our beloved Athena was a week in bed when we were informed that poor Al had the same thing in Kalamata. My pen is unable to express the tragic situation. New pangs of grief and uneasiness tore the heart of the Mother. Everything that could participate in unhappiness and sorrow had done so. Yet the worse was still to come.

Our dearest Athena was in bed 10 days when her Mother, terrified, showed me blood in her bed sheets. The doctor saw the bleeding and said nothing, as usual. Now something strange happened. The doctor called to Kalamata for another doctor's advice. The telephone message was received by a relative who didn't show up at all. The blood did not stop.

She seemed in another world. I sat by her for hours keeping the flies away. She glanced at a ring on my left hand, looked at it, then took it off my hand, putting it on hers, looked at it, raised her hand and smiled at the ring and then at me. My dear Athena, anything that is true and beautiful, anything that has value in nature, sparkled there before in the depth of your eyes.

Next day, Saturday the 21st, a day that I will never forget. I entered the room, my treasure recognized me with a smile and proceeded to tell me something. But she only succeeded in letting out an inaudible whisper while she desperately waved her hand. I was just then aware that I was losing what one's soul most desired. Athena was breathing heavily. My heart was beating like a hammer. I was waiting for a hope when I knew that there was none
 I took Nick, who was still sick, out to the next room, rigged a bed and placed him by George's side who was also sick. There I kept the poor boy company and told exactly how things were. He said, "Oh Gabriel, I think she's gonna pull through." "Me too, George."

. Then the doctor came and reached for her pulse, then dropped her hand. My head dropped. Everything was lost. Sorrow wrapped our hearts in it's cruel frosty grip. There was Mother, standing calm, inarticulate. A Mother's pain was right on her face, her eyes were fixed. Then Mother said, "I know doctor. My daughter is dead." I can't recall things in that dark hour, the darkest of my life. I caught Athena's hand and pressed it with mine, which this moment is now trembling, against my lips, and said, "Athena" was all I could say.

Profane hands grabbed me and they took me away from her. Away from my angel who was in heaven now. Away from the dearest thing to me on earth. Just then I noticed others holding

Mother for the poor lady had lost her mind. She would have killed herself if she was alone.

I could hardly stand my heart beating wildly. I did not know what to do. I entered the boy's room. Georgie in spite of his fever was sitting up. "Did she pass away?" he asked. I nodded my head gravely and answered, "Courage Georgie". "You need it", came back the answer, "'Cause Athena cared for you." Dazed as I was I did not get the meaning quickly. But slowly light came in my eyes. How blind I was before. Death revealed the greatest sentiment before me. Then everything, everything, every word, every event, and every joke. Smiling and teasings passed before my eyes rapidly like a motion picture. George's hand rested lightly on my shoulder brought me back to reality. Tears were in his eyes. Nick in the meantime awoke, realized the situation, but was unable to think. Truly both boys didn't sleep that night.

Athena was sleeping so beautifully that I tiptoed so to disturb her not. But she rested nonetheless. The wondrous soul had escaped.

Mother, poor dear Mother in an adjoining small room accompanied by some other women wept silently, as becoming a lady who knew that she had other sick children also.

Morning. They had laid her in the meantime in a rude coffin made of plain boards fixed together by a white cloth covering them. They had placed on her head an orange blossom garland and a bridal veil as is the custom when a virgin dies here.

I went and sat with the boys to keep them company. And all around was so gloomy. At least I had somebody to talk to who understood and knew me well. I tried to console them as much as I needed it myself. Once in a while a mourner would let loose and a piercing shriek went through the air. This resulted more than once in Mother's fainting. One time I had a hard time reviving her.

About 2:30 came the preacher. Everybody crowded in. I couldn't stand it and went back into the boy's room. After half an hour they took her out. The coffin passed in front of the boy's door and poor things, they sat up in bed and stretched their necks just to get a last glimpse. Pitiful looks. Georgie stammered, "It's bad enough she died, we can't even go to her funeral." I said, "I'll go George. My brother will stay and keep you company while I take care of your Mother." I then went.

Slowly and steadily the procession marched on as deeper we sank in our sorrow. My Athena, I can't believe it. Oh please somebody wake me from this horrible dream. I went by Mothers side and caught her by the hand and tried to comfort her. But no word could come out of my mouth. She looked up at me, a Saint in passion and a weary face.

Athena, soul of my soul, heart of my heart, smile once more your heavenly smile. My heart is broken. I took Mother by the hand so that she could give her only daughter her last farewell kiss. She bent over crying. Tears filled her eyes and fell on the still, pale skin. Parting forever. I bent and looked at her, nodded my head and whispered, "Good night Athena". Why? I don't know. Maybe I repeated what I had done other nights leaving her in bed. I kissed the cold lips....our first and last kiss.... Half an hour later I was standing alone by a long, round pile of sand.

Next day, Monday, The Mother and boy left for Kalamata. The reason was Al was sick down there with the same disease. After two days my family left for Kalamata too. I went down to the house of the sister-in-law of Mother where Al was confined since he returned from Athens. Alas! Things were bad too. Fate was again scratching bleeding wounds. Al's condition was serious. He seemed like he recognized me but could not utter a word. A trembled shaking of his hands and an abrupt jerking were his usual movements. I stood by Al's side a few moments and then marched across the room where Georgie was confined. The poor fellow had a high fever, all his feelings were working alright. He was glad to see me. He was good and scared by Al's fever and sufferings. Mother was there too, "I knew you would come" she said, but quickly sorrow and a new fear swept her face. Poor Mother.

As for Georgie, he was taken to the hospital. Mother objected. One child near death, and another being taken to a hospital, while there was one lying in the cemetery since a few days ago. Now you can imagine poor Mother's plight. My pen is unable to state even a fraction of what really was going on.

Mother insisted that I take Nick down to see Al for the last time. Nick was slowly recovering at a cousin's house. He was able, by this time to take a small walk around. The brother's meeting was really dramatic. It looked like Al recognized him with certain movements, while Nick bent by his bedside asked him tenderly. It was a strain for both.

The next day I was outside in the boxe (garden) when a little girl came running along the lane, "O Aleko pethane!" (Al died, is what she blurted.) It was a shock. A great shock. Poor Al, he didn't know of his sister's death. The attending relatives told us that he was fine until the night of Athena's doom. Athena would say during her illness, "I'm going wherever Al goes." She repeated it often. And so it happened, only Al followed her.

I found Mother crying with some other ladies. I don't remember what she exactly told me. I went into Al's room. The trembling had stopped. His eyes had a very pitiful look. I grasped his hand. He was cold with a pale color to it, and the fingernails were blackened already and bled also. Al, Al, speak to me! In the splendour of youth, and in the prime of your beauty, you left.

I had to think quick. I wanted him to keep company to our little Athena so she wouldn't be lonely up there in the mountain. By 4 o'clock our automobiles were ready. We stopped near the place where Nick was and he came and gave a last look. Mother succeeded in smiling for Nick's sake. He was unable to come up.

We had a hard time getting Mother up. She occasionally fainted on mule back.

It was dark when we reached Alagonia. Now came the real mourning. These things tolled on Mother and I was greatly in fear of her life. I tried to console her. At 9 o'clock the next morning the funeral started. Same march as 10 days ago. Same people, same church, same hill. And last, same graveyard next to a newly made grave.

Now Athena, you are satisfied. You have found wonderful company in these lonely spots. The olive trees above will shade you both now, while whispering breezes amoung their leaves will tell you how much we loved you.

Farewell. Farewell.

Your memory shall abide with us forever and ever. Someday we will all meet and rejoice again in worlds above.

Farewell.

This closes the book of affection.
The album of beauty and truth.
This closes the casket.
Collection of gems that were gathered in youth.
The tree of happiness is felled.
Ne'er again shall it bloom.
Underneath it our love had swelled.
A beautiful flower has met it's doom.

Gabriel Panagopoulo, 1935

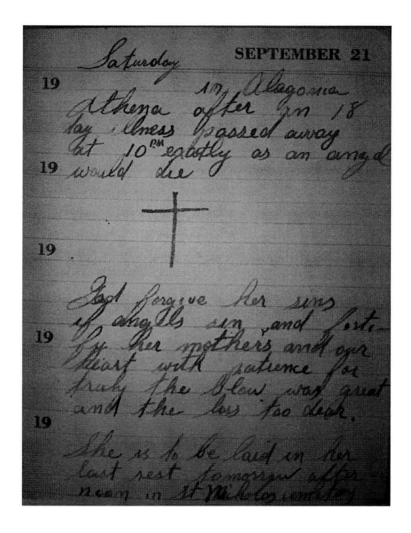

**Athena's Diary, written in Gabriel's hand
the day Athena passed away**

The passage back to California was a living nightmare. Many a night on board the ship, and for months later, I slept in the same room as my mother, and at intervals I would slap my face hard to stay awake in order to keep telling her stories, making up some, just to lure Mother into sleep and out of her fathomless sorrow. She kept crying when awake at night. Her uncontrollable grief was interspersed with "I killed my children! Why did I take them from America to bury them in Greece? Why?? Why?" Over and over this would be her idiolect "meriloyo" (mourning). (As grief-stricken as I was at the time, only upon my own daughter, Jorgi's passing over into Heaven many years later, did I truly grasp a fraction of the pain of Mother's grief.)

I share with you the graphic tragedy of our 1935 Greek excursion that you may more appreciate my mother's true heartfelt commitment to her faith. Many were the times I would spot Mother on her knees genuflecting to the floor in deep prayer seeking forgiveness and asking for HIS blessings. Mother's prayers always sought help from God in the rearing of her 2 surviving sons. With all the tragedy in her life she did not lose faith in God. Her true faith, in spite of her staggering ill-fortune, served as an example to my brother Nick and me. Her strength and determination were unparalleled.

While I am painting a picture of rehabilitation on Mother's part, do not be misled. Many a time, post World War II, 9 to 10 years later, after I would close my pharmacy for the day, I would head by my mother's house for a quick visit before setting out for my home in East Marysville. At times I would find her sitting in the darkness of the room off the kitchen rocking back and forth in her rocking chair and "meroloyoing" (chanting, mourning) endlessly over and over about her daughter and son's burial in Greece. Over and over rocking, she would sobbingly repeat, "What have I done? I led my son and daughter to their death."

When she heard me coming up the stairs she tried to change her mood, but in many instances to no avail. I would stay long enough for her to promise me she was OK and would not continue in her grief. I tried to believe her, yet I wonder if she could regain her composure. All I know is, most of the time she was a pillar of strength and lived for her two remaining sons, their wives, and her grandchildren.

Mother, like her mother, refused to move into my brother's or into my family home. She did not want to leave her house and garden. She would time and time again relive her happy memories with her husband and four children within that household. However, she did finally relent and bought a home on East 24th Street, a short block from our 228 East 25th Street home in Marysville. But as faith would have it, she suffered a fatal heart attack before taking a step into her 24th Street home. Her last breath of life was taken at Rideout Hospital on February 10th, 1958, with her home registered address 132 E Street, Marysville, California, where the walls inexplicably triggered her memory bank with cherished and treasured sounds that can only be composed by a happy, energetic, youthful family running about the home with carefree abandon, and where infinite love prevailed.

In a memorial tribute, in 1985, my wife Gaye and I went to Greece and we visited Alagonia. We went to Al's and Athena's burial site, but there was no sign of a wooden casket or burial marker to be seen. The culture then was, after due time, to exhume the bodies and study the bones of the deceased to determine if he or she went to Heaven. I do not know if that was the case. I only know the cemetery no longer existed. The Alagonia home was deteriorating, but you could still see the home as it stood in 1935. And yes, the key to the protective gate was still in its 'hidden place'.

PART TWO

The Young Adult Years

The Virtuoso

    As a youngster my mother encouraged me during my eighth grade year to take violin lessons at our grammar school. She was impressed with one of her tenants, Mr. Cosmopoulos, who would play his violin daily in his room.   Please envision a high-strung athletic kid, now 14 years old, who excelled in sandlot football games and as a catcher in baseball, with calloused hands and bruised knuckles, being saddled with a delicate instrument like a violin. If you can envision that, you will only begin to share my frustration, and I might add embarrassment, among my peers. Having no choice in the matter I relented, knowing Stradivarius himself would not want a boy to disobey his mother, and would forgive me for the ignominy I would reign upon a true violinist's virtuosity. Besides, an alternative was not an option. Mother's suggestions were stealthy metaphors to 'volunteer'! OK?!

Upon entering as a freshman at Marysville High School I was programmed to continue my 'volunteered' violin experiences by enrolling in Mr. VanCourtright's orchestra class. His reputation throughout the state as an accomplished musician and especially as an orchestra conductor was prominent. The number of accomplished violin musicians enrolled at Marysville High was not in such abundance that it was necessary to audition to be accepted into the orchestra. A glaring flaw in the program, as you will soon witness. Ergo, enter George Nicholau as second violinist in the prestigious MHS Orchestra under the renowned conductor Maestro VanCourtright. If it sounds braggadocio on my behalf, it is meant to be. However, as the saying goes, 'you can fool some of the people some of the time....' To my dismay, Mr. VanCourtright was not fooled by George Nicholau's suspect musical talent. I began to realize my shortcomings as Mr. VanCourtright would always tune my violin and direct all of the other members of the string sections to tune their instruments to mine. Why always my violin? A Stradivarius it was not. Isn't it odd that the last to suspect aural incompetence is the culprit himself? Here is how I got the message, loud and screechingly clear.

Before I arrived at the school's auditorium for our final rehearsal in preparation for a community concert, Mr. VanCourtright had informed each and every musician in the orchestra, with the exception of me, that when we came upon a particular part in the "Eggmont Overture" not one orchestra member, regardless of instrument, was to respond to his fortissimo baton theatrical cue which he would give after a short pause that was written in the sheet music. Not one peep, mind you. After I arrived and settled in my seat, the rehearsal began. The moment arrived in the music score during this last practice session, and sure enough, total silence, with the exception of a loud energetic off key screeching sound emitted from my 'Stradivarius' responding to Mr. VanCourtright's fortissimo baton. The spontaneous laughter from my peers exploding off the empty auditorium walls was deafening. Especially to my ears. Now this may be hard to believe, but believe it. I have no doubt that my spontaneous belated enjoining laughter led the whole orchestra, for once, in a synergistic mode that complimented my participation (finally) in a hilarious outstanding rendition of the MHS orchestra under the highly renowned conductor Mr. VanCourtright.

When the mirthful disruption played itself out, Mr. VanCourtright looked at me and said, "George, you portray the greatest image of a virtuoso violinist I have ever known. Your form is faultless, your bow movement is right on. You are a *visual* virtuosic asset to the orchestra. Now if I can only convince you to keep the bow off the strings of your violin, you will not only earn an A, and my deep reverence, but the esteem and gratitude of your fellow musicians."

Always fearful there be an encore of my fellow musicians' "silence prank", I heartedly complied, thus earning my A and donating my violin years later to my daughter Jamie, who did justice by it.

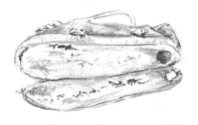

High School Shenanigans

I am now flooded with high school escapade memories. Like the time we had a high school fire drill exercise. The format was for the fire alarms throughout the buildings to be sounded and the teachers to be responsible for a disciplined student exit from the classroom to an outside area safely away from the buildings. The school bells would ring again at the conclusion of the fire drill where upon the students would go, in an orderly fashion, back to their respective classrooms.

    Simple enough. But the impetuous George Nicholau so enjoyed the outdoor liberty, that a good ten minutes *after* the class had reassembled, he came marching into his seat. The teacher, Miss O'Brien asked, "George, why are you so late getting back to class?" The self-designated comedian replied,
"Miss O'Brien, smoke got into my eyes and I lost my way."

    "George", she replied, "report to the principals office at once. I trust you can find your way now that the air is clear." Touche!

    To the office I went and reported to Mr. Pedro Osuna, our principal at the time. He sent me to the library and instructed me to write on a tablet that stated, "I am sorry and I will not misbehave again."

    "George, you keep writing that sentence until I personally excuse you."

    Being guilty as charged, there was no hesitation on my part. This fire drill occurred in the afternoon starting at 2pm. At 2:30pm I was in the library doing my penance and by 4:30pm I had several pages filled with my assignment. And yet, no Mr. Osuna. At that time the librarian came to me and informed me that he was locking up for the day and that I needed to leave. To which I replied, "I'm sorry, but I was clearly instructed not to quit writing until Mr. Osuna personally tells me to." With that reply, the librarian left and locked the doors behind him, with me still safely inside, diligently continuing my assignment.

    Around 5:30pm the janitor shows up and wants to know why I'm still in the library. I told him the same thing, "I cannot leave until Mr. Osuna tells me to."

    He went directly to the phone and called the principal at his home. Ten minutes later in comes Mr. Osuna, extremely apologetic, saying he forgot all about me and that he felt so very sorry.

I replied, "I don't blame you. I deserved the full extent of my punishment."

He felt so badly, he asked me if I needed a ride home, to which I replied, "No thanks." But I did say that I sure would appreciate a ride to the Appeal Democrat office to get my papers for the day, because the office was just about to close at 6:00 o'clock.

From that day forth I was one of his favorite students. Just goes to show you, if you do a wrong, pay the price and heed your lesson. All is well that ends well.

During my senior year I was elected student body president, and my innate impetuosity sprung into life at the end of the celebratory victory speech. As their newly elected student body president, the first order I gave (at 2pm) at the end of the official inauguration ceremony held in the auditorium to the entire MHS student body (the school day ending would be at the usual 3:20pm) was to announce to all present to take the rest of the day off.

They all exploded with a "Hooraaaaaaaaaay!!!" and headed for the exists of the auditorium, when Mr. Dawson, our new principal (Mr. Osuna became the President of Yuba College) grabbed the microphone from me and had everyone return to their seats immediately. Then he dismissed all assembled directing them to return to their respective classes. Turning toward me, he said, "George you are president of the students, not principal of the high school. Another stunt like that and you will be impeached. Understand?"

"Understood."

I had a feeling he got as big a kick out of my gesture as I did, but didn't want to acknowledge it. It is imperative that I make one thing clear. Though I was a spirited student, I was never, and I emphasize never, disrespectful to any of my teachers or administrators. Each of them liked me, but since keeping discipline in the classroom was sovereign, my disruptions had to be addressed.

For The Love of the Game

    I confess the critical motivation that propelled me from high school onto college was not academia based. It was athletics. As a freshman high school student, I was a remedial intellect at best. In grammar school I always showed up physically. Mentally I was preoccupied with sports from as far back as I can remember. I never mastered the art of studying. My mother was so preoccupied with making ends meet financially, she assumed, like my sisters and brothers, that I also was a good student. In those days there were no midterm report cards sent to the parents. Those were the days. At the end of the school year you were rewarded with a promotion card onto your next grade if you passed, or were held back if you failed. In my case, because of my age, having started kindergarten at age 6, which was later than usual, I was yearly passed on a probation status. That is, on trial, to see if I could cut it at the next level in the first three weeks of classes. If not, I would be expected to revert back to my previous school year class. Somehow through daily class exposure, for I never did prepare homework for the next day's class, I learned to bluff my way through. From the seventh grade into eighth grade I am ashamed to admit my age factor was the tipping point into the next grade. And so it came to pass through "seniority", I graduated into high school.

    It didn't take long to realize that this behavior was not going to cut it on the high school level. The D's emblazoned my freshman year report card. However, my athletic smartness excelled. Now the academic challenge presented to me was that I had to earn a minimum C- average grade to continue to be eligible for sports. For the first time in my formal education experience my books rated a high priority.

    In my sophomore year, my athletic virility kept earning high recognition and my grades improved to a C average. I was elated, as was my football, basketball, and baseball coach, Mr. Glenn Potter. Mr. Potter coached all three sports with a great track record. For me the plot thickened. I made a self-imposed athletic goal: to earn a scholarship to the University of California at Berkeley in football, the sport I excelled in most. I loved the game so much I thought life would end if I could not compete on the college level. And that is not an overstatement.

Me, in high school, playing the game I loved

The problem in my mind in obtaining my goal was not on the gridiron. It was in the classroom. To be eligible to enter UC Berkeley, a student had to earn a minimum B average in college preparatory subjects, i.e. math, foreign language, English, geography and history. That format, in itself was cause for panic.

The first thing I did was to let each of my teachers know I had to earn at least a B in their class. In addition, I would do whatever it would take if they in turn would go that extra mile to help me. I promised I would study hard, but if I needed tutoring on the side, would they be willing to assist me? To the teacher, they said they would, provided they were assured that I was studying hard. And thus an agreement was reached. However, I found out right off the bat that I did not know how to study. I tried to memorize assignments and that seemed impossible. A good friend of mine, Ted Efstratis, was an A student in high school. He agreed to help me if I would study at his home in the evenings after I finished my sport commitment practice. No problem. I must say he did teach me disciplined study habits and I am so grateful to Ted for his invaluable assistance in my hour of need.

 I would be derelict if I did not recall the time Ted and I were clowning during a study period at his home. His father warned us twice to settle down and concentrate on our lessons. On the third disruption his dad rose from his chair and came running toward Ted with a switch as Ted ran through the outside door to his backyard. I obviously was long gone out the front door the moment Mr. Efstratis rose from his chair. My understanding from Ted is that he waited a long time before re-entering the house and thus avoided the sting of a switch. The lesson learned by both of us deterred us from any further nonsense during our study hour at the Efstratis home.

 Notice I wrote the "Efstratis home" in that last sentence.

 Because his folks were going to entertain this particular evening, Ted and I decided to study at my house. It so happened Mother was not at home that evening and we were alone studying when I suggested we take a break. During the break I decided what we needed was a glass of retsina wine to rejuvenate ourselves. Ted concurred. From the refrigerator I got the bottle of table wine, and we each had a glass of wine. It served its purpose admirably. We were so rejuvenated we decided a second glass would prove great therapy. And that it did. So we decided to prolong the therapeutic effect with one more glass of wine. The problem being there was no last glass of wine in the decanter. So off I went to the barrel source of the wine. Drew out a glass for each of us and down it went. Also, down Ted went a half hour later. His head settled motionless on the book before him. Knowing Mom was due home any moment, I helped Ted onto his feet and down the 22 steps to the sidewalk where I accompanied him up and down the street until he was sober enough to drive home. That was the first and the last of our 'spirited' study periods.

Distractions notwithstanding, the bottom line was, with Ted's help and my teacher's empathy I earned all B's in my junior year. My senior year I was doing likewise but for one subject, Latin. Miss Decent, my Latin teacher, agreed to assign special homework for me to earn a B- in order for me to qualify for the University of California Berkeley entrance standards. Because of her benevolence towards me, I qualified academically, and was accepted to UC Berkeley in the fall of 1938.

My journey to Cal was made financially possible through a promised football scholarship from Cal's head coach, Stubb Allison, when he visited Marysville High School during his recruiting tour. In those days, a scholarship was akin to assistance, which was doled out in good paying job assignments to recruited athletes which would cover a good portion of their expenses. No free tuition, books, or room and board were awarded then, as they are now. In my case being awarded a 'promised' scholarship was worth noting. The quote of 'promised' is by design. The blow-by-blow tribulations of my introduction to the University of California in general, and into the football program in particular, were a happening that merits recounting.

I emphasize how through football was born the genealogy of "Doing" in my pursuit of living a happy, useful, successful life!

Narrative 1

Welcome to Cal!

    In the fall of 1938 I arrived on UC Berkeley campus a naïve, innocent 160 lb lineman who would play in the first college football game he ever *saw*! There was no TV in 1938. Just radio. As a young boy I grew up with my ears tuned to the college football broadcasts. My ambition was to become a player in a college football broadcast. I would find myself daydreaming key tackles, runs, blocks, etc., that would win the game. My aspirations for stardom were encouraged through my participation in high school football. While playing at MHS I made all conference as a guard my Jr. year, and as a full back my Sr. year. There was no doubt in my mind that I could play at the college level given the opportunity. My high school coach, Glen Potter, contacted Stub Allison, the head coach at UC Berkeley and told him he had a fellow that he should consider as a serious prospect for a football scholarship. Coach Allison was making a recruiting pass through Northern California and Coach Potter introduced me to him. Coach Allison invited me to consider UCB as my school of choice, implying I would receive financial aide. This incident took place in 1938 during the spring of my senior year. I mention the time as it becomes a factor in the ensuing fall months upon my enrollment at UC. I remember the details as it were yesterday, and I will always be grateful for the turn of events.

    The 1938 World's Fair was on Treasure Island and my brother Nicholas and my mother were to drop me off at the University on their way to the fair. Around 4:30 p.m. I was dropped off at Sather Gate, the south entrance to the campus, and begged Mom not to bother to stop by on her way home. I told her the coach would have everything worked out for me and I didn't want her to embarrass me. So I said goodbye, took my suitcase and walked through Sather Gate, and headed up toward the Campanile to the coaches' offices.

My heart was thumping hard at the time for I knew not what to expect. I remember having $10.00 spending money in my pocket for food and incidentals if necessary. When I opened the door to the coaches' quarters I saw several other athletes lounging around in jeans and like casual clothes. Boy, was I chagrined in my J.C. Penny's suit (with a belted jacket no less) and a tie, and that tell-tale suitcase! Not knowing how to act or react I just maneuvered into a corner and waited for someone from the staff to greet me. No one paid much attention to me, other than an occasional look from the other athletes. I assumed they thought I was a sports equipment salesman, considering my dress code and suitcase.

Finally, after what seemed like and eon, an assistant coach did approach me and asked if he could be of any help. I replied, "Coach Allison told me if I came to UC he would grant me a scholarship to cover my expenses." He asked me to wait a moment and he would introduce me to Mr. Allison. Upon meeting Coach Allison, he asked for my name and where I was from. I told him and he asked what position I played. I told him right guard. He sized me up with skepticism and perfunctorily said he was very busy at this time, and to please come back tomorrow.

I thanked him, picked up my suitcase and left the building. Now I must tell you there is Someone up there who was looking over me. Believe it. For here I was, with $10 in my pocket, first time out of Marysville on my own and not knowing where I would sleep that night. Well as luck (faith) would have it, I ran into Bill Blevins, a hometown buddy of mine that had received a crew scholarship the year before. He asked me if the coaches put me up for the night, and upon hearing that they hadn't he insisted I stay with him. No argument from me.

The next day, I went back to the coach's office expecting to be given a job that would cover my room and board expenses. After a long wait I was again ushered into Coach Allison's office. Again he asked for my name and what he could do for me. I reminded him that he invited me to come to Cal and that he would see to it that I received a scholarship in the way of work (that is how it was done in those days) that would cover my expenses. He fidgeted and responded that he had other commitments and asked me to come back later that evening. I left his office with real concern for my survival at Cal with only $10 in pocket and no arrangement for room and board. I went to the house where Bill Blevins roomed and asked the landlord if there was a room available that I could rent and what the rent would be. He told me there was none—unless I would consider sleeping in the attic on a cot bed. I asked how much and was told only $10/month if I wanted that set up. That settled, on my own I started making the rounds to all of the sororities and fraternities around campus, seeking a hashing job for meals. Just when I thought I would not succeed I was offered a hash job at a fraternity for evening meals. I jumped at it. Now I had a place to sleep and a daily meal.

It was now around 5 P.M. and I went back to the coach's office. After an eternal wait, an audience with Coach Allison ensued. Again, "What did you say your name was?" I told him. And, "What can I do for you?" I again informed him of the invitation he extended me to play for Cal. Visibly reflecting upon my diminutive size for a lineman he replied, "I am not sure I can help you. Possibly it would be better for you to play a couple years at Yuba College and then transfer here. I have made a lot of promises to other athletes and have been ringing door bells to place them." He didn't have a chance to say another word.

I was so angry I interrupted him and in a hesitant staccato harsh tone exclaimed, *"Mr. Allison, I came to Cal to play football. If I wanted to play at Yuba College I would have gone there. I've been ringing my own damn doorbells and got my own damn job. The next time I see you will be on the football field!!!"* He seemed stunned at my outburst. I turned around and started out of his office and before I got to the door, a bear of a paw (pun unintended) landed on my right shoulder. My knees buckled under me as he shoved me through the door toward his head assistant coach, Frank Wickhurst, and said, **"Get this kid a job. He's the type of spirit we need around here."** (The "job" was parking cars at the Claremont Hotel on weekends. I received room and board, and the tips I kept. The tips would average from $15-$20 per weekend!)

I recall reporting for my first practice with the recruited freshmen from all parts of the country (In those days it was mandatory you play freshman ball before becoming eligible for the varsity team.) Their reputation preceded them. The recruiting class was outstanding as Cal played Alabama in 1937 in the Rose Bowl.

The roster for six full teams was called out and I was still standing to be assigned when Clint Evans, the head freshman coach, asked all those whose names were not called to be ready to jump in at their respective position on a moment's notice. This was very embarrassing to me because when we were first mustered together, the coaches asked that we line up at our respective positions. When another right guard got in front of me, I just stepped out of line and re-entered the front. Little did I realize that Coach Evans had the names of the 1st through the 6th team all picked out beforehand. So there I was at the head of the line with "egg on my face", waiting for my name to be called. And it never was.

In short, I must tell you that three weeks later we had our first game and I was first string! I played in the first college football game I ever saw! And at the UC Memorial Stadium, to boot. I am really proud of that. In all honesty, the first string guard broke his leg the 2nd week of practice. And although I sympathized with him, I looked upon it as an opportunity. His break became my "break". I didn't wish it this way. Neither did I let it deter me from proving my worth as a viable first-string replacement. After all, I had worked my way up to 2nd string before his mishap. *I ended up playing more minutes in my freshman year than most all of my fellow team mates!*

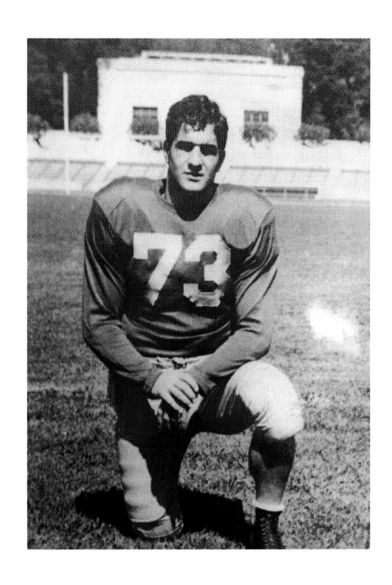

Me, #73, for the University of California Golden Bears…a dream come true

**This, and the next two clippings are from the
San Francisco Chronicle**

With my size a factor, I had to be tough…and I WAS!

Because of my freshman year record, I thought I had the secret to success. First and foremost, seek His blessings in worthy undertakings. Love what you do. Try your best and success is inevitable!

Now the proof in the pudding. I adopted this philosophy during my sophomore year in vying for a position on the Varsity squad. I prayed for the strength to do my best and I fanatically loved the game of football. I was one of the first to arrive at the beginning of practice and the last to leave the field after practice. I would work tenaciously on drills to improve my technique. I would even write notes and critique my practice of the day to find ways and means of improving. With all this resolution I was still not cutting it on the varsity level.

One day in an important scrimmage during my junior year, having made the varsity squad, a particular bread and butter play was being rehearsed and the right guard missed his assignment. Coach Allison looked at me and shouted, "Get in there, Greek!" (He could never remember Nicholau so I told him to just call me

Greek.) Here was the opportunity I hoped for. The play was called again, and guess what? That's right, I missed my block! In disgust he called back the first string guard and I was out!

That night in a state of complete depression I reviewed my notes on fundamentals, on my desire, on my attributes, and was still distraught as to why I failed to prove my worth in that window of opportunity. Then like a bolt from above the answer came so loud and clear I couldn't wait for the next practice to begin, and those to follow.

The genealogy of doing was born. Remember, I believed that if you invoked His blessing, loved what your were doing, and tried your best, you would be rewarded with success. And if that were not the case, it seemed to me there really wasn't anything more you could do to succeed. Sounds logical, doesn't it? It never crossed my mind that this formula might prove inadequate. Yet there had to be something illogical with being assuaged with failure because "you gave it your all". For under these guidelines subconsciously I found myself pleased with the fact I gave it my all, rather than focusing on my failure in the end. There must be a flaw in my adopted formula for success if faith, love and trying didn't in fact lead to success. Although it worked wonders up to and throughout my freshman year at Cal. Where was I missing the boat?

Once again that proverbial inquisitiveness within me came to fore like dawn transcending darkness. There was a critical last rung missing in my philosophical ladder of success. It is that gargantuan step one must mentally negotiate, which elevates one's state of being self-satisfied from the plateau of trying one's best, to the summit level of *doing that which one must do to succeed!* Accept no alternative to self-satisfaction. I cannot overemphasize this enough. It is the *doing* that counts in the end! Giving it your all doesn't hack it if it does not get the job done. It is a sad commentary but a true one that the real world does not reward tryers, only the doers.

This became my newfound mantra: First seek His blessing in any worthy undertaking I embarked upon, love what I must do, give it my all, and DO it! Nothing less should appease me. Transcend the effort barrier to the plateau of success. I was going to become a doer in my exciting life of dreams. Above all, I would continuously enjoy the pursuit! And I had to always remember, it was <u>my</u> life I was enjoying.

It was not my intent to downgrade the virtues of faith, love, and trying my best. Rather it was to italicize the importance of *doing* as the end product of my undertaking. Faith, love and giving it my all were essential precursors to doing!!

Now back to the football field for the laboratory test of the crucial evaluation of the doing philosophy. Once I adopted the doing goal, I was satisfied with nothing but success in that which I was committed. Within two weeks of that realization I was promoted to first string. In the crucible of the trenches I cared not about fundamentals, or trying my best, or how long I practiced. These assets, although essential, were but a means to an end. Not an end unto itself. They meant something to me only if they contributed toward getting the job done. I, instead, focused on success. I passed or failed. Period! No reconciliation on my work ethics, or that I tried my best. That did not satiate my conscience. Only *doing* would suffice.

From that day forth, my face was one big scab from ear to ear, with my nose carrying the brunt of the attack. I made up my mind that a square yard of terra firma on the scrimmage line was my territorial responsibility and no one, but no one, was going to trespass! Unless by design. How I accomplished my mission was not paramount. That I *accomplished* it, was. Those days, football was not the specialty sport it has evolved into today. A lineman played both offense and defense. I loved the format, for it gave me one hundred percent control over my "real estate" responsibilities. God, it was fun! Sure, you would lose a battle now and then, but not the war.

Since then I have embraced this philosophical approach in my daily pursuit of living a happy, useful, Christian life. It has allowed me to jump in where otherwise I would never tread. If I committed to a worthy project, I would do it. Risk of success was not a factor. Pragmatism was. Looking back on some of my accomplishments, I do wonder about the liberties I took with the pragmatic factor. Many a time I seemingly bit off more than I could chew. Yes, I not only chewed it, I digested it!

Still another example of the importance of doing was my opting for a pharmacy major while playing football for Cal. What made this challenge so difficult was the mandatory per semester unit load I had to carry. This element was compounded daily by the distance I had to negotiate between the respective campuses. The pharmacy school was located at the medical center in San Francisco.

To succeed in both my chosen major and football, there required a myriad of sacrifices and ingenious arrangements. I commuted daily across the Oakland Bay Bridge to the UC Berkeley campus for football practice. I missed key classes for which I had to make special arrangements for make up sessions, and had to plan around traveling time for away games and skill meeting sessions for strategy preparations…on and on. But only upon reflecting back do I realize it was quite a feat. At the time I never gave it a second thought. I believed I could do it. It was a worthy cause. I applied my philosophy for success and *did* it!

Cal Memorial Stadium

Living The Dream

That's enough pontificating on the essence of doing. I would like to share some comic occurrences during my exciting college football adventure.

Frankie Alberts, Stanford's star quarterback in the innovative "T" formation offense, (initially introduced at Stanford by Coach Shaughnessey) was a freshman the same year I started at Cal. When we played each other it was ticketed the "Little Big Game" back then because in 1938 freshmen were not eligible for the varsity team. Nevertheless, believe me, the game was played with the same intensity as would be played in the varsity "Big Game" later that same Saturday afternoon. On a particular play, quarterback Alberts faked a handoff to his half back starting off tackle, and ran backwards and towards the sideline looking to run or to throw a pass down field. Playing linebacker on defense, I was not fooled by Frankie's fake hand off. My intent was to keep a perfect collision angle between him and myself and the out of bounds line that limited his escape from me if he chose to run. His receivers were covered, and I, having great momentum built up, and anticipating the point of explosion, literally flew through the air to crush Alberts who's escape maneuver was handicapped by the out of bounds line. Frankie, the fox, abruptly stopped, and stepped sideways out of bounds rather than pressing forward aggressively, thus nullifying my angle of approach. I ended up sailing through the air knocking over two Stanford subs near their bench with Alberts literally standing there smiling at me. Frustrated, I was so angry I got up shouting across the field to our coach, Clint Evans, and begged while making a fist to just let me bust him one. The scene just made Frankie laugh all the more, and damned if I didn't join him, with an explicit jovial "oh hell" expletive.

During my varsity escapades I had a comparable funny incident, only this time it was on me, the instigator. It occurred in the Cal vs Oregon game played at Oregon. The game was being played in a heavy rain that afternoon, and the field footing was compromised. Oregon featured a big two hundred and thirty pound All American tackle. Fortunately I did not line up opposite him. Bob Reinhart, our two hundred and twenty five pound All American tackle did. The play I am about to describe had Oregon in punt formation. I rushed the kicker to no end as he kicked a beauty far down the field to our safety, Walt Gordon Jr. He fielded the ball, bobbled it, and the next thing I know all hell is breaking loose with both Oregon and Cal players mixing it up with fisticuffs over a loose ball. I of course, while running back towards the action, was raring to join the fracas. I'm five yards away from the action when I hit a mud puddle that threw me off balance. First it threw my upper body backwards and to keep from falling I lunged forward crashing my helmet into what I thought was a truck. It was the Oregon All American tackle in a braced position. My helmet was buried into his chest. The next thing I knew, he placed his hand on my helmet, tipped my head back and looking down from a foot above me said,

"You don't really want to get involved do you?"

I quipped, "Who me?" "Hell no! I was running for our huddle."

He produced a friendly smile, and I just shook my head to clear the cobwebs. I'm sorry I do not remember the tackles name, but in my book he was an all American Guy on and off the field.

That year, for our game with USC at the Los Angeles Coliseum, we boarded a Pullman train late on Thursday night after practice, in order to spend Friday night in a hotel in Los Angeles. At nine o'clock on the train to LA the coaches ordered lights out, and we headed to our assigned Pullman bunks for the night. I had a lower bunk, and after about twenty minutes, not being able to sleep, I crawled out of bed and tiptoed to an adjacent lower bunk, gingerly pulled back the curtain and Whap! slapped my surprised victim on his stomach – a move that violently reflexed him up, causing him to bump his head on the upper bunk. Of course I was long gone before he recovered to see who the culprit was. Five minutes later, still awake I did the same stunt with the bunk behind me. Same results. Same escape. Now the disruption awoke several of the team members and our line coach, Bob Herwig, a former all American Center on Cal's 1937 Thunder team. Coach Herwig shouted for us to "cool it and get some sleep". Another ten minutes of insomnia and I thought I'd give it one more try. This time I would strike the curtained bunk across from me. This I did, and a Goliath-sized hand quickly clenched my wrist. It was Bob Herwig's bunk. From the previous commotions he suspected I was the culprit.

"Greek," he angered "get your ass back in that bunk – and if I hear one peep from you before 7 am you will not only be off the team, you'll be off this train!"

I experience peaceful insomnia the rest of the night. I always did have a hard time getting to sleep on the night before the game. I would fantasize key plays I would make the following day. In today's world I would parrot a recorded DVD, revisiting replay after replay in my mind, during a pre-game night.

During my senior year I recall in the Cal vs UCLA game in Los Angeles, when the gun sounded at the end of the game, with Cal the victor, the opposing center picked up the football and started to run towards his side of the field. I chased him down, tackled him and tossed the ball back towards our side of the field. (The custom was for the winning team to be rewarded the football and I wasn't about to be denied our prize.) This caused a rumpus and the two teams were swinging at each other in a post game free for all. I mention this to emphasize all I could hear were knuckles bouncing off my helmet and shoulder pads, reminding me of a hailstorm. The reflex thing one does in such circumstances is to put his head down and randomly fly his fists. Usually it lasts about a minute or two at the most and no one is hurt, except for a possible sore hand, as was the case with me.

More football shenanigans.

I "borrowed" a five-pound, and a ten-pound small disc free weight from our training quarters and secured them in my football locker. At different times during the season there would be bulletin board postings to weigh-in before practice. We were to report to the trainer, and he would list our weight on a chart. On those rare occasions, I would use one of the weights, depending on how much I weighed that day, and slip it under my weigh-in shorts, under two jock straps worn backwards for support, and get on the scale, always with my body in an oblique position with my back away from the trainer's eye. I doubt he ever suspected anything, but if he did he did not make a point of it. This I did, because my actual weight was between 163 – 167 lbs, and on weigh days I would use either the five lb or ten lb weight; which ever would put me over 170 lbs. You see, when I became a starter, I did not want to call attention to my borderline weight, for I was already being touted as one of the lightest varsity guards in California's football history. Considering the bulk of the post WWII athletes, that obsolete statistic probably still stands today. My weight as a starting lineman for Cal would, however, qualify for the weight of one's thigh by today's standard weight for a lineman! I mentioned that I doubted the trainer suspected my shenanigan. Wrong.

An incident occurred later that convinced me the trainer was on to me, but pretended not to be as he charted the scale weight. At the start of my senior year, the first game was a double header with St Mary's and Santa Clara University. On the Friday night before the Saturday games, after the training table, and dinner, there was a film critique of the two teams being shown to us by the coaches, and I felt nauseated with a pain in my side, but I thought nothing of it. At the end of the session, I headed back from the Berkeley Campus to UCSF where the school of pharmacy was located hoping a nights sleep would relieve my symptoms. That did not occur. Instead my symptoms were escalating. I was vomiting and the pain became severe. Around 11:00 pm I got out of bed and reported to the emergency center at UCSF hospital, telling the receptionist I needed something to settle my stomach and relieve my pain, for I had a game to play the next day. She stuck a thermometer in my mouth, read it, and got a hold of the on-call doctor to examine me. Acute appendicitis was the diagnosis.

"George" he said "we must operate at once, and hope we can remove your appendix before it bursts."

I signed the necessary paperwork, and he immediately performed the appendectomy without complications.

The game with St Mary's and Santa Clara was that Saturday afternoon and I had no way of letting the coach know I was in the hospital. My teammates said Coach Allison was ticked off when I was a no show at Memorial Stadium without an explanation. On Monday I had the doctor inform coach Allison of my emergency appendix situation.

While at the hospital, after the first day of recuperation, I contacted Dan Mc Carthy, a teammate, and asked him to come by the hospital the next day and get me out of there. The operation was on Friday night, and on Monday I *escaped* from the hospital and rehabbed on my own. The operation, as explained to me by the doctor, was preformed by a new technique that involved splitting abdominal muscles rather than cutting them for access to the appendix. This method, new at the time, would accelerate healing by weeks. With this assurance, in my mind, I became ambulatory on day one. That is on Sunday. I started walking the hallways at the hospital. The nurses did not approve but I was determined to get up and about at once. Each day away from hospital restrictions, I was more and more active. I recall the following Monday, a week after leaving the hospital, I would walk-jog the San Francisco hills near the UCSF center. Each day I would increase my pace. On the next Monday, 17 days post operation, I went to our trainer, and he was surprised to see me. I asked him if he would tape my appendix area with sponge packing to protect it from uniform irritation. He emphatically said "No way!" Unless he had a clearing from the doctor himself he would not tape me for practice. He was adamant. When he left the taping area I picked up several rolls of tape and left the training quarters. At my locker I taped myself as best I could, placing a protective sponge pad over the appendix scar. Put on my uniform and reported for practice. That coming Saturday –3 weeks post operation- USC was on our schedule to be played in LA and I wasn't going to miss that game. I reported early for practice and did some warm ups and jogging and stretching when Stub Allison, our coach, blew his whistle for the beginning of our scheduled practice session. He spotted me and said "what are you doing here, Greek? Didn't you have an appendectomy?"

"No coach" I lied "I had an attack and I'm ready to go"
"Great" he said "Glad to have you back."

I was happy the way things were going during our pre scrimmage routine. Near the end of the practice session the coach gathered us together and laid out the scouting report for our scrimmage session. When he called the names of the first team players, mine was called. Now is where the rubber hits the road. An all out scrimmage! I was on the offensive team and the first play called was an off tackle trap play where I pulled and blocked the defensive trapped tackle as he crosses the line of scrimmage. I've got to tell you, with the quick pulling out from my offensive stance, and moving towards the tackle all in one motion, the sharp pain I felt was amplified several fold when I collided with the unsuspected trapped tackle. I never made a sound but I instinctively put my hand on my self-bandaged area and it seemed to be intact and I felt no blood. What a relief. The elation of relief was like the feeling I always experienced after the first contact in a regular game. From that moment on, I discarded what discomfort and pain I experienced during the scrimmage. In my mind again "all's well that ends well". To this day I believe coach Allison called that first scrimmage play to check me out.

That Saturday afternoon I played in the Cal vs USC game in Los Angeles and my name was broadcasted over the radio now and then during the game. Unbeknownst to me, the doctor in San Francisco who operated on me heard my name over the radio and was dumbfounded that I would be playing football three weeks after an appendectomy. Monday I went to my locker as usual for practice, and I was shocked to find my locker completely bare. I rushed to the trainer and asked if he knew what the score was. He said, "check with your coach." This I did and coach Allison was livid.

"Do you realize the compromised situation you put me in? You told me you had an attack not an operation. Your doctor called me this morning and wanted to know what the hell was going on! I told the doctor you said you only had and inflammation and not an operation. Without a doctor's clearance you lied and jeopardized me and your teammates. You are off this team!"

I panicked and headed to San Francisco to see the Doctor. I had to wait about an hour before I got to visit with him. I begged him to examine me and if he was satisfied that I was absolutely OK, would he please call coach Allison and clear me for team participation. He agreed to do so, and I must admit he was very, very thorough in his probing physical examination. When he finished his exam, scratching his head in disbelief, he commented "There is always a first" and he said he would talk to coach Allison for my clearance. Thank God Coach Allison forgave my falsehood and he reinstated me on the team.

Do you recall my earlier remark, when I wrote I suspected the trainer was on to me regarding my weigh-in trick with the free weights? On Wednesday, reinstated, I went to my locker and sure enough my football uniform was in place as were the *five and ten pound free weight*s.

As I am recalling matters of levity, an incident that happened at our last Big Game practice may be of interest. Coach Stub Allison whistled the squad together after our scrimmage that afternoon and delivered a pep talk, looked at his watch and remarked,

"We have fifteen minutes more of practice to burn, any suggestions?" I raised my right arm up and he acknowledged "Yes Greek."

I responded, "Coach, how about we choose up sides and hit the showers?" with Big Game tension at its peak, everyone broke out laughing, and the coach looked at me and said, "Not a bad idea Greek. You hit the track."

Hell it was worth breaking the ice of the Big Game anxiety and I headed for the track.

"Forget it" he shouted "Hit the showers!"

I mentioned earlier that I played in the first college football game that I ever saw. TV broadcasts did not exist, only radio, play by play broadcasts. I have another first to relate. It was our first freshman game, and we were playing San Francisco State College at Cal Memorial Stadium. San Francisco State won the toss and elected to receive. On the kick off of my first game, I ran full speed into the SF player who fielded the kickoff. His knee caught me in my solar plexus knocking the wind completely out of my lungs. The tackle caused a fumble, I was told. The thing I do remember however, was the trainer over me, trying to get my lungs full of air as I was hearing the rooting section yelling "Greek Rah, rah, rah, Greek Rah, rah, rah" etc. You know, that was my only " time out" during my freshman year. In fact, I do not recall having an injury time out on my account during my whole college career! Wounded many times, but not cited for a time out. However, this was not so in practice sessions. I sustained a broken nose that was forced back into place by our trainer. After the season I had it operated on. During the season I wore a single protection bar, in vogue at that time, on my leather helmet (plastic helmets were not yet in vogue) to protect my nose only to cause more damage. The bar across the helmet got caught on the turf during practice when I attempted a submarine tactic on defense. It caused my helmet to come forward over my forehead with such a force the bar ripped my lower chin away from my jaw-bone. It took twenty-three stitches inside my mouth to get my chin back in place. I still did not miss the practice the following day - or a game. I broke the thumb on my left hand during a scrimmage. All these mishaps happened in practice. Mishaps notwithstanding, I did not miss suiting up for a scheduled game. All said and done, I was a fortunate football player

A passing unforgettable thought regarding my football experience at Cal. During my senior year, before the Big Game at California Memorial Stadium, the team was going to celebrate a Father's Day dedication by having each player on the squad, with his father alongside, jog to the middle of the field before the game, and the father and son together would be announced to the crowd. I was the only player without a father, and this, because of the circumstances, was the first the players and coaches knew of it. I was about to trot out there alone teary eyed, knowing my father was by my side in spirit, when Dr. Harkness, the team physician got by my side and asked, "Greek, I would be honored to be your father for this occasion." I couldn't speak a word. I grabbed his hand and we jogged out together. The announcer, instead of announcing Mr. Edison Nicholau and son, announced , "George Nicholau and father."

I am certain my tearful eyes were not noticed in the stands. I was ever grateful to Dr. Harkness, for his compassionate generosity, even though I knew my father was right beside me.

Epsilon Phi Sigma

Enough football stories, and onto the social aspect of my collegiate life. For starters, I always bragged to my children *"I enjoyed my college experience so much, that if I had to relive it- it would kill me."* That's how active and dynamic I was during my college years. It was a blast. (Yet, it was also a demanding commitment that demanded more sober hours than leisure good-time hours if I was to academically survive.)

I will now focus on social events that preoccupied my time. A good place to start is the day my roommate, Ted Efstratis, and I were walking on campus, on a beautiful fall day, from the

Campanile towards Sather Gate, the entrance to UCBerkeley from Telegraph Avenue. As we were approaching the gate, to the right of us was Wheeler Hall, a large lecture Hall for various classes. The Hall was noted for its Wheeler steps where students would bask in the sun while cramming for a class. On this particular afternoon I noticed one student above all the others. She was a strikingly beautiful Mediterranean female. There were no books to be seen about her as she was leaning back resting on her elbows on the next step above. With her olive skin, radiant face framed by a captivating coiffure, and glamorous sexy symmetry, she resembled a day-dreaming Goddess sunbathing at a Grecian temple. Captivated, I looked towards Ted as we were passing by, and remarked in Greek,

"Kita Prama" – translated "Look at that!" before we could take another step she retorted,

"Sas aresi?" in Greek – "Do you like it?"

Stunned, I stopped in my tracks, looked towards Ted and said, "Ted, if there are such beautiful Greek girls on this campus, we've got to do something about it so we can get to meet them!"

We approached the "Goddess" and I introduced myself. I'll be darned at this writing if I can remember her name, and Ted is resting in heaven, so no help there. We had a great visit. I got her phone number and promised I would get in touch with her, and I did. Through my football exposure, there were many Greek students from various parts of the State that I came to know. Among them was an LA contingent headed by Harry Pappas, Sam Menzelos, Gus Nickandros, and several others I cannot recall at this writing. From the Bay area there was Nick Petris, who was to become a power player in the California Senate. His brother Gus Petris, Nick Elefther, Solan Scordalis, his brother Alex, Georgia Francescis, Katherine Glafkides, and the Ellis sisters, Mati, Zoe and Sophia. Names, names I can't remember all the names. No problem remembering faces. From Stockton, Paul Christopulos; from Fresno, Eli Skofis. From the Marysville area, Georgia Changaris,Ted Efstratis and myself.

We were all part of the founding members of the Epsilon Phi Sigma club. I invited all the names I just wrote and others I can't remember to a "Greek Town Hall" gathering on campus at Wheeler Steps. The genesis of my idea was to discuss the forming of a social Greek Club that we may be better acquainted with one another. The meeting was very successful, and thus was born the Elenikos Fitikos Silayous – Epsilon Phi Sigma- the "Greek Friendly Society"!

To my knowledge this society still exists. An ongoing scholarship fund has been raised through the Epsilon Phi Sigma efforts that to this day, 60+ years later, still monetarily honors qualified needy Hellenic students attending one of the University Campuses to further their education.

Let me share with you the tone of Epsilon Phi Sigma celebratory social happenings. Lake Merit is located in Oakland, a couple miles south of the campus. Many were the times we would chip in and rent the facilities for a Saturday night Gala. The theme was Greek-American, i.e., there would be Greek dancing mixed with American dancing. There would be Greek sing-a-longs led by one of us, and there would be American sing-a-longs over the rippling moon-bathed waters of Lake Merit. Our parties would, at times, last the night and go on well into Sunday A.M. There was libation, not intoxication, or misbehavior. All the Greek girls were respected and treated via Greek culture standards. Several mornings after partying as a group, we would all go to the Greek Church in Oakland. Our reputation in the Greek Community of Oakland was exemplary. We, as a club, would be invited to some of their civic doings. The Epsilon Phi Sigma venture was so successful, chapters migrated to other University of California college campuses in the state. I am, to this day, proud to have been one of the charter founders of Epsilon Phi Sigma. Many successful accomplished Greek college students are alumni of the Epsilon Phi Sigma experience.

**Epsilon Phi Sigma
The Greek (literally) Fraternity I co-founded
I am on the far right hand side, back row**

Near Misses and Other Antics

During my junior year, 1941, WWII hit the scene. Having volunteered and been accepted into the V7 Navy program, I, along with Sam Menzelos and Ted Efstratis, applied for work at the Richmond Todd California Shipbuilder's Corporation. We were still enrolled at UC Berkeley, so we applied for the swing shift from 4 pm to 12 midnight. (The swing shift schedule allowed us to earn some money while helping the War cause and still attend classes.) The shipyard was operating 24-7 at full blast building Liberty ships to carry our troops and supplies into the battle zone of the war. My resume qualified me as a timekeeper. A misnomer for a "spy", whose assignment was to cruise around the yard entering ships under construction, and observe if any of the employees were sloughing off when they should be working. I was not comfortable with the job, as I did not like reporting delinquents to their superiors. Workers knew who the "time keepers" were, because we had a band on our right sleeve broadcasting our duty. I suffered this humiliation for two weeks before I asked for a reassignment. (As timekeeper, I experienced two close calls when a hammer, first, then a chisel "accidentally" slipped from workers hands a deck above me while I was making rounds on the ship.)

I was transferred to the "frame slab". This job required that I strike a twenty-pound sledgehammer onto a two-inch diameter tool head with a flat four inch bottom. This tool was attached to a four foot long bar, at the end of which a slab foreman or one of the other slab-men, would at a given pace, move the tool along a twenty to forty foot white red hot U shaped steel beam coming directly out of a special steel heating oven. The resulting U shaped steel ribs were used to form the frame of the Liberty ship. There was a perforated steel slab deck upon which the U shaped steel beam slid from the oven. The beam was white hot! A timely rhythm was absolutely imperative while you and a fellow sledge slinger alternately smacked the moving target. The sledge slinger and the tool operator, to protect singeing of their face and eyes, wore heat protective celluloid masks during the task. Coordination between hammerers and the person advancing the tool was critical.

Having briefly explained the operation, let me tell you, I thought myself to be a pretty powerful guy, what with my football conditioning and all. Well, power and strength, just like in football, was a prerequisite but not the solution to being an accomplished sledgehammer slinger. My first go at swinging a 20 lb sledgehammer was an eye opener. Better yet, a stomach opener! I swore I pulled every muscle in my stomach when I tried to sling the sledgehammer forward over my right shoulder from its back position. The foreman, a great guy, laughed at me and quickly got up and took the sledge hammer away from my hand and completed my assignment on that first beam out of the oven. Then he took me aside and showed me the importance of leverage in slinging a sledgehammer. He ordered me to go off in the corner of the slab and practice hitting a stationary "tool' every time a steel beam came out of the oven. This was to develop a rhythm in timing with those doing the real thing. When he thought I was ready to be activated, he called me over and said, "The next slab out, you are on" It was a ball. I had the knack and the rhythm automatically kicked in. It seemed effortless (I wish I could always copy that feeling with a golf club. When I do, I play really good golf!) Anyway, I soon got so I could get fancy, and whirl my sledge hammer a time or two around my body before landing it on the tool head, and still be in rhythm with my slugging partner. That maneuver classified me as the "Around The World Slammer". No one else on my shift was able to do it. I had mastered the technique when bored with routine hitting.

When I told Ted about my experience at the shipyard he applied for a job at the yard. I recommended him to my foreman and he was hired. We both, along with Sam Menzelos, who also worked at the shipyard, but not as a sledger, worked the swing shift. With this schedule we did not miss classes although we did have to adjust our free time for studying. Sam Menzelos was our transportation to and from the yard as he owned a 1936 Chevy Coupe. Obviously this job was during the spring semester, not during the fall football season. The pay was terrific. It financed my senior year at Cal.

One evening Ted and I were the dual sledge team. We were moving along really well when my sledgehammer, due to sweat, flew free from my hands during my return motion to the target. The free sledgehammer "missile" was hurling across the U beam at waist height, when Ted's reflex reaction brought his hammer down out of rhythm and struck my flying hammer on the wooden handle, knocking it clear on the slab rather than across it. This could have been a disaster had Ted not reacted the way he did. Another catastrophe averted! Someone up there was looking out for me…or, more so, Ted!

I wasn't always the *sole* recipient of a friend's benevolence. There was a time or two when I had guardian angel status. One such a memory was when Sam Menzelos and I worked the swing shift before Ted joined us. Sam was living with his widowed mother in an apartment near the University. He had, as mentioned earlier, a '36 Chevrolet coup and that was our transportation to and from the shipyard. I would meet him at his apartment around three thirty and off we would go to the Richmond Ship yards. After our swing shift, he would go directly back to his house while dropping me off at mine on the way. I lived a couple of blocks from Sam's apartment. One Friday night, after work, we both decided we would go into Oakland to a bar. I believe the name of the bar was "The Two Mile Bar", for it was two miles from the campus, a fact that made it legal to serve liquor. It being a Friday night, and our fifth surviving day of work (we did not work on weekends for that was study time), it made sense to both of us that a bit of libation was in order for relaxation before we had to hit the books all day Saturday and Sunday. The problem was, a bit of libation for one, may be a lot for another. And so it was with Sam. After a stint of imbibing, Sam thought we should head for home. It was now about 1:30 a.m. I agreed, and when we got to the car he looked at me and said,

"George, can you drive?"
"Yes, why?"
"Well," he offered "I can't. Here's the keys."

We got into the car and headed for Berkeley and his apartment. By the time we got to Berkeley, Sam was completely out of it. I mean a Zombie. I could not take him home to his mother in this shape, so I took him to my apartment. I took off all his clothes, drew a cold-water bath and placed him in it. He let out a screech and was shivering, but I wouldn't let him out of the tub until I thought he was sober enough to take home. After 6 to 7 minutes in the cold tub I got him out, and instead of getting him dressed again, I put my robe on him so that he would be ready for bed when I snuck him into his house. The plan seemed to be moving along as I had anticipated, except for one thing. Sam was still incoherent and wobbly. I used the house key on his car keychain, opened the door to the apartment, and stealthily got him to his bed.

Softly I kept asking, "Sam, tell me where you put your clothes when you're in bed, so your mother won't suspect anything if she wakes up before you do." No answer.

Again, "Sam where do you…" He mumbled something but I couldn't make it out. On the next try, I heard a sigh, but not from Sam. It was his mother with an outburst from an adjoining bedroom.

"Vre, vanta sto krevati, ke fevya apo etho "– colloquially translated "put them on the bed and get out of here." I threw his clothes on the bed, and was long gone before Mrs. Menzelos got out of her bed. Many times afterwards, Mrs. Menzelos would look at me with feigned animosity. Then say , "Efharisto Yeoryio" – translation "Thank you George".

A Sucker Is Born

A couple of happenings I am about to reveal make me a leading candidate for a promising customer for the sale of the Golden Gate Bridge. The Barnum and Bailey Circus philosophy of "daily a sucker is born" would be the proper classification for my naivety.

In my junior year at Cal, 1942, I purchased my first automobile, a 1932 two door Cabriolet Model A Ford. I bought the car from a newspaper ad. The car was in dire need of repair. It cost me 100 dollars. From my shipyard earnings, I could afford the bargain. The first thing I did was to buy car upholstery material, and with the help of Ted Efstratis, spent a weekend of our study time reupholstering the car. Believe me, we did a terrific job. The car had no exterior body damage, which was a rarity. The next order of business was to overhaul the engine. It ran, but.... I elicited the help of my friend Peter Angiledes, an engineering major at Cal with a background in auto mechanics. He assisted me in the overhaul project. I bought the necessary parts – rings, bearings, gaskets, etc., for a total investment of under 40 dollars. Imagine what that would cost today. A very close friend, and Cal graduate, Nick Elefther, lived in Richmond, a few miles north of Cal, and he allowed me to work on the car at his home. After a week's effort under the tutelage of Angiledes, the overhaul repairs were completed.

My love of cars began early on

The car ran terrific except for one minor knocking sound that Angelides discounted as being of no significance. Of course, he was right, but George the perfectionist, a misguided perfectionist, would not enjoy peace of mind until he got rid of the knocking.

Now I've got to tell you, for a total investment of under $200, I had a good-looking automobile coveted by my fellow classmates. I used it for my commuting to and from UCSF, Richmond Shipyards, and for dating – its primary intent. I also made two trips from Berkeley to visit my mother in Marysville. Like I said it was a real doozy, a conversation piece among my buddies. Cabriolet, no less!

I started this automobile novelette with a self-imposed sucker implication. The validity of that classification is irrefutable. One evening, I started from my Berkeley apartment headed for Oakland's Broadway theatre to see "Gone with the Wind", when I noticed a hitchhiker thumbing for a lift at the corner of College and Broadway. I picked him up, and told him I could give him a lift to the theatre. He commented on the car, being impressed with its appearance. I thanked him and volunteered,

"I overhauled the engine too, but I'm concerned about a little knock". He listened and commented,

"Now that you mention it, I hear it. It sounds like your main bearing may be loose."

"Oh, is that what it is, because I replaced that bearing", I responded

"I'm sure that's it. I'm a mechanic working at the Ford dealership in Oakland. Roy is my name."

"How much would it cost to have them repair it?" I inquired.

He said, "Mechanics earn good hourly wages and it would be significant, but I could do it on the side for ten dollars, if you bought the gaskets and a new bearing - if it is necessary to replace, which I doubt."

"Hey, that sounds great. When can you do it?"

He offered, "I'm not doing anything tonight and there is an auto part store, Goodyear, that is open until 9 pm, so I could get the parts if you want me to do it tonight"

"Really", I reacted, "lets do it."

"I got an idea" I continued, "I'm headed to the theater to see *Gone with the Wind*. If I give you 7 dollars for a gasket and a main bearing, if needed, could you finish the job tonight?"

"No problem'

"Good, here's the game plan. I'll give you 7 dollars for parts and ten dollars for your labor now, then you leave the change for the parts under the front seat along with the key and I will pick up the car at the parking lot across the street from the theater on Market Street in San Francisco tomorrow afternoon. I have an 8 o'clock class at the UC Medical Center on Parnassus, and tomorrow afternoon is the soonest I can be free." (I cannot believe my naiveté, but believe it I must.)

"That sounds good to me", Roy commented. "I'll have it finished easily by 8 pm tonight and I'll drive to the lot across from the theater in San Francisco, and bus myself back to Oakland by 10 pm", he enthused.

Now I know why 'he enthused'. I got out at the theater, wished him luck, and thanked him for rushing the job. I have always preached to my kids "you can't live a lie." If I am destined to be a sucker, I'm not going to go half way! In this instance there is an authentic realm of truism in the saying, 'what you see in me is what you get' <u>from</u> me. In this scenario, Roy, saw a car in me, and a car he got from me. You see, the following afternoon there was no 1932 renovated Ford Cabriolet in the designated parking lot. Not only that, but I kept insisting there must be a 1932 Ford parked there, all the while the attendant was in the process of reporting me to a police officer as a prowler casing the lot! I explained my dilemma to the officer who arrived, and wanted him to make out a theft report. He told me, from my remarks, the report would have to be made in Oakland where the crime occurred. Upon parting I couldn't help seeing him shaking his head in complete disbelief.

Off to the Oakland police station I go.

When I got there I asked the lady clerk, "Where do I report a stolen automobile?"

She said, "You're in the right place" and called for the officer on duty to come forth. I noticed another gentleman leisurely sitting in a chair nearby the counter where I was to file my complaint, but did not give him too much thought at the time.

The officer's inquiry follows as best as I can remember it. Of this much I am sure, there is no way I can embellish what I am about to describe and make it more entertaining than what actually took place. Here goes.

"Your name?" inquired the officer.
"George Nicholau"
"Your address?"
"Whitehouse apartment, Berkeley California. Phone…"
"Your complaint?"
"A stolen 1932 Ford Cabriolet."
"License plate number?"
"Ah – I don't know – I just bought the car last month and I never memorized the license plate."
"Where was it parked when it was stolen?"
"It wasn't parked, a hitch hiker stole it."
"At gunpoint?!"
"Oh no, he was thumbing for a ride at College and Broadway when I picked him up."
"Did he threaten you?"
"No."
"Well, get to the point, how did he steal it?"

All the while this conversation is taking place the gentleman sitting nearby was becoming more and more interested in the report.

"You see officer, the car needed mechanical repairs, and he told me he was a Ford mechanic, and could do the repair, parts and all, for under 17 dollars. He also volunteered that it would cost a lot more at the Ford Garage."

"And you hired him?" he interrupted.

"Well I guess that's what I did. But I made arrangements for him to leave the car at a designated parking lot in San Francisco after he repaired it. And then I would pick it up the next day in the afternoon. I made this arrangement because I had an 8 o'clock class at the Medical Center in San Francisco."

"Son, let me take it from there. No 1932 Ford Cabriolet at the parking lot, right?"

"Right."

"George, I doubt if we are going to have any luck getting your car back, but we will do our best. Do you have the pink slip with you?"

"No, it is in the glove compartment of the car."

"The pink slip should be filed *away* as proof of ownership of the car, not left *in* the car," he offered.

"What's the name of the person from whom you bought the car?"

"I don't remember. I gave him 100 dollars and he gave me the key and the pink slip to the Ford. And that was it."

"Well the fact he gave you the pink slip tells me he was on the up and up. Of course you signed the pink slip as the new owner before putting it in the glove compartment." He saw a facial look of a complete questionable gesture as my chin dropped, eyes fixed with a furrowed frown staring straight ahead into space.

"Don't tell me you didn't sign the pink slip before filing it in the glove compartment?"

"No, I didn't know I was supposed to. When he gave it to me I just put it in the glove compartment as proof I was the owner of the car"

"George, for your edification, I'm going to review with you the context of our dialogue and you be the judge as to its' authenticity before signing the report.'

"You came in here to report stolen car. You don't know the license plate number. You left the pink slip in the glove compartment of the car. You never signed the pink slip. You don't know the name or address of the seller of the car. The vehicle was not stolen from a parked area. You gave the key, and money to a stranger named 'Roy', and instructed him to leave your repaired car in SF at a parking lot with the change, mind you, and the parking lot ticket with the key under the front seat of the car. Have I missed anything? Oh yes, the SF police officer directed you to Oakland to file your report. Can you describe the smile on the officer's face as he was telling you where to file your complaint? Don't bother, I can imagine. I have your report on record. We will do what we can, but don't hold your breath for positive results. All that Roy has to do, if he is so inclined, is find a buyer for the car and sign your pink slip as he being the owner, and give it to the buyer, who I am certain will sign the pink slip as the new owner unaware of any shenanigans, and enjoy his good fortune in another part of the state as an innocent foolproof owner of the 1932 Ford Cabriolet."

Now, as all this dialogue was taking place, the strange gentleman who had been seated, was now standing at the counter spellbound with a look of disbelief on his face. He seemed to become more and more interested in the circus he was witnessing. I assumed he was a detective on the force being taken in by the bizarreness of the report. Wrong. When the officer finished his questioning and comments, he bid me thanks for the signed report and went back to his desk shrugging his shoulders and shaking his head in disbelief. The stranger then took over the inquiry.

"I think I know you. I heard you say your name was George Nicholau and a student at Cal."

"That's right," was my curious response

"You are a guard on the Cal football team. Your nickname is "Greek", right?"

"And your name?" I enquired

"Rosenthal, I'm glad to meet you Greek," he said

"The pleasure is mine," and I left the station.

The officer who took my complaint was clairvoyant. I never did get my 1932 Ford Cabriolet, newly upholstered, overhauled engine, with I suspect, the still impotent telltale slight knock. More disconcerting to me, I never received an anonymous thank you for the 17-dollar "tip" I gave to the gifted "legal owner" of my beloved 1932 jewel. C'est la vie.

Oh, yes, Mr. Rosenthal was the sports reporter for the San Francisco Chronicle. I still have a copy of his column, filed somewhere, that was published in the sports section of the San Francisco Chronicle, describing my stolen car fiasco. The essence of his column was his questioning if The Greek always wore his helmet during football practice.

In my collegiate years, saddled as I was with a limited memory, a lesson learned was soon a lesson forgotten. Shrug your shoulders and read on. In the spring of 1943, I wanted to go home for the weekend to celebrate Greek Easter. Most times it was celebrated on a different Sunday from Western Easter. There had been times in the past when I was 'broke', and I would thumb my way home. However, the thumbing experience was always cumbersome and uncertain. For this particular Easter voyage, I had the total sum of three dollars that would buy a one-way ticket to Marysville on the Greyhound bus. A round trip ticket, I found out, at the Oakland Bus terminal, was $4.50; a one dollar and fifty cent savings. Being a spendthrift and brilliant negotiator, I managed to parlay a dollar and a half ticket savings into a fifty dollar loss in the process of orchestrating a collateral arrangement with a ticket seller at the Oakland Greyhound Bus station.

I pleaded with the ticket clerk to sell me a round trip ticket, and I would be able to give him the extra $1.50 when I got back. He said he was sorry but that he could not help me. I tried talking him into it, but to no avail.

Finally, I said, "Evidently you don't trust me, can I trust you?"

He replied, "Sir, I don't have the authority to undersell the price of a ticket. It has nothing to do with trust." At the time, I was wearing a gold Swiss wristwatch I bought from the Payless Drug Store catalogue advertising Christmas gifts. I was desperate to save $1.50, so I made the following proposal.

"If I leave my wrist watch with you as collateral, will you personally lend me $1.50 till Monday?"

He looked at the watch and said, "If it means that much to you, OK."

I gave him my watch and asked him to write his name on the back of my half of the ticket stub, as a receipt for the return of my watch when he was reimbursed for his $1.50 loan. This he did. When I got back to the Oakland station on Monday, I could not find the teller with my watch. I asked for the manager and he told me a Mr. So and So, (I don't remember names) whose signature was on the back of my ticket stub, quit on Sunday, and he knew nothing about a wristwatch. I showed the manager my ticket stub with the information, and he was sorry, "but there's nothing I can do about it." Case closed. Watch gone. One round trip ticket from Oakland to Marysville and back, for a few ticks on a $50.00, 15 jewel, 14 karat Gold, Swiss wristwatch on a stranger's wrist. It wasn't, I am happy to report, a self-winding model, so every morning when he winds it his conscience will haunt him. Don't you agree?

Now I must share my philosophical lesson learned from the past two "stings", of which I was the victim. Instead of brooding over my loss, I truly honored my gain! ~ yes, that's right, my gain. You see, I figured my probity was not compromised, but the two culprits who preyed on my naiveté sabotaged their honor! Through these two ill-intentioned incidents the value of trust was more so ingrained in my mind for life. Say what? Well, isn't it amazing how often in one's lifetime, negative happenings become the genesis for a positive impact on one's character? Lesson learned. In fact, I had learned this lesson years ago in one of the many rap sessions with my Dad: Be a trustworthy person, do nothing that will discredit your integrity and you will always be respected among your peers. However, in my case, it also wouldn't hurt to be a better judge of good character and respond accordingly.

The Prankster

A ritual celebration enjoyed by members of Cal's football team, sets the strategy of my "Saturday Night Dance at the Savoy" a.k.a. Harmon Gymnasium. After one of the rival home games during a season with USC, UCLA or Stanford, played at Memorial Stadium, the UC student body hosted a Big Name Band celebrity ballroom dance in Harmon Gym. It proved to be a popular venue for the whole UCB student body. Several of the team members would attend the dance. My game plan at the dance followed a set routine I hit upon my junior year, and it served me well through my senior year. My strategy was to wear my Big C award sweater, canvas the dance floor for an eye-filling candidate, and approach her for a dance.

When my request was favored, I would dance along for several bars of music and suddenly flinch to a complete stop and place a hand on my ribs and say, with my Big C sweater as a clue, "Oh wow, I'm sorry, that was a tough game this afternoon."

"Are you on the football team?" would be a common response to my moment of pain.

"Yes I am, and I want to dance with you, pain be damned!" that format set up the evening for me. The girl I was dancing with would broadcast to her friends that she just danced with a Cal football player. I kept a stealth eye in her direction after our dance and if any of the girls she was talking to looked enticing to me, I would casually walk over and ask for a dance. I met a lot of wonderful winsome girls at the "Saturday Night Dances at Harmon Gymnasium". After all, I did pay the price on Saturday afternoon in Memorial Stadium, pre-dance time. Right? An aside – at my present age I don't have to prove it- but I was an enjoyable piece of work on the dance floor. Take my word for it.

As you shall see, my sophomoric pranks were not limited to the dance floor. For example, the Big Game in 1942 was played in Palo Alto in the Stanford Stadium. We won the game and as a team we were in a festive mood. The team had our bus driver stop at a bar in Palo Alto after the game. It being the last game of the season, and sans the coaches' presence, we began our celebration. The Saloon had a thirty foot long bar on one side of its depth and a number of 20 gallon barrels of various wines with spicks in them displayed on the opposite side of the bar for bulk wine sales to be taken home.

Envision a 50+ squad of rowdy, celebrating football players within legal age, (it says here) swarming the bar, covering it from end to end. With two bar tenders going at it full bore it still took a while to get everyone served. While this was taking place, I went to the 20 gallon barrel of wine stacked closest to the front door, picked it up off its dispensing stand (thank God it wasn't near full – but it was heavy) and headed for the bus which was parked nearby. When I reached the bus, the bus driver would not allow me to put it on the bus. About this time the guys were coming back to the bus and they had no more luck than I did with the bus driver regarding the barrel of wine. So I went back to the Saloon with the barrel. I stealthily placed it inside the front door and took off for the bus that was waiting for me.

I still don't know how good a prank it would have been if I had gotten it on the bus. As it turned out, the team ended up in San Francisco at the St Francis hotel as guest of a prominent alumni booster, partying until the wee hours of Sunday morning.

I want to emphasize, I did not, as I am certain most of my teammates did likewise, break training rules set by our coach during the season. We were on an honor system, and to my knowledge not one squad member was disciplined for a rule infraction. I close my football reminiscing with the following declaration. I unequivocally honored our training rules. I loved the game so much, that when I was active, I daily thanked God for the privilege of blessing me with the heart and body that allowed me to play the game at the PAC 10 college level. The game was therapeutic for me during my stressful academic pursuits.

The Courting Days

      I will now chronicle the multi-courting days of "The Kid". (A nickname my son-in-law Chris bestowed upon me when he first entered into the Nicholau clan due to my youthful outlook on life…and it stuck.)

      But I digress. The name of my collegiate heartthrob was Pauline. Pauline Paris was one of four sisters and a brother: the children of Mrs. Anesti, a widow who remarried Mr. Anesti before I met Pauline. The Paris-Anesti family was a most loving and beautiful clan. The family name warranted respect within the Oakland Greek community. I met Pauline through a function of the Epsilon Phi Sig club. Our serious relationship was fostered through meetings at the Oakland Greek Church on Sundays and on other civic sponsored Greek functions. Although we saw much of each other, we still kept our options open for making and accepting other dates. Knowing I had three more years of college commitment in order to complete my pharmaceutical degree, coupled with Pauline's popularity in the Greek community, it seemed to be the logical approach to our mutual courting arrangement; I might add for both of us an uncharacteristic bohemian approach. As gallant as it appeared on the surface, I would be lying if I did not, at times, regret the fact we were steadfast pursuing our relationship in this manner, yet I have always maintained, God moves in mysterious ways.

      They say timing is everything when it comes to decision-making, and that impacts the direction and the status of one's life. The declaration of WWII following the infamous Pearl Harbor

Attack on Dec 7th 1941 found me in the final days of my junior year at Berkeley. It played a profound part in the mutual parting of ways between Pauline and me.

World War II placed me in a position to make, on short notice, a very serious decision. My choices were 1) wait to be drafted within a month, or 2) immediately enlist in the navy V7 program. The V7 voluntary enlistment allowed a college senior university student, which I now was, to finish his senior year and graduate before having to report for duty at the Northwestern University located in Chicago. Upon graduating from college, he would then immediately enter the V7 program at Northwestern University as a midshipman. After three months of concentrated officer's training, and if you survived the physical ongoing challenges with daily-abridged academic tests, and of consequential importance, exhibit a salient Navy officer's decorum while at Northwestern University Officers School, you were commissioned an Ensign in the USNR. I opted for the V7 program and was accepted. Having graduated from Cal and upon receiving my officer's commission three months later, I was assigned to active duty. My orders were to report on a yard class minesweeper at Pearl Harbor as the executive officer, second in command to the captain.

While I was participating in the V7 program, the second, and more consequential boy meets girl saga of 'The Kid' was about to take place. Upon graduating from the UC School of Pharmacy, I had two weeks leave before I had to report to the Northwestern University V7 Naval Academy. In that time I immediately took and passed the California State Board examination for my California Registered pharmacy license. Also while the subject matter was fresh in my mind, I took the Nevada state board exam, which allowed reciprocity with all the other states in the union with the exception of New York and California. I did this for security reasons. Having now qualified for California and Nevada, I would be eligible, after the war, to practice my profession in any state of the union other than New York. I felt empowered that I had earned universal control of my professional future, should I choose to practice in 47 of the 48 states, at that time, of the Union. Alaska and Hawaii had yet to become the 49th and 50th states of the United States of America.

While at Northwestern University in Chicago, I inquired about the Greek Orthodox Church in the area, and attended Sunday service. As was the custom of the Greek communities throughout the states during the war, there were sponsored welcome gatherings for the Hellenic boys and girls enlisted in the various armed services.

At one of those social events, I met Jane Ellis. We struck it off in a friendly way from the very beginning. It wasn't long after my attending several Hellenic social functions that I was invited by Jane to meet her family. The Ellis family, like Pauline's family was active in the community and highly respected by their peers. Being what seemed like a million miles from California, isolated in the service, I found myself visiting the Ellis family often during my limited leave from duty. Soon our dates during those three months escalated into a more serious relationship to the point of mutually agreeing to go steady.

While I was serving in the south pacific war zone, we kept our relationship ongoing through letters. This led to a commitment from me after the war that upon my discharge from the navy I would go back to Chicago primarily to discuss the seriousness of our intentions. This I did. We both felt upon our reunion, we should get engaged. I returned to California, and soon afterwards, Jane with her mother, followed on a prearranged date. A formal engagement announcement and celebration followed, and all seemed to go well. Wedding invitations were printed with guest lists on hand, when a drastic turn of events ensued.

In reality, I must admit Jane's mother, and to some extent Jane, were unpleasantly surprised to find on their first visit that our home was in the lower section of town, in a second story of a building over a saloon. I had warned Jane of this fact before their visit, and at the time it did not register to her as an important issue. The truth of the matter is, I did not then, nor do I now, blame either Mrs. Ellis or Jane for their initial shock. In fact, I was prepared for it. What I did expect, however, was upon meeting my mother, my brother and his family, our Greek community, and my college friends, they would accept and appreciate my home environment. Evidently this was not the case. It appears Jane's parents and Jane, I assume, although I could be mistaken on Jane's position, were formulating plans for me to move to Chicago where Jane's father was in the process of closing a deal to purchase a neighborhood pharmacy as a wedding "prica" (gift). This is commendable of her parents, for what parent does not wish the best for their child. However, this alerted me to the reality of our relationship.

After our engagement, I had interviewed for several pharmaceutical positions both in Marysville and in the bay area. Immediately following the war, registered pharmacists were in great demand. I was in the throws of making an exciting decision that I was eager to share with Jane. However, before I could do so, I was apprised of her father's pharmaceutical investment itinerary.

The very next day I phoned Jane and asserted my position of seeking employment in California. Her reaction and response was so devastatingly negative with the thought of her moving to California, it took the wind right out of my sails. Under the circumstances I suggested we call the whole thing off. Silence on the other end of the phone, then click! An hour later, I answered the phone and there was a compromise proposed by Jane. She would move to California if I promised to take a bay area pharmaceutical position that was waiting for me to accept. With her ultimatum, I was convinced it would be in the best interest for both of us to call the marriage off. It was clear to me that the relationship between her and my mother was uncomfortable, and I did not want to have to compromise my love for one over the other. Plus, the ultimatum was dictatorial in my mind and that was not a foundation that either one of us should endure. Ending the engagement turned out to be beneficial for both of us later on in our lives. Jane, met and married the right person for her. She has a daughter, who like my daughter Edie, studied voice and has preformed professionally. Details of my good fortune leading to my darling wife, Gaye, will follow later in my memoirs.

Football and Pharmacy
Time To Walk The Walk Off The Field

    At war's end, upon being honorably discharged from active duty, I again seriously pursued my profession. I had no apprenticeship experience other than my high school days when I worked as a stock boy in the local pharmacy. Yet I had a dream of how I wanted to practice my profession. I did not aspire to practice in a "general retail" pharmacy. I envisioned a clinical professional setting for a pharmacy. This concept was an innovative, daring approach in the forties, particularly in rural communities. My dream was to open a pharmacy with doctors in a clinic environment; to be an integral part of the professional medical health care team. It was a bold calculated risk at the time.

    I had several lucrative offers pending in a retail pharmacy, but chose to gamble, testing my dream on its' merit. Accordingly, I made an appointment with one of the founding doctors of our local clinic, Dr. Hoffman, to share my ideas and concept for a pharmacy. To my surprise, he was very receptive and suggested I return the following day for further discussions. I did so. That meeting went like this: "George, are you eligible, licensed and board certified to practice pharmacy at this moment? If so, how much capital do you need to open a pharmacy in this building? How long will it take? And can you design a functional dispensary pharmacy in a twelve foot by fifteen foot office area?" This meeting took place in July of 1946 and lasted ten minutes. Without hesitating, I answered in the affirmative on all queries, except the time and capital needed. On those issues I told him I would be back within a week with plans and a capital estimate. We stood up; we shook hands, and Dr. Hoffman said, "Go for it!"

    As soon as I left the clinic building, I realized the severity of my commitment. I started trembling, wondering where do I go from here? I hadn't filled one prescription as a registered pharmacist—let alone priced and stocked medications, or designed and managed my own Pharmacy! I tried to recall my lab sessions. The apothecary weights vs. metric system vs. the lb, etc. Compatibility of chemicals and their order of sequence for compounding various formulas, inventory of drugs, chemicals, compound equipment, scales, current laws and regulations, etc. This all rained upon me in an avalanche of concern, and priority. Could I get a pharmacy in a 12x15 square foot area? I certainly didn't hesitate to say I could. The more I reflected on all of the challenges awaiting me, the more I trembled.

Then it occurred to me. Was all this philosophical jargon I bought for myself through football just a figure of speech or the real McCoy? I distinctly recall making the following pledge to my coaches and fellow squad members at my senior football awards banquet:

> "In the course of my life, whenever confronted with a prodigious challenge, I will look at my Big C medal and know I will succeed. For this I thank my coaches, teammates and especially the sport of football!"

With that flashback in mind, I took a deep breath, and said a prayer and started doing! I knew I loved the opportunity. I knew it was a worthy venture. I had but to do it. So, I bit the bullet. Few meaningful things have happened in my life that caused more exhilaration and excitement, sprinkled (down pour is more like it) with fear and trepidation over my "chewing and digesting" that bullet.

First and foremost, I visited the Dean of UC Pharmacy School in S.F. I laid my dilemma before him and asked for advice on how to proceed. He pointed out the dangers and pitfalls of opening and managing a pharmacy without on-hand experience as a registered pharmacist. The risk factor in both competence and in financial survival was enormous. He asked if I had a design plan drawn up for him to review. I did not have one. Was I up on the current laws and post war plethora of new drugs flooding the market? On their pros and cons, incompatibilities, etc.? On and on he queried me on the business and on the technical end of the profession, as well. Finally, he congratulated me on my enthusiasm but strongly advised that I not take on such a venture at this point in time. The odds of failure were overwhelming, and the odds of patient error would be imminent.

I thanked the Dean for his sincere and valuable advice and left his presence wondering what now? Well, to my surprise I felt even more determined to succeed. I relegated his advice to that of a detailed, competent, scout report: Obstacles that I must overcome with a pragmatic game plan. Being aware of the pitfalls is the first step to conquering them.

I lost no time in going from the dean's office to a leading professional pharmacy in a S.F. medical building. I introduced myself to the owner pharmacist and related to him my mission. I asked if I could spend a day or two observing his operation and taking some measurement of his Rx bench. Being a UC Pharmacy alumnus, he had kept track of my football exposure as a pharmacy student and was very happy to help me in any way he could. His input was invaluable.

Next, I introduced myself to the president of McKesson and Robbins, a Sacramento area pharmaceutical distributor, and asked for guidance in opening a pharmacy. Specifically, I was interested in an initial inventory list, pharmaceutical equipment, and store design ideas, etc. The reception was cordial and cooperative. I received extraordinary attention in all facets of my project.

Now that I had an inkling to the specks for a pharmacy work bench along with a base inventory of essential chemicals and drugs, plus the California store licensing procedure, I interviewed and negotiated a contract for the actual remodeling of the 12 x 15 space into a professional dispensary.

All of the above was done within a week of my interview with the clinic doctors! I gave the doctors a to-date progress report. They, being favorably impressed, deposited monies in the bank for immediate and current expenditure. Thus, The Marysville Clinic Pharmacy became a reality in September of 1946.

Becoming a reality and becoming a successful business venture entailed two separate challenges. The former was to research and obtain the parts of the puzzle, which to date, was accomplished as it is written. The latter was to successfully manage the contingencies of the outcome! All the physical essentials for a business venture, i.e. location, store design, lease, inventory, etc., were in order. However, the labor personnel to operate the venture was on hold.

    Not to worry. The Good Lord again intervened, and presto, there, least unbeknownst to me, came the love of my life to the rescue. It so happened, during that particular point in time, Gaye Bravos was between semesters during her graduating year from Yuba College, and volunteered (I emphasized volunteered) to help me arrange the stock and get organized for opening day. Not only that, but with her father's encouragement, she willingly stayed on during her vacation period as my right hand in operating the Marysville Clinic Pharmacy. Yes, I could have managed it on my own, but oh, what relief to have her take charge of all the nuances that go with the initial grand opening of a business.

My angel, Gaye

Envision, and I am not exaggerating one bit, as you see from the above picture, a very attractive, always stylishly dressed, beautifully proportioned, angelic girl, whose goal was to graduate with a teaching credential from San Jose State College. Further envision her volunteering to work by my side in an hour of need, and emphatically denying one penny for her efforts. Now you know why there was no way that angel was going to escape from me, if I could help it.

Not only did I help it, I proposed and made it happen! Thank You Lord for one of the many blessings I will eternally celebrate!

Gaye and Mother

While I do not hesitate to credit the Good Lord for many of my fortuitous happenings, I would be remiss if I did not emphasize the critical role my Mother played towards the fulfillment of our marital vows. You see, unbeknownst to me, Gaye shared with Mother her true feelings towards me. Of course Mother thought the world of Gaye, and together they plotted~ I use the word advisedly for lack of a more definitive
term that would adequately describe the matchmakers
marital sting ~ and for their success I am ever grateful!!

Pauletimi Aglaia Bravos, "Gaye"

Our engagement picture
Gaye's Mother, Lula Bravos, Gaye, Me,
and my Mother, Despo Nicholau

Gaye with her brothers, George and Ted, and her Mom, Lula Bravos

The best decision I ever made

What's more, Gaye was and is a ballerina when it comes to dancing. Many were the dance parties we attended where I had but the first and last dance…"Goodnight Sweetheart"… with *my* sweetheart due to her popularity on the dance floor. Yet, I'd have it no other way. After all, I was a pretty good hoofer myself.

Now that you have been formerly introduced to my Gaye, I will resume my account of the embryo years of the Marysville Clinic Pharmacy. Upon opening the pharmacy, with Gaye's volunteering effort, I was so inexperienced I didn't dare hire permanent help of any kind, as I did not know what to expect. I visited our community college and sought help from the business department for setting up my books for P and L statements. I do recall that weeks before opening, I bought a supply of carbon copy paper to distribute to the nine doctors who comprised the clinic staff at that time. I asked them to make available to me a copy of every Rx they wrote. At night I would go to their respective offices and collect the Rx copies and practice reading them, filling them and pricing them. Many of the prescriptions I could not decipher until I became more familiar with their handwriting and drug nomenclature. I recall experimenting with my scales for compounding prescriptions. That was a revelation in itself. I thought a 5 grain aspirin tablet should weight 5 grains!! Of course it weighed more due to other innocuous ingredients necessary to manufacture the tablet. After a few panic moments I resolved that dilemma.

      I mention all the above to impress upon you just how inexperienced I was. Yet I would not relent. I knew somehow, someway I was going to get the job done I was bound and determined to do it. I would not be denied. I made it a point to cross each bridge as it presented itself. I trusted in God that all would go well. I absolutely knew what I was doing was proper and not at the risk to a patient. The rest is history. Over a million prescriptions and 41 years later I retired from my beloved Clinic Pharmacy. I also founded Safesave Pharmacy in Yuba City in 1961, and it is still going strong. I turned the store over to my faithful and very trust worthy pharmacy <u>friend </u>Ernest Low in 1987.

      I do believe now is as good a time as any for some literary thoughts on 'reality'.

Narative II

THE ABSOLUTE OF REALITY IN MAKING SMART
CHOICES DURING YOUR LIFESPAN

     Having enlightened you on the utmost chance for success through the subject of DOING, I will now address the vital element of REALITY plays in the pursuit to live a happy, useful, Christian life.
     During WWII, while stationed in Honolulu, I was the executive officer on the minesweeper USSRUFF, before being ordered on a minesweeper in the Philippines. I was approached to try for a spot on the active enlisted Navy football team operating in the South Pacific waters. During the latter stage of the war, the armed forces were recruiting university and pro football players who were in the service to form an inter-military league. The sole purpose of the league was a diversion to boost the morale within the armed forces. Games were scheduled in the various war zones. Those chosen to represent their units were given time off from their primary assignment to participate in the program. Boxing matches between Navy ships' personnel waiting further orders, and shore personnel likewise, were also a popular morale booster.

I felt singularly honored to have been recruited, and gave a cursory Yes! to the invitation. The love and enthusiasm I had for the game factored into a knee-jerk, yes, no-brainer decision.

But wait! Upon further consideration a mind-blowing reaction flashed within my mental faculties. Mentally, if anything, I was over qualified. But, physically, now that's another story. For the first time since the genesis of my "Doing" canon, I experienced an underlying thought that challenged the validity of the "Doing" edict, without giving due consideration to the prerequisite essentials to succeed in one's chosen goal.

Hence, an eye opener; upon sensible review in the truism of doing, it was with certainty that I realized in this instance, at my size, weight and age, I was not gifted with the God-given native stature to compete on that level. Don't take my word for it. I'll let you be the judge.

My innate profile follows: height 5'8", weight 168 pounds, speed average. Those numbers, for a lineman, albeit with my heart and desire unlimited, would pale in comparison to the endorsements of proven pro athletic linemen blessed with 6 feet plus height, >250 pounds and above, speed of 4.7 to 5.2 seconds in the 40 yard dash. They were also blessed with great heart and desire, which separated them from other physically eligible gifted recruits. Under those circumstances, it would be totally illogical for me to believe that my Doing doctrine, in itself, would enable me to succeed. My cursory yes response was doomed to failure.

Ergo- heart, desire, and love—all essential assets to the successful pursuit of one's dreams, must now incorporate the silent critical element in the Doing edict, REALITY! With reality aboard, poor choices are vastly minimized.

So, one must incorporate the essence of REALITY within the doing creed in one's life's cafeteria of choices; whether they be in a physical venture, or in an academic stratum. Go forth in a realistic manner in the pursuit of life's rewarding dreams. With HIS wisdom and walking in HIS light, one must exploit his God-given choices that challenge one's intellect to it's fullest.

During my senior year at Cal in the midst of WWII, the last game of the season was scheduled with the US Air Force football recruits stationed at Moraga, the home of the then St. Mary's College football team. Ironically, playing right tackle on the Air Force line opposite me was none other than Larry Lutz, weighing 235 lbs, height 6'1", who incidentally was my freshman coach at Cal. How about that! (Memorial Stadium was packed. Military personnel matched the student body in the stands, while the civilians occupied the rest of the seats).

The initial greeting between us was bizarre; fraternal, but brief. The ensuing combat was fierce and combative with no holds barred. I was singularly intent to prove to him his coaching acumen paid off. Yet, at the same time, the truth be known, the REALITY dictum proved relevant. This was evidenced when right after the game, while still on the field, we both became civil again, and Larry praised me with "Good Game, Greek", which was somewhat embroidered with a wink of an eye. The hidden message being "I taught you well, but…"

Vi Botary, another Cal All American, played halfback on the Air Force team. The one time I had a clear shot at tackling him, I carried a bruised face the rest of the game. This was brought on by the continued pumping of his legs against my face before he went down—five yards after my initial contact! Another endorsement of REALITY in my adventuresome life. Reality, an inherent precursor to success, is immune to personal pride. I knew I had to respect it's importance within the "Doing" concept, and then my life's smart choices would ultimately excel.

Bottom line: Honor the process of making REALITY choices. Retire pride to the back burner of your brain cells. Keep on simmer your common sense cells to initially ignite wise REALITY choices at your beckoning. That approach will enable a worthy, yet seemingly impossible commitment, to become possible, then probable, and in the end, doable.

Anchors Aweigh!

To refresh your memory, I volunteered in the Navy sponsored V7 program, which allowed a college student to finish his/her college degree if there remained just one more year before graduating. Having graduated from UCSF pharmacy school in the spring semester of 1943, I immediately reported to Northwestern University in Chicago, Illinois as a Mid shipman for training to become commissioned an officer in the United States Naval Reserves.

Upon successfully completing my midshipman schooling, I was commissioned an Ensign. I volunteered for submarine duty, but was assigned to a minesweeper. The ship to which I was to report, the USS RUFF, was stationed in Pearl Harbor, Honolulu, Oahu. It was a yard class minesweeper staffed with two commissioned officers; a lieutenant, the captain, and a commissioned executive officer. I was ordered to replace the current executive officer who was ordered back to the main land for duty.

Let me put this into perspective. A land lover, registered Pharmacist, whose extensive naval experience was (other than midshipman academia) an occasional canoeing on Ellis Lake in Marysville, California (a good 120 miles from the Pacific Ocean) and who had never seen, let alone boarded a navy ship (other than being transported from San Francisco to Oahu on an aircraft carrier) was ordered for duty as an EXECUTIVE Officer on a minesweeper!! I was welcomed aboard by the current executive officer on his way OFF the ship. He had stat orders, the moment I reported on the ship, to leave for San Francisco.

  The captain of the USS RUFF, Lt USNR Mr. Peach lived in Hawaii, and when the ship docked after its early AM sweep of the channel into Pearl Harbor, he would turn over the ship to this veteran executive officer and head for his home. When the captain is off the ship, the executive officer is the acting captain. Ergo, Ensign Nicholau reports for duty on the USS RUFF with the rank of surrogate Captain! Now, I was well read in the protocol, etiquette, and responsibilities of a Navy Officer, but starting as an executive officer was a bit much even for me. Thank God for my "doing' philosophy, for it kicked in during my hour of need (panic). The first order I gave to a steward was to have the chief petty officer report to me in the Captain's Quarters. When Gregg, the chief petty officer, came forth I returned his salute and ordered him to carry on with his normal duties until I became better acquainted with Captain Peach's routine. He acknowledged my order, and I hibernated in the Captain's quarters for the rest of the day. The following morning, I met the captain and shared with him my orders to the Chief, and informed him of my inexperience. He was very understanding and for the first week he ordered me to observe him and ask any questions I wanted to ask. He volunteered to stay aboard during the day, so I could observe his daily routine with the crew, in the granting of liberty, meeting out discipline, if necessary, ordering special duties that needed to be attended to, etc. He ordered me to pay special attention to the *Conning* of the ship: the orders and sequence of orders to be communicated from the Conning tower to the engine room for maneuvering the ship. This I did studiously, and I must add I was a fast learner. At weeks end, I felt comfortable when the captain headed for home after we docked for the day. Comfortable, but not totally competent, as you will see. A learning curve is still a curve that has to be mastered. Although I was headed for the peak, I still had a long way to go.

For starters, one of the subjects imbedded at Northwestern was the imperative cleanliness of the crew's living quarters aboard a ship. Of course, that included the ship's galley and heads (kitchen and toilets). During my midshipman's training, the officer of the day would wear white gloves and do his inspection, expecting them to be spotless at the end of his routine. Our beds were supposed to be so neat, you could bounce a coin off the top blanket. Fail an inspection, and your liberty privileges would suffer. With that mindset, I would do my routine daily inspection when the captain would leave the ship under my command when we were docked.

In my first couple of inspections, I was appalled at the low standard of cleanliness I encountered. To correct the situation, I began denying liberty privileges until the galley, heads, and living quarters of the crew were midshipman-grade clean! It took a full week of spot inspections around the ship before it met my expected standard of cleanliness.

With that being so, three things became alarmingly apparent. First, the USS Ruff was the cleanest A.M.C. minesweeper stationed at Pear Harbor. Second, the crew morale was fast demoting from an efficient, easygoing bunch of men into grouchy, unhappy sailors. Third, and most crucial in significance, was a noticeable inefficient launching of the minesweeping gear. To the extent, one morning the captain called me into his quarters before leaving the ship and asked me for the cause of the launching snafus. It took three weeks for this meeting to be a necessity, as the effectiveness of our daily mission was gradually deteriorating. He ordered me to get things back in shape and to do it now!

With that responsibility on my shoulders, I gave one of the smartest orders during my whole career as an officer. I ordered the chief petty officer of the crew, Gregg, to meet me in my quarters at eleven hundred on that very morning. Eleven sharp he was in my office standing at attention in full dress uniform, which incidentally exhibited more stripes up his sleeve than I cared to count. I gave the order "at ease" and asked him to take a chair. The following is a verbatim dialogue that took place between us.

"Gregg, how many years have you served in the Navy?"

"Fourteen years, Sir." was his response in an affirmative authoritative voice.

"Chief, I'm just completing my fourth month." My remarks caused an inquisitive look on his face, wondering what I was leading up to. I acknowledged his silent query with the follow up, "Until I counter my present order, I give you full authority to deny or grant liberty to any crew member. Further, I order you to give a high priority in getting all mine sweeping gear in efficient operative condition. If you encounter a personnel problem beyond your means to settle, refer the sailor to me with your recommendation. Unless I sense an overt cause of injustice, I will heartedly back you up. Are you clear with my orders? Do you have any questions as to the intent of my orders?"

"No Sir, the intent of your orders will be done."

"Good. Let's get this ship as efficient as it was before I came aboard."

Within a week, under Chief Gregg's leadership, the USS Ruff was once again a happy, thoroughly efficient minesweeper. Captain Peach congratulated me on the complete turn around of attitude and efficiency of the crew. I let Gregg know how the Captain felt and congratulated him for righting a wrong in a short order. To boot, the living quarters of the crew did not fail an occasional inspection under a more realistic standard. Flexibility has not been one of my shortcomings. I never question one's motive for agreeing to see things my way. Say what?!

This past experience propelled my learning curve of a commissioned officer in the USNR, i.e.; Be aware of priorities under your command , and lead by example through appropriate channels to excel in a given mission. Be knowledgeable and fair, but firm in all dealings with your crew.

The Bell Tolls for ME

I hinted above that I was a fast learner, and I was. Too fast, particularly in the incident I am about to relay. In lay terms, each time an order is given from the conning tower to the engine room, a bell alerts the engine room of the order. The engine room then acknowledges the order by repeating it up to the conning tower. To dock a ship, the speed and approach angle is critical to avoid excessive forceful contact of the ship with the dock, or with an adjacent ship one may be docking along side. It is not uncommon in the process, to give anywhere from four to six orders, or more, from the conning tower, each activating a bell response before the ship is docked. The less bells heard in the process, the more respected is the conning officer. The bell count begins after the first 'stop all engines' order is given in the docking maneuver.

    The following conditions all play a role in the reason for a bell order to the engine room; water current, force and direction, wind, angle of approach, present speed, whether the ship has one or two propellers, and tonnage. All docking orders are registered in the ship's log. A perfect dock is registered in the ship's log as a "No bell" docking. A rare specimen on one's resume, if attained at all. I took pride in having had several one-bell landings, but still no 'No bell' landings. The crew was aware of my proficiency and they kept encouraging me to go for the No bell record. Low and behold, after several months of trying, I succeeded! The crew seemed more elated than I. However, having done it once, I was committed to a repeat, to prove to myself it wasn't by accident. Two weeks later a turn in events put that goal on the back burner. Here is what took place.

Upon completing our sweep of the area, the captain, Mr. Peach, as was his custom, went to his quarter, giving me control of conning the ship. The channel leading into Pearl Harbor would begin about two miles out, (I'm guessing a the distance) marked with restrictive buoys on each side of the channel within which the ship must navigate. Before heading for the channel to return to our docking area, Gibson's Point, located in Pearl Harbor, all minesweepers would retrieve their magnetic and manual gear beyond the first set of the buoys. Once all the gear is retrieved, we would check for any destroyers, cruisers, carriers or battle ships heading for the channel. If one of the above ships were spotted we would wait, and follow it into the now swept channel of Pearl Harbor. Because of our limited speed, it was a taboo to go before them into the channel. On this particular morning, I had just retrieved all my gear, and was headed for the channel opening. It was a foggy morning, but visibility was still adequate to the point where I saw no vessels approaching the channel from a concerned distance. I entered the channel and sailed along as usual until I got about halfway home. Then all hell broke loose. Approaching from the rear was a big cruiser. At once I ordered 'full speed ahead' to get further away from the cruiser, but to no avail. It was gaining on me. (Because of the buoys' restriction I could not maneuver to either side of the channel). I ordered 'flank speed ahead', which meant give me all you got and do it now! Still the cruiser was gaining. I'd hoped the cruiser was aware of the gravity of the situation, for each time its bow would raise up and come back down into the ocean, I could see it knifing my little AMC in half. By now the USS Ruff was vibrating and the captain came topside. I had just ordered the crew to put up three balls on the mast to signal to the cruiser we were in the process of sweeping the channel- although we were not-which obligated any ship near us to stay a given distance from us, so as to not be in danger of an exploding mine through our efforts. That maneuver caused the cruiser to slow down, and we escaped intact. I logged the whole incident as I lived it, and the captain praised me for my reaction to fast approaching cruiser. The reason for the impending crisis was heightened due to the difference in speed between the minesweeper and the cruiser. It was heartening to know I did not panic under the trying circumstances.

Having been stationed in Hawaii for several months, I was due for a change of orders. However, I fast-forwarded my orders from the Hawaiian Islands to the Philippines area with a bang.

As you recall, I mentioned I was a fast learner. In fact I was too fast. Here is what I mean by too fast. Since my first No bell landing, I was bound to repeat it to prove to myself that it was no accident. I succeeded on my second attempt, no less! My reputation was approaching an "old salt" among my crew. However, I soon encountered a "speed bump". I was ordered to dock our ship next to her sister ships now docked at Bishop's Point within Pearl Harbor. To do so, it was necessary for me to make a 180 degree turn maneuver to approach a proper angle for the docking. Recall the ship speed is critical moments before the docking. Too fast, and you must give a signal to the engine room to back off. Too slow, the ship floats uncontrolled and you must give a signal to the engine room to start the engines. Judging the critical speed of the ship before it starts to float, or before it goes too fast for a No-bell landing, means you must give the first 'stop all engines' order at the exact time you feel the ship will have enough inertia to respond to rudder orders. This will assure the proper speed and angle of approach to the docking target whether it is next to the dock or an adjacent ship.

This particular day I approached Pearl Harbor sailing north into a formidable North wind. Therefore, I delayed my initial order to stop all engines in order not to lose steering speed for the 180-degree turn maneuver and still have the critical speed needed for the remainder of the docking procedure. At the proper moment I gave the 'stop all engines' order with just enough headway speed to make the 180 degree maneuver without another bell order. So far so good, but wait. Now the north wind and current were behind me, and the ship's momentum was appreciably picking up speed as I was approaching the side of the sister docked minesweeper. Forget the no bell effort.

I ordered 'back 1/2 speed'. But still the ship was approaching too fast for comfort. I ordered 'full back speed', but the wind and current still had a positive effect on the approach speed. Finally, I gave the 'flank back order', the ultimate capacity of the engine. The ship vibrated. The captain rushed topside and observed the activities. To exacerbate the situation, there were several captain gigs docked just ahead of the space allotted for my ship to dock, against the docked sister ship, so I knew if I did not react at once, I would crash into all those captain gigs. I gave a 'hard left rudder' order to increase the angle of approach towards the sister ship, preferring to have it absorb the shock, rather than annihilate several captain gigs. Having given a 'flank back speed' order, a 'hard left rudder' order, and 'fenders over the side' order to help absorb the shock, I looked at the Captain and asked "Do you have any other suggestions?

"Just one" he offered, "Brace yourself."

Now the ship was literally crawling about one plus knots but still the tonnage mass of its glancing blow against the sister ship ripped up several yards of railing on both wood framed ships before coming to a halt about ten yards short of the captain gigs. Pleased with the end results, compared to the potential disaster that loomed before me, without hesitation, I ordered over the loud speaker "secure all gears and all liberty party ashore", implying just another routine docking. Which of course it was not.

The captain looked at me and said, "George, you're one of a kind. Log the incident, and write up a report for the base commander. Make an appointment and present it to him!" This I did. I made an appointment, and damned if the base commander wasn't a Cal alumnus. I handed him my report with the comment, "Commander here is a blow by blow description of my docking fiasco."

"Greek, good luck on your next command." By golly, he even knew I played ball for Cal, because how else would he know to address me as "Greek". Two weeks later, I had my orders as an executive officer on a YMS minesweeper, a larger class than the

AMC sweeper. A promotion no less! Off I went to Morotai in the Philippines, a launching site for the Japanese mainland.

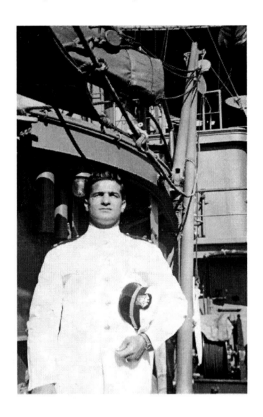

An interesting sequel. Years later I was a guest of Jim Kourafas in a Golf invitational at the San Joaquin G&CC in Fresno. While enjoying libations in the card room with several of Jim's cronies, personal WWII stories were the topic of interest. In due time I shared my No bell experience, and I'll be damned, unbeknownst to me, if the retired Lieutenant Commander at Pearl Harbor who ordered my YMS order in the Philippines was among us. He verified my story and with humor added he would have ordered me into Tokyo if a YMS was stationed there. Rest assured my reminiscing is not a figure of my imagination. They are unembellished facts as I experienced them.

Leaving Honolulu for the Philippines theatre was an interesting happening in itself. To say it was a harrowing start would be putting it mildly. At Gibson's Point in Pearl Harbor, directly across from where the minesweepers were docked, there was a big aircraft carrier docked, facing the exit direction in the channel. I was to board this ship for transportation to Morotai. I received my orders at 15 hours on a Saturday afternoon and I reported aboard the carrier by 1am Sunday. My last day in Honolulu was going to be a memorable one. One of the officers invited me to his home on the far side of the island where he was celebrating his first year wedding anniversary. Of course I accepted and joined him at his home where the party was in full swing. Suddenly, it dawned upon me, it being 2400 hours, I had just one hour to get from the far side of the island to Bishop's Point and report aboard the carrier. I pleaded to the host to please call for a cab, as I was desperate to get to Bishop's Point before 1 a.m. He made the call, and the dispatcher said all cabs were busy and that there was a backlog waiting for transportation. Panicking, I asked him to call the Shore Patrol and register a complaint.

"Tell him you have a sailor who refuses to leave your house". I emphasized he say sailor, not an officer, to assure him of a positive response. This he did, and the shore patrol was surprised upon arriving at the home to find an officer to be the culprit. However, when I explained the dire circumstances of the situation, he agreed to get me to Bishop's Point on two conditions. First, I would have to sit in the paddy wagon cage with the other inebriated sailors. Second, he was instructed to drop off the sailors in sequence to their ship location in Pearl Harbor, and therefore, had no control over the time it would take to get me to Bishop's point, as that would be the furthest distance in his route. Having no alternative, I got into the paddy-wagon among the celebrating wayward sailors. The first remark I heard was from an intoxicated sailor seated across from me, in a sarcastic voice, "S_ _ _ , a stoned sailor can't even dodge an officer in a paddy wagon ride to his ship!" All the eyes of the 'crocked' sailors now focused on me. I countered in an exaggerated slurred, drunken tone, "Sailor, I feel damned proud to have earned the right to be in your company on my last trip on this island." – under my breath I said "I hope". Anyway, my soused dialect and the gravity of my comment broke the ice, and from there on we were a big happy ("inebriated") family, joking and singing, as we were being shuttled, one at a time, to various ships stationed in Pearl Harbor. I arrived at Bishop's Point at 1:30 A.M., a half hour late according to my orders. Thank God, the carrier was still docked across the channel from where I stood. I was preparing to swim for it, when the officer of the day for Bishop's Point approached me, and inquired what I was up to standing at the edge of the channel. I told him I had to be aboard that carrier, and it had to be now, as I was already 1/2 hour late to report aboard. "Come with me and I'll get you transportation across the channel" he offered. And that is how I dodged a bullet honoring my orders into the Philippine war zone.

Upon my arrival in the Philippines, the Minesweeper I was ordered to serve on hit a mine itself, while I was on my way there. I was ordered to dispose of it in deep waters before serving on another Minesweeper

Oh Karithia!

    I'm forever grateful for having made the ship in time, for more than the reason outlined above. It was on the carrier crossing the Pacific Ocean to Morotai, that I had the honor of making the acquaintance with one, Christopheredes, whom at the time was the middleweight champion of the world. What brought us close was the fact that he was Greek, and I was exposed to the sport of boxing early on because our home in Marysville was across the street from a boxing arena, owned by Cal Herman, a prominent promoter in the thirties. I used to spend a lot of my youth in the arena getting boxing tips from Eddie, a trainer and caretaker of the facility. There was a parking garage next to the sports arena, and I recall parking Max Baer's big Lincoln automobile. Max Baer was the heavy weight champion of the world, and it just so happened that he was featured as a referee on that night's boxing card. I received a one-dollar tip from him!

    Back to Christopheredes. With my limited boxing background (incidentally I did enter into several boxing matches at the Cal Herman facility, retiring with an unbeaten record) I would occasionally go into a shadow boxing routine with Christopheredes, and he would tease me along. In this way we had fun breaking the monotony on the trip. Christopheredes was a non-commissioned officer, put in charge of boxing exhibitions while stationed at Morotai, our destination.

    Off the shores of Morotai, the horizon was dotted with the silhouette of several anchored transport ships in preparation for the impending Japanese island invasion. From this array of ships, Christopheredes would find the personnel to put on weekly boxing exhibitions on Morotai every Friday night. It was a coveted attraction to all armed forces. Many navy marines, air force, and army personnel from the anchored ships headed for the boxing matches on the island. The island personnel and stationed ship personnel would start gathering at the site of the boxing ring around 1400 hours for the start of the boxing exhibitions beginning at 1800. Reserved in the front several rows would be seating for the top brass personnel – admirals, captains, etc. and one, George Nicholau, now ranked a Lieutenant JG in the USNR, who was assigned a reserve seat next to the promoter of the event, Mr. Christopheredes! Accordingly, I would make a last minute presumptuous entry to my reserved seat, after all the brass were seated in front of the several thousand service-men in an amphitheater setting. Christopheredes advised me, if any one of the brass approached me, to volunteer I was one of his past sparing partners. Although I noticed some high brass intrigued eyes fixed on me, no one approached me for my autograph.

    Now here is the reason for the reciprocity of my good fortune with Chritophoredes, other than our close relationship on the carrier. Not being a commissioned officer in the navy, Christopheredes was not allowed into the officer's club. I corrected this remiss by loaning him one of my shirts with the lieutenant J. G. bars attached, and presto, "officer" Christopheredes Lt. J.G. accompanied me into the officer's quarter for a bit of libation. I first used this approach when stationed in Honolulu, when my cousin Nicholas Nicholau was stationed in Pearl Harbor as a noncommissioned Military Police officer. It worked wonders at the Bishop Point Officer's club for Nick and myself. So once again I used this hoax for the third and final time. After the Christopheredes expeditious promotion to rank of Lt. J.G., I had the honor to "commission" Dan Mc Carthy, my fellow pharmacist and football teammate at Cal, when he too ended up in Morotai in preparation for the invasion of Japan. (Dan was a New Zealand citizen and was not eligible for the draft. However, when I was commissioned and had one week leave, I asked Dan to join me at my home in Marysville for a going away celebration. Unknown to his parents who lived in San Francisco, and to me at the time, Dan, while in Marysville, volunteered and enlisted in the US army as a private at the Marysville, California P.O! As a registered pharmacist, his civilian future was limitless, yet he chose to fight for a worthy cause and for his adopted country, the USA.) A singular happening in a "small world" during a big war. An aside.

Lt Governor Leo McCarthy was Dan's brother! Many were the times we spent celebrating evenings together in San Francisco during Dan's and my pharmacy years. Dan's father was the proprietor of a very popular cocktail lounge located on Market Street, and a prime booster of the governor of California.

Gads but I get side tracked! Back to Christopheredes. On a day I drew the Officer in Charge duty for the base at Morotai, I was checking the log and I came across an entry of a Greek merchant ship docked off shore. I used my binoculars and spotted the Greek flag on the ship. I immediately contacted Chritophoredes, and invited him to join me as I intended to pay a "social" visit aboard the ship that afternoon. He eagerly accepted my invitation. I commandeered a captain's gig and off we went towards the Greek merchant ship. Upon arriving at the ship, I saluted the deck officer and asked permission to board the ship. Permission granted. I asked the officer to take us to the captain. When I met the captain, I, in Greek, introduced myself and my guest Mr. Christophoredes.

"Mr. Christopheredes" the captain exclaimed, "the middle weight champion of the world!" And from then on the king of Greece would not have been more welcomed aboard this captain's ship. Now, all this exuberance and dialogue was in Greek, which magnified the exhilaration exponentially. We were invited into the officer's quarters, and hors d'oeuvres of the Greek variety from feta cheese, Kalamata olives, loukanika sausage, tarama, skordalia, dolmades, to lamb ribs, graced the dining room table. To tease your appetite, they also served retsina, the vintage Greek wine noted for it's high alcohol content, as well as its turpentine flavor caused by the tree pitch added to the fermenting process. Once one becomes accustomed to the unique bouquet, it grows on you to become the wine of choice. Especially so when accompanied with Greek cuisine.

While stories were told and celebrated around Christopheredes' boxing adventures, the Captain kept our respective glasses filled to the brim, before we ever had a chance to empty them. This went on for a couple of hours when I suggested to Christopheredes we had better head back before it got too dark. He looked at me with a dazed facial expression. I repeated myself, and still the frozen look off into space. I reached over and tapped his shoulder to snap him out of his trance, and his head came straight down landing on his arms folded in front of him on the table. I mean he was out of it, period! Now I was in a real bind, and wondered how I was going to manage this dilemma, when the captain, seeing my concern, said "don't worry, I'll have him up and about in a short amount of time." Again, I remind you all conversation was in Greek. I emphasize this for it lends flavor to the happenings.

The captain ordered two of his crew to take Christopheredes to his bed quarters and called for the chef to come forth. When the cook arrived, the captain apprises him of the situation, and the cook acknowledges his understanding of what is expected from him. The captain then says to me "George, don't worry, we'll have him ready to go in a few minutes." True to his word up comes Christopheredes 20 minutes later, I won't say bright eyed, but sober enough to be ambulatory. I asked the captain what his secret was. He told me the chef sliced a red onion and placed the slices on his testicles, keeping them in place with a towel for about 15 minutes, and it did the trick. What say I – live and learn. I hope not the hard way. As I have mentioned before "All is well that ends well."

Fast forward post war to 1985 when the National AHEPA lodge was sponsoring a 5 day golf tournament in Corfu, Greece, that year. A close friend of mine and a Cal classmate, Harry Pappas, and his wife Agape, invited Gaye and me to join them for the AHEPA sponsored golf tournament. We accepted the invitation and what a surprise was awaiting me. When, after playing golf, we got to our reserved table situated among the several hundred attendees representing several states in America, we were seated two rows back from the elevated podium, where the dignitaries from Greece, and top delegates of the AHEPA lodge were seated. Also seated there was the main speaker for the evening. His name? Christopheredes, the Mayor at that point in time, of Glifada, a city situated just outside of Athens. I was flabbergasted to put it charitably. Having been served our dinner, before taking a bite, I excused myself from the table, and went to the podium, leaned across the table and greeted Mayor Christopheredes, at the same time asking him if he remembered me, George Nicholau. He gave me a cursory polite acknowledgment, and I was aware he really couldn't place me in his mind. He probably ventured I was one of his loyal followers during his boxing hay days. I sensed his uncertainty, and commented in Greek "You don't really remember me, but do you remember the red onions on your testicles?" (in Greek it does not sound sexual). Phonetically translated, "Then me thimase alla themase ta krimithia sta karithia?!"

"George!" he shouted, and jumped up from his chair, reached across the table and grabbed my hand in a wild handshake, all the time saying, "It is you, it is you!!" "Let's get together after the banquet."

"Of course" I agreed.

When he was introduced as the key-note speaker as the mayor of Glifada, and the former middleweight champion of the world, the applause was deafening. When the hall became quiet, and all were seated again, he began,

"Before I speak on the topic of the evening, I want to introduce you to a fellow warrior, who befriended me during the war while we were both stationed in the Philippine Islands. "George Nicholau, will you please stand. This man was my perfect host during our short stay together on the Island of Morotai. George, if you have time to visit me in Glifada, I'll see you have the key to the city." Just goes to show you, what goes around, comes around.

As he spoke you could sense how he earned his World Boxing Championship belt. His message was inspirational, delivered with such enthusiasm you could feel the vibes in his words. Between thunderous clapping you could hear a pin drop onto the floor as he captivated us with his quality leadership message. His worthy opponents in the ring need not bow their heads for succumbing to his relentless attack in his pursuit of victory. I consider it an honor to be counted among Champion

Christopheredes' elite group. I am so "thankful for the memories", to paraphrase Bob Hope.

I am in the middle, Christopheredes is far right

A Farewell To Arms

For no apparent logical reason, a morale-building incident comes to mind. It occurred during my decommissioning of the yard minesweeper in WWII that I referred to earlier. The ship was docked, missing its stern at an island port under the Australian flag. On the island there was a recreation center where sports equipment, from boxing, baseball. soccer, football, etc. could be obtained by military personnel, while awaiting the invasion orders into Japan.

The playing field was extensive and several games from the personnel of the various docked ships would be in process during the day.

It was during one of our recreation periods that our chief Petty officer, David, forgot his last name, a powerful individual, got into an altercation with a much less physically endowed sailor of our crew. He was punishing his small adversary when I intervened.

"Dave that's enough. You are taking advantage of a smaller man. Save your skill for someone your size."

The chief was still fired up and shouted, "If you weren't protected with your officer's rank bars…" he stopped there.

"Dave" I said "for the sport of it, I'll remove my rank bars and jacket and put the gloves on with you for 2 minute rounds, one minute rest between rounds, until one of us says uncle. This way it becomes a recreational outing for both of us". The word spread pretty fast, for by the time we signed out for the gloves, there must have been over a hundred sailors from the recreation field forming an imaginary square ring for us to box within. A sailor volunteered to time the rounds. In round one, before I knew what happened Dave rushed me with a wild haymaker connecting on the side of my head. My feet buckled under me and the next thing I realized, I was on my knees. I had the sense to stay down for a few seconds to clear my head and then got up thinking defense. With my ingrained boxing skills, I was able to block his haymaker attack and counter with straight left jabs to his face for the rest of the round. Round two was some of the same; left jabs to the face with occasional right thrust to his body. His attack was negated by my continued blocking of his wild haymaker bar room swings. In round three, I threw several right hands to his body, with constant left jabs to his face. By the end of the round his face was totally bruised, but David wasn't about to say uncle.

Before the fourth round started, I walked over to David's corner and said, "Dave, how about calling it a draw. You knocked me down, I can't knock you down, but I am getting some hits in. You've proved one thing to me. I am privileged to be in the company of a shipmate with your heart." Dave didn't say a word. He offered his gloved hand in token agreement and I shook it enthusiastically. All who were witnessing the match were clapping as we returned the gloves to the recreation center office.

Naturally athletic, I enjoyed boxing, too

From that day forth, the morale on the decommissioned YMS was 100 percent improved. Everyone was talking about the recreation encounter. Several of the crew came to me, in the presence of David, and gave us both the thumbs up salute. I acknowledged their gesture with a blink of my eye, and chief Petty Officer David would just laugh.

A natural born thrill-seeker (aka show-off)
Diving off the topmast was a favorite past time

The swan dive was my specialty

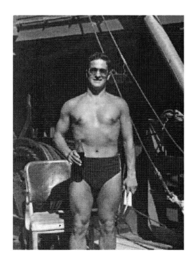

Here I am celebrating, post dive

As my commitment to the Navy was coming to a close, I realized that somewhere along my line of duty, I accrued an inguinal hernia, and opted to get it repaired at Treasure Island, before my discharge. I logged in at the Medical facility on the island and a date was set for my operation the following morning at 9:00 a.m.

I recall asking the doctor if he would allow me to see the operation, as he was going to give me a spinal anesthesia. No problem. If I was sure that's what I wanted to do. I assured him that was so. I recall the spinal anesthesia being given and the doctor probing to be sure that I felt nothing in the hernia area. That being so, he started the operation by making a 4 inch to 6 inch cut and out oozed fat cells and blood from the area. My color changed from rosy red to carnation white, as I watched the fat cells and blood decorating the proximity of the knifing. Up went the screen barrier to block my view, with the Dr. commenting, "So what's new?"

By 10:30 a.m. the doctor was gone, and I was moved to my bed to recuperate from the trauma. At three o'clock (1500 hrs) the nurse documented in my medical file that I was not resting in bed! Having recovered completely from the anesthetic effect of the operation, around 2:30 (1430hrs) I snuck out of bed, out of the hospital, and went for a two block walk to the officer's club, where I enjoyed a couple of beers before returning to my hospital bed around 3:45 (1545hrs). This too was recorded in my hospital records.

The doctor checked me out the following morning. He found no problems, but said, "I advise you to stick around for another day, unless you want to sign an early release." I felt great, but decided the meals and officer's club visits were rated 4-A. So I stayed the extra day. And that constituted my final official tour of duty as a U.S. Naval Officer. Incidentally, no complications.

When I did leave the hospital, I stayed in the Bay Area for several days. One evening when I was making the rounds in the bars on Market Street, I ran into an acquaintance of mine whom I knew to be an exceptional football player during his high school years in the Sacramento area. He was drafted into the army when he graduated from high school, and had just been discharged in San

Francisco and he was making the rounds of the Market Street bars on his own. Gus Manolis, the person I am referring to, while in the service, was assigned to a base featuring a football team, and he volunteered to try out for it. He not only made the team but beat out a Stanford All Conference graduate who played the center position on the army team.

Being an alumnus of Cal, I asked Gus if he would be interested in playing for Cal. He told me he sure would, but would not meet the entrance qualifications because his grades were mostly D's and C's and some F's in high school. Also, he was recruited by Oregon State on a scholarship, and thought he would go there. I told him service men who wanted to go to college after their discharge were given special consideration, and that was why he was being accepted at Oregon State. Would he rather go to Cal if I could get him accepted with some benefits to help him along? He said, "Sure!". So I told him to hold off any commitment until he heard from me.

The very next day I went to the Cal football coach's office and introduced myself to Pappy Waldorf, the current coach at Cal. I filled him in on Gus's football background. He was All-Everything in the two high schools he played for, and the fact that he beat the Stanford graduate in the army caught Pappy's attention. He referred me to one of his assistants and asked him to see what could be done. In the end he said he could get Gus an athletic scholarship if he could get admitted to the University. To be eligible, Gus would have to take 12 units and pass them with a grade of "C" or better. Six in the spring session and six in the summer session.

Gus was eager to take on the challenge. Now mind you, this is a kid with more D's and F's than C's during his high school years. Get this. He took the 12 units, and earned a B+ average! He enrolled at Cal and received a football scholarship. Unfortunately he suffered a career ending knee injury that cut his playing days short. Pappy Waldorf respected him so much, he kept him on scholarship and appointed him as a student coach during Cal's two Rosebowl teams in the 50's. Gus, upon my recommendation, went on to coach at Yuba College, and from there, Chico State.

Gus lost his life while volunteering to search for a reported missing boy in the Chico mountains. He passed over from a severe heart attack. I was privileged to be the Godfather of one of his sons. I mention Gus's relationship for two reasons. First, to emphasize my total commitment to Cal's football program over the years, and of equal, if not more importance, the close friendship between Gus and myself that was sparked by the game of football. I forgot to mention, I was Gus's best man at his wedding to his wonderful bride, Anne Karneges.

Living Room Gridiron

This is a good time to let you know how proud I am of having served four years on the University of California Council for the nine campuses, and four years as a member of the BIG "C" Society Board of Directors. Just to have played a part, matter not how miniscule, of that great university, UC Berkeley, rates a featured bulletin in my personal resume. My close associations with the University post WWII years, presented me with the opportunity to meet and host, in our home, many interesting Cal associates, namely Pappy Waldorf, Dee Andros, Pete Elliot, Paul Christopoulos, Dave Maggard, and Ed Bartlett. The occasion for our socializing at our home, varied from Greek Easter celebrations to golf invitationals to discussing recruiting strategies.

The recruiting visit with Pete Elliot and Dee Andros bears detailed coverage. Elliot, the head football coach at the time and Dee Andros, an assistant coach, were responding to my invitation to meet two football prospects I believed were PAC 10 quality players. Dee Andros was of Greek descent and I had Gaye fix dolmathes with avgolemono sauce (meatballs covered with grape leaves in an egg lemon sauce), and a Greek salad; tomato, feta cheese, red onion and cucumbers with vinegar and olive oil dressing. Both coaches ate heartily and Dee thought he had died and gone to heaven.

Following dinner, the two coaches and I relaxed in our living room hashing over my notes recommending the two prospective recruits. While we were discussing their merit, we were casually sipping retsina, which was served in a specially designed decanter. The decanter had a separate area for ice to keep the wine cold, while not diluting it. It also featured a pouring spout for the wine. After discussing the pros of the two athletes, we moved on into offense and defense strategy. At that time I was involved with coaching Yuba College and Yuba City High School football teams in a volunteer assistant capacity. My primary responsibility was to plan defense strategy from scouting reports and to then discuss my strategy with the respective coaches for a final game plan. I also coached line fundamentals, both defense and offense.

One night I had an epiphany regarding team conditioning, which would at the same time create a defensive havoc for the opponent. I asked and received permission from Matlock, the Yuba City head coach, who later, under my recommendation became the Yuba College head coach, to put my plan to the test during our contact practice session. The plan was as follows:

*****The following paragraph (or two) is devoted to football stratagem of which you may skip and not offend me one iota.*******

The offense would line up with one primary goal in mind and that was to fire straight out taking on the nearest lineman in his path. From a standard T formation the quarterback would read the block of the linemen and hand off the ball either to the right half back or the left halfback, (both halfbacks are expecting the ball). The full back, responding to the handoff, would lead the ball carrier back into the hole created by the line. The backs were instructed to run to daylight full speed ahead whether they had the ball or not. The quarterback, after his hand off, would run straight back and look down field to see how the defensive backs were responding to the play. The right and left end would dart for the line backer on their side and block him head on.

All the while discussing my plan, we were sipping retsina. The go signal for the offensive team was on a given "hut" after setting by the quarterback. There would be no huddle after a play. The go-hut was broadcast to the line by the second number of the first teen number barked by the quarterback, i.e. "et 31-14-22-hut, hut, hut, hut" - exploding on the fourth hut. Again - "set 48-12-26-33-hut, hut," exploding on the second hut. Now the ends, remember, were to fire on the linebacker on the go signal – EXCEPT when the quarterback started an offensive play with the 50's. In that case the two ends start for the linebackers and fake their blocks. While the cornerback was reacting to their fake they then would explode down field on a pass route. The quarterback would call the 50 series when he thought the cornerbacks were ripe for the fake. The rest of the offense would fire off and still block for the run. In the 50 series ("50-14-20-hut,hut,hut,hut") the quarterback faked the handoff to either one of the backs expecting the ball just as before, only in this case he would fade back as always but throw the ball to the end who was most open. Remember, we're still sipping wine. Also, remember, this practice session will be the 10 minute conditioning closing drill for the offense and defense. As all the offensive and defensive players would have to rush to wherever the ball carrier is tackled, without a huddle. The players would have to get immediately set up and start a new play. No rest between plays. A no huddle offense is very common today, but back then, unheard of. On the onset the ball would be placed on the offensive 30-yard line, and no rest for either team until the offense scored. Repeat the sequence for the full 10 minutes of contact action. The players not involved would be hitting the track on alternate nights, as the whole squad would previously do for conditioning. This doesn't only get one in condition, but does it so under game conditions.

Welcome back to the story.

Yuba City won two close ball games by going into this no huddle drill during the closing minutes of the half time, and at the end of a game. In one game, the final play, the quarterback called a

50 series, after three straight ahead line plays were called, and threw a 40-yard touchdown pass to our right end.

As for the retsina part of this experience, let me put it this way. By this time in our meeting Elliot, Andros, and Nicholau were in offensive and defensive positions exploring different techniques in blocking one another in the middle of our living room. I mean no holds barred explosions, each coach proving his method to be the best. What finally rescued us from demolishing the living room furniture and one another, was my last attempt to pour the wine from the decanter into coach Dee's glass, when no matter how steady I tried to be, I kept pouring the wine onto the carpet instead. We were all three stunned at what was taking place when I finally discovered I was trying to pour the wine from the top of the decanter from where it had been filled, rather than from the wine spout from where it should be served. By the time the top of the decanter got to his glass the wine was pouring out of the spout below onto the carpet. Thank God retsina is not a red wine and the damage to the carpet was negligible, but of significance to the imbibers. Coaches time out – coaching strategy over.

The sequel to the story is that two weeks later, Cal used the no huddle offense with great success. Possibly modified, but essentially the same. The irony is, as in isolated instances in the real world, the genius for the no huddle offense was born with a primary purpose of a conditioning tool, and it ended up with an added feature of an offensive scheme.

Dee Andros went from Cal to become head coach at Oregon State, and from there to become Oregon State's Athletic Director.

On a personal note, during my volunteer coaching at Marysville High, Yuba City High, and at Yuba College, no team I was associated with finished below second place in their respective league, with several first place finishes. A Yuba College team – I believe it was 1956 - Bobby Haas was the quarterback- played for the State championship that year. Of course the head coaches and their staff were the determining cause. I do feel, however, that I was a contributing factor.

PART THREE

Nicholau Construction Co.

I will now document the adventures of a self-licensed home contractor, whose only qualifying credentials were the fact that he was a Registered Pharmacist at his apothecary at the Marysville Clinic Pharmacy. Period.

I had bought a lot in east Marysville in a coveted district with the plan of building a home there when it was affordable for me to do so. With two daughters, Gaye six months pregnant, and myself making do with a one bathroom, one bedroom, combination dining room - living room, small kitchen apartment built over a garage, *affordability* be damned. Time had come to shove. I had to bite the bullet and get our house built. We would economize in other ways. I shared my thoughts with Gaye and she agreed we had no other choice. With that finality I went forth gung ho on getting started on our new house. This occurred in the year of our Lord, the summer of 1953.

  First off I contacted my good golfing friend and building contractor, Elton McDaniel, and apprised him of my plan. I asked if he would be willing to bid on my house blueprint plans. He said he would, but cautioned me, at this point in time the building market was flourishing, and to be prepared accordingly. I hired an architect and drew up the plans for our home. Gaye and I were adamant in what we wanted in the size and style of our house. Finally, when the blueprints reflected our dream, we forwarded them to Elton for a bid. His bid burst our dream. True, I was forewarned, but that didn't diminish my shock one iota. You see, I was daydreaming in the twenty thousand dollar neighborhood, and the best Elton could bid was in the forty thousand dollar neighborhood.

  Spinning off my grandmother's grit and my mother's fortitude to triumph over seemingly insurmountable objects, I refused to be dispirited in the pursuit of building our dream house. I decided that I would become my own general contractor and sought bids on the various phases associated with building a house literally from scratch. I interviewed carpenters with house building experience. Fortunately, a very capable carpenter, Mr. Binninger, was between jobs awaiting a call from a licensed general contractor when he agreed to work with me. In essence I agreed to pay him the going set hourly fee, and give him free reign in the hiring of a helper as needed. It so worked out his brother, also a carpenter, became available two weeks after the beginning of the project. I, being the surrogate "general contractor", excelled as the coolie laborer of the team.

  My primary responsibility as a general contractor was to supply all the material as requested by Mr. Binninger in a timely manner. This I did by shopping around the various suppliers over all of Sutter and Yuba counties and as far north as Oroville, 30 miles away, seeking the lowest bid I could on basic needs such as nails, lumber, mortar, etc. I also, along with a family friend, the aforementioned Bill Callas a.k.a. "Woodchopper", dug all the trenches as laid out by Mr. Binninger for the cement foundation. Rather than strategically placed cement foundation blocks for support of the house, I opted for solid lines of cement upon which to build. Much more work, but greater stability. Besides my labor rate was "dirt" cheap. Pun intended.

    What is not intended was the obstacle of hardpan that greeted my prying shovel. I had to revert to a pick to break the hard pan so the shovel could remove the dirt. So I contracted a dynamite specialist to strategically dynamite areas of the plotted land to make its development feasible!!

    The frustration as general contractor/pharmacist, was unrelenting. Yet, I found myself "enjoying the pursuit' constantly reminding myself how much I was saving in the long haul. I contacted several suppliers for the various needs such as windows, doors, brick-layers, plumbers, electrical workers, hardware supplies and roofers. Whatever it took, I shopped diligently and thoroughly always measuring reputation against price until I settled on the most affordable qualified supplier.

    I was pleasantly surprised many a time on the differential figures on the bids I received. Much had to do with the supply and demand among the bidders at the particular time of my request. Bottom line, the savings were appreciable and well worth my effort. I could sympathize with a true general contractor as it would not be cost effective for him to do likewise, considering the number of projects he would be overseeing at one time. The general contractor had to maintain good interrelationships with suppliers so that they would keep abreast of his ongoing demands. You see, I had the luxury of time and a single project that made my approach not only feasible, but profitable for me. Time not being of the essence, the suppliers were allowed the luxury of delivering their product at their convenience, which favored me in negotiating a more competitive price.

All the above maneuvering and involvement on my part allowed me to finish the house, less ideal furnishings, without compromising the blueprint plan for twenty four thousand dollars!! That's right- a good forty five to fifty percent savings over Elton's very competitive general contractor's figure! Taking into account the man hours I put into the project, on some weekends working 16 hour days until 2 am nailing hardwood floors, or roof planks, I conservatively estimated the average hours I worked, including after my pharmacy work days, would factor into a good seven day, twelve hour per day work week. That alone over the three-month period that it took to build the house would amount to a substantial labor-dollar savings. As president of my self serving GNU, an acronym for General Non Union contractor, I vetoed any thoughts of a strike that entered my mind. And many did! Add the competitive bids I garnered and you will see another meaningful savings contributing to the forty five to fifty percent estimated savings on the finished project. What I am leading to, is that the Elton McDaniel bid was very competitive, but not financially do-able. My daily involvement and zero cost self-labor enabled me to go forth on the house project.

Did you notice above, where I singled out bricklayers, not bricks, as a needed item for the construction of the house? I had the bricks from the demolition of the E street homestead, which I will detail a bit later. This was yet another factor that contributed to the dollar savings of the finished house. Incidentally, the bricklayer I hired was from Oroville, between jobs, and available at an appreciable savings. Being apprised of the job by the Lumber Yard, he approached me for work. He did an outstanding job. Another welcomed gift, solely due to good timing.

It is important at this time to praise Gaye, my better half, for her invaluable contribution, and for her extreme patience during the three-month construction period. As the grisly general contractor dove into his high priority contractual obligations, he bossily demanded much from his secondary, "coolie" laborer, his darling, lovable wife Gaye. This, he solicited even though she was seven months pregnant with our third daughter, Jamie!

One of her tedious assignments was creosoting all of the 2x4 twelve foot boards along with the 2x6 lumber boards before they were placed over the solid dug out cement foundation. This was necessary to prevent termites from chewing their way into the wood floor. Also, at the most inopportune times, she was asked to get this, get that, go here, go there, hold this, hold that, on and on, I'm sure you get the picture. This she did like a trooper. To her credit, she did not flinch from her responsibilities. All this was done on top of her household and motherhood demands for our two young daughters and the one due in two months!! Does anyone doubt me now when I boast of being married to an angel on loan from Heaven? Albeit her incentive to do what had to be done was to get out of her 700 square foot restricted "palace".

I did experience close calls while on the job. One in particular occurred during the 1961 remodeling phase when I was nailing planks over the roof joists, making a solid base for the sheeting and the finishing roofing shakes to be applied later. The design of the roof called for a 4 ft by 2 ft opening at the west edge of the added on family room to accommodate a brick chimney over the large fireplace foundation. I was on my knees as the on-the-job contractor, nailing the planks in their order starting from the peak of the roof, working downwards to the gutters edge when I escaped being impaled by exposed reinforced steel rods sticking up 2 feet in the fireplace cement foundation under the fireplace chimney's opening in the roof.

As I was working down towards the roof's edge focusing on tightly placing each five-foot plank, I forgot all about the fireplace opening. I was judging my distance to the end of the roof by focusing on the place where the gutters would be attached to it. The next thing I knew I was airborne in a free fall through the designated fireplace opening in the roof, heading towards the exposed steel rods, when luckily I was able to grasp the last joist of the opening, saving me from being impaled by the vertical exposed steel rods. Through my innate athleticism, I was able to hang on and climb back to the top of the roof. There is no substitute for youth! Not until I got off the roof and relived my experience, did I realize the gravity of that life-threatening situation.

Now that I have outlined the original building phase of the house, let me familiarize you with the financial aspects of the project. With my blueprint in hand, I went to the Bank of America in the summer of 1953 and asked to speak to the loan officer. I shared with him my plans to build the house, and asked for a twenty thousand dollar loan. He looked over the blueprints, evaluated the location, and said "No problem, who is your contractor?"

When I told him I was contracting it myself, he looked somewhat shocked and said, "Under those circumstances, I cannot approve your loan". Disappointed and disheartened, I left the bank wondering "now what". That day I reported to my pharmacy thinking I'll just have to wait until I save enough to build our house. An unfortunate delay, but not the end of the world. What little savings I had accrued from the war, and from working in the shipyards before reporting to the Navy, and from my pharmacy savings to date was all deposited in the Bank of America, and I assumed if they wouldn't finance me no one else would.

I have always maintained the Lord does move in mysterious ways. And my loan seeking experience plays that edict out. By chance, a doctor at the clinic, familiar with my dilemma, suggested I visit a newly locally owned savings and loan establishment located on Fourth Street in Marysville. With nothing to lose and possibly something to gain, I took him up on his suggestion.

I made an appointment with the loan officer of the Marysville Savings and Loan and presented my blueprints and the location. He was impressed and proceeded to get the paper work started for the loan. The problem was, he didn't inquire who the contractor would be until we got to the part of the paperwork where the question was finally asked. When I told him I was contracting it myself, he too, denied me the loan. Disheartened, I left the Marysville Savings and Loan even more depressed than I was after my rejection from the Bank of America.

Speaking of the Lord's secret ways, that very afternoon I sat at the counter of a coffee shop with my disappointment evidently apparent in my solemn mood, when Mr. Aaron, a pillar of the community, and unbeknownst to me a founding member of the Marysville Savings and Loan, sat next to me. He knew me from my newspaper days and later from my football experience at Cal. While sitting next to me he introduced himself and asked,

"George you look dejected, what's up?"

"Oh, Mr. Aaron," I said, " I've been trying to get a loan to build my house and I have had no luck."

"Did you try the new Marysville Savings and Loan?"

"I did just today, and no luck."

"What's the problem?" he inquired.

I told him, "As long as I am contracting it on my own the loan officer could not approve my loan and I can't afford to have a general contractor build it for me. So there I am."

"George, what are you doing now for a living?"

I told him, "I founded the Marysville Clinic Pharmacy in partners with a few doctors when I came back from the war in 1946."

"George", he said "will you do me a favor?"

"Of course, what can I do for you?"

"I want you to go back to the Marysville Savings and Loan tomorrow and tell the loan officer to check with me when you get there. Will you do that?"

"I sure will Mr. Aaron. Do you work there?"

"Good, I'll see you tomorrow, have a good day and stop worrying" was his reply.

The above dialogue is as close as I can recall of that meeting at the lunch counter that summer day of 1953. The rest, as the saying goes, is history. I not only received a loan, but one of a low interest rate. Thank you, George Bailey, I mean Mr. Aaron, it certainly is "A Wonderful Life."

So exceptional was the loan that if I wasn't so cash-culturally indoctrinated, I would have made money conservatively investing in the market instead of seeing how fast I could pay off my loan. I do not recall the term extent of my loan, (I believe it was for 15 years), but I do know I paid it off within five years. Every extra dollar I had went into paying off my one and only outstanding debt. I do not regret my doing so even though in hindsight there was no financial justification for my prepayments on the loan. In fact I would have gained much more financially had I paid off the loan in monthly installments and conservatively invested the balance! I consider my financial debt-free approach to be a byproduct of my undying memories of the Great Depression.

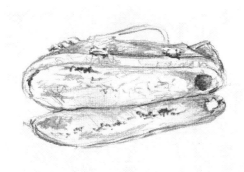

While in a contractor mood, I will move on to the extreme back yard overhaul I undertook years later. Again, I dusted off my retired general contractor's license hanging in the pharmacy and took on the project as though I was an old salt at "home improvement and yard projects". Nothing had changed over the years. Confusion and tantrums were my temperament of the times.

I got bids on sprinkling system equipment such as sprinkling heads types and underground pipes, both in steel and PVC composition. I bought a book on the ratio water pressure to sprinkler head size, type and distances between sprinklers, etc. Oh yes, more hardpan barriers - much more than the foundation experience. I went through not one, but two leased ditch digger machines because of the hardpan. Again, a dynamite specialist was called onto the site, saving hours of hard manual labor digging though the hard pan to lay the underground water pipes. The good news at this writing is that the system is still satisfactorily functioning more than 50 years later. Yes, periodic repairs and upgrades were made over the past several decades since the system has been in place. So what's new? At the outset it functioned through ten manually operated water valves. It now is upgraded to an automated electric time clock valve system. I accomplished this feature with literally a near mile of underground wiring to the ten valve stations located throughout the front and backyards, leading from the master timer clock situated in the garage.

  The raised kidney shaped garden area, the three gazebo designs, and fireplace pit you see in our backyard, are the results of bisexual coolie laborers consisting of Gaye and myself and our kids too. Our late-comer grandchildren dodged a bullet on this project. But not for long. There were occasional operations when they were called to duty, and their help was deeply appreciated. As I keep repeating, after all, they are the greatest.

  Years later, even though I had filed my "general contractor's license" deep in my closet office, I did have occasion throughout the years to again dust it off for house improvements such as remodeling the kitchen, and installing parquet hard wood floor throughout the kitchen and family room of the house. I did electrical upgrading with the help of my brother Nick. I updated all windows with double-paned Pella windows, replaced the glass sliding doors with Pella glass sliding doors, on and on. Upgraded the toilet, light fixtures, marble floor entrance-way, outdoor lighting yard system… Enough? Not so fast. As the family grew, space shrunk. In the summer of 1961 out came my general contractors license again as I undertook the project of adding on twelve hundred square feet of living space. My plans called for adding on a master bedroom, extra hall closets, a twenty by thirty foot family room, large fireplace for family room, and an extended outdoor cement porch. A major undertaking that, at that time, even with me as the contractor, cost almost as much as the original house. Just the thought of that undertaking and I am really ready to change gears into another subject matter. And so I will.

The backyard that Gaye and I built...from an empty dirt lot, to this.

Notice the gazebos in the top picture. We built those too.

Christmases Past

At this point in my memoirs, and for no logical reason, I am flooded with my youthful experience with Santa Claus! (I wanted a lighter, more jovial topic than the hard labor of my career as a contractor, and I think this fits the bill quite nicely.) What a difference one generation plays in society's culture. Each generation, in it's own way uniquely welcomes Santa Claus into their lives. There just is no wrong way to celebrate Christ's gift to mankind.

Allow me to first recollect the Great Depression era during my soul-stirring, electrifying Christmases. We had an annual Christmas tree in our home. The tree was decorated with enthusiastic heartfelt passion. Simple, yet artistically adorned with the usual string of lights and ornaments. Snow-like glistening ribbon traversed from the top to the bottom limbs of the tree. Strategically placed cotton puffs were added on several of the tree limbs accenting the snow effect of the natural habitat from where the tree was harvested. With the exception of the scarcity and banality of the ornaments, when compared to modern ornaments, there was no significant difference in the decorated tree.

But what was under it tells another story. During my youth Santa Claus was limited in how much of a child's Christmas wish list he could honor. The Great Depression also took its toll on

Santa. What he did was to critically evaluate one's list, and with careful management pick out what he thought would be fair to the multitude of good children's wishes according to their needs. That way no good child was left off his long inventory list. The good news to that approach, as far as the Nicholau family was concerned, not one of us four children was without a Santa Claus gift under the tree on Christmas morning. Albeit one gift each, it served its purpose in rewarding our good behavior. Four children and with rare exception, four wished-for items adorned the space beneath the tree.

As for myself, I challenge any of my daughters to have experienced a more exhilarating feeling than I did when I received a spring wind-up street car from my list. Symbolically, the message from Santa was that he acknowledged I was a good boy. That meant a lot to me. Our six daughters, thanks to God's blessings, the second American generation of the Nicholau clan, were not so restricted. On Christmas morning the packages under the tree resembled an avalanche of colorful paper, wrapped boxes of various sizes spread out in piles all across the floor beyond the Christmas tree branches, far reaching to the opposite wall of our living room! The common denomination between the first generation and the second generation of gifts was not measured in quantity. The paradigm Santa went by was his seal of approval on our daughter's good behavior 'year-end report card', just as he did during my generation. Be a good child and he will do his best to affordably reward you accordingly from items on your list.

EXTRAordinary Miracles on 25th Street

I like what I am about to recall so much, I am putting my remote brain changer on hold to stay the course and focus on priceless happenings during the youthful celebratory holiday seasons beginning in the 1950's within the George E. Nicholau family.

I thank God for blessing me with a memory that affords me the privilege to reminisce, on call, the enduring happenings of which I will never tire. Presently, I am so self-entertained in my recollections, my only wish is that I can pass on to you the realistic exaltation I experienced at the time of those happenings. The exhilaration I am reliving this very moment just thinking of them is priceless. I am sprouting goose pimples with the thought of what I am about to dash off.

    For starters, I shall never forget Dessi's Christmas recital at the tender age of 10 years. "T'was the night before Christmas and all through the house…" How innocently her hand and arm jesters were theatrically complimentary to her face expression and voice intonation while standing erect on the hearth of our family room fireplace. Her theatrical performance gave deep meaning to the classic Christmas Carol. Sheepishly, I secretly looked towards Gaye, and sure enough, she too had a glassy eyed look, with a tear caressing her cheek as we applauded Dessi's performance.

    Nor shall I ever forget Dorre running to the front window looking across the street, literally shouting, "I saw him! I saw him!!"- meaning Santa Claus of course, just leaving the roof of the fireplace chimney of our neighbors house, the William Hust family, at that time.

You see, minutes before at approximately 4:15 Christmas morning, I was busy arranging the kid's Santa Claus gifts under the tree in our living room when I heard movement and voices coming from the adjacent hallway that led into Dessi and Dorre's bedroom. Their room featured a large window facing the Hust's house directly across the street. This alerted me that Dorre was up and addressing her sister to wake up! Afraid that Dorre was going to rush into the living room to see what Santa left her, and that I would be caught "with my fingers in the cookie jar" subbing for Santa Claus, I panicked and rushed to the front door of our house, adjacent to the daughter's bedroom, opened the front door, and slammed it shut with a loud BANG!, shouting....

"Dorre!, Dorre!, quick, look out your front window! Santa just left our house heading across the street to the Hust's rooftop!!! Hurry, hurry, before he leaves the roof!!!" The next moment I heard Dorre shouting, "I saw him. I saw him!" and it was so convincing that for the moment I experienced a spirited, soul-searching feeling for Christmas, that to this day has not been duplicated. Nor can I find the words to adequately describe that happening. Dorre swears to this day she did at that moment see Santa Claus - that is how strong her belief of Santa Claus was!

I cannot forgive myself for lacking the literary talent to record my feeling in such a way that others would experience like vibes about Santa Claus and Christmas as I experienced through the innocence of my daughters. Their naiveté was total. It certainly put into perspective how real Santa Claus is in the innocent eyes of the beholding. Each of us in our toddler years should be so privileged to share a like happening during the Yuletide season.

Just once would suffice for life. My fondest wish is that each of my daughters blessed with children may experience everlasting memories of comparable happenings with Santa Claus. This thought should in no way compete or conflict with the true spirit of Christmas: the celebration of the birth of our Lord Jesus Christ. Children should not be deprived the prerogative of their formative years to mature from adolescence to puberty into adulthood progressively. Thus, graduating from the tinseled world of aberration into the spiritual world of reality. Santa Claus is for real, and a child should not be robbed of his or her Santa Claus encounters.

Sadly, as I am putting my thoughts and reflections to pen, the world is wrought with religious and political conflict to the extent that a whole generation of various ethnic groups will be fortunate to survive, let alone enjoy the thrills and excitement of witnessing Santa Claus's treasures. My heart truly bleeds for those boys and girls should that come to pass. I pray that the world comes to its civilized senses before it is too late.

Where There Is A Need, There Is A Means

Which brings me to the saga of Santa's bicycle presents to my daughters. Each of my daughters, the angels that they were, and are, received a bicycle from Santa Claus on top of our roof!!! Either partially jammed into the brick chimney or leaning next to it!! Along with the bicycle was a note personally written by Santa, congratulating each of the girls for being such good children that they earned a bicycle.

The bicycle epic deserves detailed editorializing. It all started when the 2 oldest daughters. Dessi and Dorre were 8 and 7 years old. They both wrote, in a letter to Santa Claus, having outgrown their tricycles, what they most wanted for Christmas was a bicycle. In the letter they bragged what good girls they were, and for him to please do his best to get them a bicycle. Their mother and I discussed their letter and I felt they were too young for a two-wheeler bike. They had received a tricycle the previous Christmas. Besides, with 5 girls at that time, I had other priorities for them and reasoned the bicycles could wait for another year.

Their mother, however, kept informing me how important it was to them to have Santa reward them for being such good girls. Gaye was leaning in their favor. I kept firm insisting not this year. Finally, after "due process", i.e.; Greek culture for what the man of the house says goes, Gaye was convinced to forget the bicycle gift and have Santa leave other gifts, such as a doll and a toy or two, for the two older girls. (Boy has my Greek culture done an about face of late, and I thank God it has. Oh, the power of true love.)

    Their younger sisters were too young at the time to become involved with bicycle requests. They verbalized "Betsy McCall" dolls, "Revlon" dolls, doll clothes, toys they spotted in a Sear's Christmas catalog and more. Each implying to Santa in their scheming way they were good girls and deserved no less. Gaye, on her own, bought a yard tent (more like a teepee) with camping and cooking equipment for the older girls to make up for the bicycle absence. Mr. Scrooge, *a.k.a.* Dad, upon ruminating over Gaye's reasoning and picturing the emotions of her arguments in favor of the bicycles from Santa Claus relented, unbeknownst to her, and did the aforementioned about face concerning bicycles for Dessi and Dorre. I stealthily ordered two bicycles through my pharmacy outlet to be delivered on the 23rd of Dec to the Marysville Clinic Pharmacy. Upon their arrival, I hid them in the back of my stock room, so that neither Gaye, nor my daughters would see them should they choose unexpectedly to drop by the pharmacy for a visit, as they were prone to do occasionally.

    As Christmas Day was approaching, Gaye would bring up how disappointed the girls were going to be when there were no bicycles under the tree. I falsely poo-poo'ed her emotional concern in order to cover up my shenanigan surprise.

    On Christmas Eve, after convincing the girls to go to sleep, (for Santa would not pay a visit if they were awake,) and after we, too, went to bed, Gaye remarked, "You will wish Santa brought them a bicycle. And that's that. You'll see."

    It was now 12:30 am Christmas Day.

    My response. "Merry Christmas". Scrooge at his best.

    Well, wouldn't you know it, that night it literally stormed, raining cats and dogs, as the saying goes. At three a.m., while Gaye was zzzzing in her usual and customary deep sleep, I snuck out of bed. I got dressed, used my brother's gifted 1957 Chevrolet pickup, and drove to the pharmacy. I placed the bikes into the pick up and drove back to the house.

Now the fun begins. It was my intent to stealthily place the bikes on the roof, as I perceived Santa would do, with a note from him praising them for being such wonderful girls. In the note Santa would also explain to them that the bicycles were not next to the Christmas tree in the living room because the bikes would not fit down the chimney opening. "Santa" hoped that they would be truly surprised and elated after their initial disappointment, when eventually they would spot their bicycles on the roof.

My game plan was simple enough. The misbehaved weather be damned. I forged ahead. I placed a garden ladder leading to the roof from the porch area gaining a four foot advantage next to the brick wall of our bedroom wing. I climbed the ladder with a bike in tow to the roof's edge and shoved the bicycle up onto the slanted shake roof. Here is where things went astray. I got on the roof myself, hoping to gingerly tiptoe up the slanting roof, as I had mentally planned with the bicycle, placing it on the apex of the roof next to the brick chimney. Then, I planned to retrieve the second bike and prop the handle-bars in the chimney opening. With that accomplished, I was to nonchalantly sneak back into the bed from whence I came, with no one, especially Gaye, knowing the difference. I had anticipated the bicycle spectacle to be visible from the street fronting of our house. I could not wait to witness the surprise of the two Nicholau daughters, and their mother, when they first spotted Santa's bicycle on the roof. For the girls, that Christmas scene would be awesome.

Then *reality* set in. I anticipated the adventure to be simple. In reality it proved to be otherwise at 3am Christmas morning. What I had not planned on was a blistering cold stormy winter night. I had the audacity to envision my mental mode of operation, in ideal climate, time and again in my mind's eye, without one negative thought of how I would pull it off. What a gross miscalculation that proved to be.

That stormy Christmas morning, I had minimum trouble getting the bicycles from the ladder onto the edge of the roof, but when I climbed aboard myself, it turned into a whole new ball game. Because of the rain on the soaked, moss-covered, steep shake roof, I could not stand up to tip toe with a bicycle in hand as mentally planned, for my feet would slip from under me. So, I lay flat on my stomach, and literally crawled along, up the steep graded slippery shake roof heading for the chimney. All the while pushing a bicycle ahead of me. Having reached my destination with one of the bicycles I became overly confident. I almost did myself in. I stood up thinking, without a cumbersome load of a bike handicap, I could save time by walking upright while retrieving the other bike laying at the edge of the roof. An almost catastrophic mistake! My footing slipped from under me, and I catapulted uncontrolled - resembling a bobsled racing down a snow bank on my back - with my feet leading the way- gaining speed towards the edge of the roof. Luckily the heel of my shoes caught the metal gutter, and with innate athleticism kicking in, I managed to stall my fall from the roof.

Having survived that peril, I gingerly proceeded to crawl with the second bike up the slope of the roof, and placed it with the handlebar, as planned, jetting into the chimney.

Having miraculously avoided any telling mishap, and priding myself at being a fast learner, I managed to *crawl* back to the ladder, without incident, and climb down the ladder to the porch. I then removed the ladder from the wall putting it back into the garage, and re-entered the bedroom. I dried myself off, but still shivering, climbed back into bed without Gaye suspecting that I was gone for 1 1/2 hours. It was now 4:30 a.m. Christmas Day.

A 20 to 30 minute plan, due to the stormy conditions escalated into a 1 1/2 hour adventure. The George Nicholau Way is never easy. Giving in to the inclement conditions was not an option....My way, or no way.

As was the custom in our home, Gaye and I would get up around 5:30 or 6:00am on Christmas morning before the kids awoke, and wait with our 16 mm movie camera to capture their spontaneous expression of joy on film for posterity.

That clear Christmas morning, the rain having subsided, and with Dorre's exuberance having witnessed Santa Claus atop our neighbors' roof a few years prior, our two eldest daughters rushed into the living room where our yearly Christmas tree was on display, to embrace their expected Santa Claus bicycles. Shocked at the bicycle's absence, the look on their faces betrayed their counterfeit elation and the sincerity of joy for the many other gifts that Santa Claus had brought them. The "I told you so" look I got from Gaye was absolute.

   The disappointment was so genuine, I almost faltered by asking them to check our roof. Luckily, however, my sinister entity prevailed and I let the event play itself out. All the while I followed them around with my movie camera on the ready, should they dash outside to play with some of Santa's toys. It was imperative to me that I capture their reaction, when by chance, on their own, they spotted Santa's bicycle gifts next to the chimney. Unexpectedly, in the interim, cars in the neighborhood drove by, and the automobiles would come to a screeching halt, while kids and adults alike, stared in disbelief, at the Nicholau chimney where Santa had crammed Dessi and Dorre's bicycles!

   Finally, around 11 am, Dessi, Dorre, and the other daughters, having exhausted their excitement and elation over Santa's generosity, went out to the front lawn where Gaye had set up Santa's teepee so that they could play in it. I followed like a shadow of theirs making believe I was interested in taking pictures of them in their tee pee tent. All the while I was anxiously waiting for one of them to spot the bicycles on the roof. Sure enough it happened. Words fail me to do justice to their spontaneous reaction. Suffice it to say, they were so hyper with joy that they were jumping up and down with arms flailing uncontrollably in all directions. Their antics of jumping and gesturing made me wonder if they suddenly were under the spell of their tee pee tent. All the while during their theatrical exaltation they were yelling almost in unison "I knew it! I knew it! Look Dad, my bike! My bike!!" shouted both Dessi and Dorre. All of this was captured on our 16 mm camera for posterity. We have looked at it several Christmases since, and still react as though it is happening for the first time.

   An added plus. To this day, I don't know if the kids' elation such as it was, came close to the sigh of relief I witnessed in Gaye's eyes, when she too first spotted the bicycles on the roof. I do know for a fact, neither Gaye nor the children could have expressed more exuberance than I stealthily felt that Christmas morning. It truly is more blessed to give than to receive. Especially when plotting a surprise gift.

On following Christmases, in succession, the bicycle ritual was repeated by Santa Claus to reward the "good" Nicholau daughters with comparable ecstasy- I quote good – because I am biased. First for Jamie, then Terre, and finally for Jorgi; each in turn wrote their letters to Santa Claus and knew come Christmas morning they would spot their bicycles next to the chimney on the roof. Our neighbors likewise, expected no less. Their expectation was accompanied by the sound of screeching tires from the first-time passers by.

Each daughter's initial routine on Christmas morning was predictable. Perfunctorily scan the Christmas tree, then dash out the front door to spot their bike perched on the roof. Their genuine spontaneous cry of joy was stealthily captured on celluloid by the hidden "master" film director- yours truly.

Following Dessi and Dorre's Santa Claus bicycle episode, Santa's request for a "volunteer" helper was answered by Gaye. And a good thing too, as it turned out to be a blessing. Although the weather was not a factor in Jamie's and Terre's turn for Santa, it proved hazardous for Jorgi's turn. It did not rain, but it was so cold during the wee early hours of Christmas morning, the roof was covered with a thin layer of black ice. It looked normal on the shakes- but what a deception! It turned out to be a real challenge for Santa to maneuver Jorgi's bicycle next to the chimney without Santa Claus literally sliding off the roof – sleigh, reindeer and all. Suffice it to say, Santa and helper managed to survive the challenge, although a couple of close calls were experienced.

Last, But Not Least….

Obviously, after 5 daughters receive a Santa Claus bicycle, Edie, the sixth and youngest of the daughters, expected the same. The irony however, is that by now, Dessi and Dorre had outgrown their Santa bicycles, having them replaced with a standard size bicycle, with their mini sized Santa Bike stored in the garage. Jamie and Terre are now also ready for a standard bike this year. With five sub-sized bicycles ready for garage storage, and two already purchased standard bicycles, for Jamie and Terre , I rationalized enough is enough! Our garage could rationally be confused with a Sear's bicycle display department.

With this mindset, I approached Gaye suggesting we forsake a bicycle on the roof for Edie, as she would have several to choose from in the "Sear's" section in the garage. I argued, Santa could get Edie some other meaningful gifts to express his love and reward for the sweet "good" baby girl of the Nicholau clan. Gaye, wisely cautioned me, that Edie would be terribly disappointed, but to honor pragmatism, left the decision up to me. As usual, Gaye had a knack, and still does, for letting me be the man of the house on "push come to shove" arbitrations.   Three guesses how many of my decisions favored Gaye's wishes. One guess would suffice. A 90% estimate would be conservative. And for that, I am ever grateful.

Edie's Christmas, as I like to refer to it, aka the "Miracle on 25th Street" went as follows. The always-present camera was on standby to register the exciting facial and body language expressions of the girls. The five eldest daughters did not disappoint Gaye's and my expectations. Santa Claus had the girl's individual fireplace socks filled to the hilt. Christmas wrapped packages encroached the living room floor space to an alarming degree, making it impossible to walk through the room without the danger of stepping on a gift, or five. The 5 girls were flinging Christmas wrapping paper all over the living room floor reconciling their Christmas list inventory.

Edie, however, quickly and superficially, mentally inventoried the tree, as though it was a prerequisite to rushing out the front door and onto the lawn, where upon gazing at the fire chimney on the roof, she would see Santa's bicycle gift. Oops! NO BICYCLE!! What?!

The disappointment on her face told it all. I tried to console her by telling her that Santa Claus wanted to please her with special gifts and toys he personally picked out. Gaye, bless her, joined me in consoling Edie.

After what seemed like an eon of time, Edie seemed to accept her plight and became preoccupied with Santa's toys. (An aside. Surprisingly, I had two phone calls later that day from my neighbors wanting to know why Santa boycotted our home on this Christmas Day!)

Ironically, that Christmas we hosted all of Gaye's and my family members for a Christmas celebration. As the morning wore on and our guests began to arrive, I became more and more depressed over my faux-pas regarding Edie's Santa Claus bicycle. By 12:30 it became unbearable. I just knew I had to right a wrong. I stealthily snuck from the house, not revealing to Gaye or anyone what I had in mind. In fact, I wasn't sure I could accomplish the "miracle" I was entertaining. I rushed downtown, riding up and down D Street looking for an open store that stocked bicycles. They were all closed. Of course they would be, but I was so desperate, I was looking for that proverbial needle in the haystack. At last, I did spot the haystack: A Capital Western Auto chain store with the needle staring at me in the form of a bicycle on display in it's window. But the store was closed! Surprise, surprise. I knew the proprietor of the store. He was a golfing buddy. I grasped at my one hope for salvation. I went to my pharmacy, picked up the phone, called his house and asked, no, frantically pleaded, is more like it, if he could please meet me at his store in 5 minutes and sell me the bicycle displayed in his window?

"George", he countered "Isn't it Christmas for Greeks too? We are just about ready to sit down for Christmas cheers. How about I get the bike for you first thing tomorrow morning?"

Rudely ignoring his plight while tactfully focusing on mine, I persisted to the point he felt obligated to accommodate a friend when I explained in detail the circumstances of my pleading. We met at the store, I bought the bike, and thanked him profusely, letting him know I owed him one. He was gracious in his rescue effort (The way I felt I know I would do the same for anyone in my shoes.)

OK, phase one of the miracle plan accomplished. Now, how do I get it onto the roof, in mid afternoon, where Santa would have placed it had I not interfered? Remember, a house full of guests were visiting at home.

To sneak the bicycle onto the roof without being seen would be the finishing challenge of the "miracle". This could be covertly done by placing a ladder secured from the garage against the bedroom wing brick wall. There I could not be seen from the back yard, or through the long wall of sliding glass windows of our family room where Christmas merriment was in full swing. From this vantage point it made the job of getting the bicycle onto the roof more risky and challenging, as it was a longer climb on the ladder with the bike in tow, yet it allowed me the luxury of a stealth operation. That is, if I was able to maneuver the ladder to it's destination without being seen.

Fortunately, with due caution, I succeeded in getting the ladder from the garage around the front of the house and in place without incident. With the Lord's blessing I successfully accomplished the final phase of the miracle without incident. The bicycle was placed next to the chimney along with a personal Santa Claus note. This note, like those to her sisters, not only praised her for being a good girl, but gave a believable reason for the delay. (I have been told Edie still treasures Santa's note, more than any other Santa gift she had received, and forty years later, can recite verbatim the apologetic reason for the delay.)

Mission accomplished. With the bicycle's handlebar partially jammed into the chimney on the roof I nonchalantly reentered the house full of guests to join in the ongoing Christmas festivities. The above machination took only 1/2 hour. With a rejuvenated spirit, I mingled among my guests as though I had never left. Indeed, I doubt I was even missed, as no one enquired about my absence. So much for the self-eminence we place on ourselves. With the bicycle safely placed on the roof and the gala of the Christmas spirit being uninhibitedly celebrated, it was just a question of time before the bicycle would be spotted by someone at the house. My fondest hope was that it would be Edie. It didn't turn out that way, yet it detracted not one iota from the elation she experienced.

It was approaching 4 pm when the some of the guests started to leave the house. Edie along with her sisters, Gaye, and I, followed the guests out the front door to the yard when one of the guests spotted the bicycle and quizzically commented, "What's a bicycle doing on your roof jammed into the chimney?"

Of course, camera at the ready I captured Edie going absolutely bananas. She was so thrilled and happy, one had to believe Santa knew best how to surprise the youngest of the charming, beautiful, Nicholau girls, and thereby not rob the last of the six daughters of her moment of true Christmas spirit. All she knew for certain was that there was no bicycle in the morning on the roof, and there was one there on the roof in the afternoon.

She was jumping for joy and shouting for me to please hurry and get her Santa Claus bike down.

I said, "I will, but how? You know I don't have Santa's reindeer and sleigh to help me".

The profound one theatrically volunteered while still animated, "Why not use that ladder I saw leaning against your bedroom wall?!!!"

"Of course", I bluffed. "What an idea. You're right. There is a ladder there. I used it to clean the bedroom windows last week and never put it back in the garage." (I could go to hell for lying, but Lord, consider the circumstances!)

To this day, I am not sure who was hoodwinking who, and I could I care less. All I do know, and will never forget, is the unabridged happy reflection on Edie's face. A priceless reward for my efforts. So what, if indeed hers was an Oscar performance? Big deal! It wetted my appetite for great expectations that I knew were forthcoming from the theatrically talented one. And it came to pass. Her artistic resume has exceeded my greatest expectations of her professional operatic endeavors, and her outstanding voice teaching accomplishments. Edie has numerous students who currently sing throughout the world. (Tuesday 9-01-06, Edie reviewed this script and swears she knew nothing of my involvement with her Santa bike. She claims that her ladder comment was offered in sincere innocence. So there!)

The EIGHT of us (only the six girls pictured here) actually piled into the Porsche, and took a ride to see SNOW falling in the foothills. I'd never advise this today. Back then the 'seatbelts' were Gaye's arms.

Oh, The Games We Played….And The Home It Made

There are so many more cherished, fun doings that occurred in the Nicholau home when the girls were growing up. These daily happenings nourished our love and friendship for one another, making our fond memories more fertile and genuine as time passes on. My mind is now flooded with so many light hearted, whimsical moments, I am overwhelmed with gratitude for the abundance of blessings bestowed upon me and my family during their adolescent years.

I remember a particular "Guess What" game we enjoyed at the dinner table. It was hilarious and a super outlet after a day at work or at school. It went like this. We would each, individually and silently, study every item on the dinner table until we settled upon an item which we believed could not be identified by merely giving the first letter of the word that the item started with. No matter how clever the item would be, one of us, after a hilarious round of guessing, would solve the riddle. Then it would be the victorious guesser's turn to pick an item on the table. I remember when I said it starts with an S and knew no one could possibly guess it. Wrong. Jorgi came up with the current item after many hilarious frustrating guesses – *shadow*! It was the shadow of my arm cast on the table. Wow!

How about the hide and seek game we played throughout the house? I can still hear lamenting OLLY-OLLY OXEN FREE, when one of my six daughters hid so well none of us could find them.

A perennial favorite, "spook hall", as we affectionately named it, would be played in our totally blacked-out 35-foot long hallway. The girls would start out on one end of the pitch black hallway, and I would be lurking somewhere between them and the other end. At times it was so quiet one could hear a pin drop. The whole idea was to quietly, without being grabbed or 'found out', sneak to the other side of the long, scary hallway. At times, out of the blue I would let loose a growling, horrifying sound that would emanate from nowhere in the pitch darkness, and that would scare the girls to pieces. Or, without an inkling, I would grab one of them just when they thought they were safe and clear, and it would scare the dickens out of them. The recovery laughter would prove belly wrenching!

Or, when I pretended to be a car, with one of my young daughters on my shoulders to be the driver. My head was their (and my) only steering wheel, and they would place their hands on my ears and steer me through the house. I would go at a steady pace exactly where they turned my head, and many times it would be into the wall. I would continue bumping into the barrier until they turned my head for clearance. I vividly remember them laughing so hard at my dilemma; I would feel the ripples in their stomach as I kept bumping into the barrier. Thanks a lot.

I will never forget the in-house bicycle episodes. This whimsical happening I will describe in minute detail, if for no other reason, than to relive it as I write it. It begins with my decision to ride my bicycle to work, which was a three-mile jaunt. It was fifteen to twenty minutes one way, depending on my mood and traffic.

First off, you must understand, being the only male of the household, and the father of 6 dynamic, spirited, mischievous, loving, youthful daughters, made me King of the Roost. I could do no wrong! And they would enthusiastically react to my eccentricity. Mar Mar, (an affectionate acronym for mother) a.k.a. Gaye, would just shrug her shoulders in disbelief.

At the end of my work day I would ride my bike home, and upon approaching my house, about 30 to 40 yards from our driveway, I would let out a loud, ear-piercing whistle that could be heard blocks away. My daughters were expecting that whistle from 6 pm on, and knew what they had to do in response.

Upon reaching our home I would ride my bike up the driveway, through the breezeway, and on to the gazebo area, around the raised kidney shaped planter, up the ramp onto the porch, heading straight to the four foot wide sliding glass doors of the family room.

Without hesitation, my daughters would be there to open the door just as I approached it, allowing me to continue nonstop, and without the least bit of deceleration, through the family room sliding doors, heading north into the dining room, and on into the entrance hall, do a hard left through the <u>carpeted</u> living room, dodging furniture, through the door leading into the kitchen, on through the kitchen, back into the family room. There I would do another hard left heading back to the brick wall of the family room from whence I first entered the house. The girls would follow exuberantly behind me, giggling all the way. I would then nonchalantly get off and park my bike in the family room. By then the girls were screaming with laughter, and that set the mood for the evening in the Nicholau household. Gaye, my loving angelic wife- on loan from heaven – would shrug her shoulders and wonder aloud, "when will he grow up". Heck, I was enjoying the present so much, that I never gave a thought to "growing up".

It became obvious then that much of the credit for our happy home fell on the shoulders of the angel I married. And at this writing she still has a permissive knack of flowing with the flow, when it comes to the theatrics of her seven babies - of which I play the perennial Scaramouch!

Through "Mar Mar's" tolerant understanding- tolerant being a gross understatement- we turned a three thousand eight hundred square foot, coveted neighborhood, luxuriously furnished house, into a fun abode for the family. Conventional behavior be damned. The family's antic's converted a house into a fun living place we affectionately call home!

What Mothers Must Endure

There were also quite a few life-threatening happenings that go with the territory of parenting, and as usual, most of the burdens would fall on the mother's watch. This clearly not due to parental dereliction, rather due to the 24-7 job description of being a loving, attentive, doting mother. When our most lovable Dorre was born on July 28, 1952, she was a twin to her brother, our son, Edison. They were seven-month premies, and Dorre weighed 1 and 1/2 pounds at birth. Edison was born with a lung infirmity that did not respond to that day's medical expertise. Rideout Hospital had only one incubator, and another was borrowed from the County hospital in order to accommodate both babies. Dorre survived. Edison passed on into Heaven after 12 hours of earthly life. Because of the low percentage for Dorre's survival, Gaye and I rushed her to Sacramento to be baptized – a luxury that did not exist with Edison. I thanked God for his life, albeit a mere 12 hours. From day one of Edison's demise to this current day, I pray to God to bless his soul with peace in Heaven. Gaye, on recovering from the difficult delivery, aware she was carrying twins was not only unaware of Edison's death, she did not ever see him! She did witness Dorre, before being put under anesthesia during the process of delivering Edison. Gaye had to stay in the hospital for four days before being released to go home. In the interim, Edison had already been buried.

Dorre was born with an innate desire to survive, for when first put into the incubator her color improved and her legs were kicking the top of the incubator. Weighing only one and one-half pounds at that time, she set a low weight record for survival at Rideout Hospital. Immediately upon being baptized, Dorre's health response was miraculous. Gaye and I both felt total relief, knowing she would survive. What a blessing God presented to us to allay the pain of Edison's departure into His care.

At this writing, Dorre is a professor of anesthesiology at UC Medical Center in San Francisco. She decided to go to medical school and earn her MD and specialty degrees only after earning her PhD in Genetics. She owns a beautiful home in a desirable neighborhood in San Francisco, a walking distance from the Medical Center. Dorre enjoys the love and support from all of her sisters, their spouses and her niece and nephews, as she likewise loves them. All of the sisters' love and respect towards each other makes for a model "mutual admiration society". Of course Gaye and I love all our daughters with equal zeal, and feel their reciprocal love. Family wise, it just doesn't get any better than that!

    Here is another example of the many I could write about, under the title Oh What Mothers Must Endure. It took place on Dorre's first day home form the hospital. Dr Belz, a pediatrician practicing at the Marysville Clinic, where I too was practicing my pharmaceutical profession, prescribed iron drops because Dorre was growing at such a rapid pace her blood was delinquent in iron. At the hospital she was getting an iron supplement through timely blood transfusions. Her prescribed dosage of iron drops at home was to be administered orally through placing the drops into the nipple, before it was secured onto her prepared milk formula feeding bottle. In this way, she was assured of getting her prescribed daily dose of iron, no matter how much of the milk formula she would otherwise take from the bottle.

    What happened on her very first dose resulted in a life threatening experience. Gaye followed the doctor's directions on how to administer the iron by placing the desired dose from an eye dropper into the nipple, and then having Dorre suck it into her mouth where upon afterwards she would take the now empty nipple, screw it onto the formula bottle to wash down the iron with the milk into her tummy. But before she could put the nipple onto the bottle, Dorre was choking and turning blue gasping for air. Gaye, panicking, grabbed Dorre by her ankles, held her head down trying to clear her passage-way into her lungs. At the same time she phoned the clinic, three blocks from our house, screaming "it was an emergency." Dr Lerch, the pediatrician on call responded immediately by leaving his office to make an urgent 'house call'. In the interim, while Gaye was coping with Dorre, her sister Dessi, ten months old, was vying for her mother's attention by placing buttons she found into her mouth, all the while looking up at her mother for her reaction. Here was Gaye, in a contorted position, holding Dorre by her ankles and the phone held at her ear by her shoulder, while frantically fishing buttons out of Dessi's mouth with her other hand. At that moment, Dr Lerch rushed up the stairs of the apartment responding to the emergency call. When he got to the bedroom of the apartment, Gaye had just placed Dorre on her side on the bed and a black fluid spilled out of her mouth as her color was returning to normal. Dr Lerch thoroughly examined Dorre and found no mitigating health problems from the hazardous ordeal. When Dr. Lerch left the apartment, Gaye picked up Dorre to comfort her, and for the first time during the episode, was shocked to see where Dessi had vented her lack of attention. Dessi had emptied all four drawers of lingerie from a dresser in the bedroom. To this day, she wonders what Dr. Lerch thought of her housekeeping standards. It is imperative to note that Dessi developed into the most considerate, unselfish person a sister could ever hope for. She set a high standard of decorum for her younger sisters to emulate.

Still another jolting experience Gaye endured, merits being told. Edie, the youngest of the sisters, was not yet one year old when it happened. Gaye, earlier in the afternoon, had taken the other five daughters out to Peach Tree Golf and Country Club for their Saturday swimming lessons, and was on her way to pick them up with baby, Edie, cuddled next to her in the front seat of the Chrysler station wagon. At that time car seats and seat belts for infants were unavailable. At the end of the Simpson Lane paved road there is a 90-degree left turn onto Dantoni Road leading to the Peach Tree Club House. Gaye, always a reserved driver, and especially so with a child in the car, approached the turn with due care. Yet, in the process of making the turn, the centrifugal force, unnoticed by Gaye, slid Edie on the leather seat towards the passenger door striking the door handle in such a freak way, that it flew open and Edie was tossed out of the car onto the Simpson Lane road! It all happened so quick, Gaye was first unaware of the mishap until she saw Edie screaming through her rear view mirror, lying on the road with a car approaching. She slammed on her brakes, rushed out of the car as the approaching vehicle also had stopped. Edie was crying up a storm. Gaye, distraught, picked Edie up and profusely thanked the driver of the other car for stopping in time. She immediately drove to the Clinic where the pediatrician examined Edie, and but for a facial scratch found no other physical damage. Of course, you couldn't prove that to Edie, she was still screaming during the whole examination. Dr Lerch's final comment was directed to Gaye "Your daughter is fine, but you look awful!"

Gosh, one memory triggers another. I must mention this happening to further impress upon you the parental anxieties that go with the territory. This time I was the culprit. I was heading for the back yard from our family room. I opened the glass sliding door, walked through it facing the yard, not bothering to slide it shut behind me. Jorgi, seeing me heading for the yard, rushed from the dining room area through the family room to follow me out to the yard to pet her favorite cat. Terre, seeing the door left open, closed it while Jorgi was petting the cat. Jorgi, knowing she had left the door open, turned around to rush back into the house running full bore smack into the now closed sliding glass door. The sickening, piercing sound of Jorgi's forehead hitting the closed door was followed by the thunderous crash of broken glass. Such was the force of the collision. Jorgi suffered deep cuts at the base of her nose, and on her arm and leg. There was blood everywhere, adding to the trauma. To the clinic we rushed where she was stitched and released. The doctor on call, Dr. Grant, did such a good job stitching her up there remained no tell-tail scars of the incident.

Another close call was when Jamie, like Edie before her, also slid toward the passenger door of our station wagon where she flung it open, and then proceeded to hang on the door for dear life. The car was moving at a very slow pace, and Gaye was able to stop and Jamie pulled herself back into the car and shut the door.

Those two life-threatening close calls in the car were the genesis of the "Nicholau In-The-Car-Zone" code: Lock the doors, use the now available seat belt, do your cross, and remain seated while the car is moving.

Aside from the alarming emergencies, there were a myriad of happenings that were dealt with on a daily basis. Like the time our daughter Terre was in kindergarten and the class lined up to march out of the classroom for recess. As she was moving along, she was running her hand along the table by her side. It so happened there was a nail sticking out from beneath the table's edge and it caught Terre's hand causing a deep gash across the palm of her hand. To the clinic Terre went.

On another day, playing in our back yard, Terre stepped on a metal rake, puncturing the bottom of her foot. To the clinic Terre went for a tetanus shot and bandaging of her wound. Again a nail accident happened to Terre. This time she was helping her mother by removing a chair from the kitchen to the dining room only to have the culprit nail cause a deep gash above her knees. To the clinic Terre went for repair. Terre's mishaps seem trivial in hindsight, but not so at the time. To this day Terre's reputation precedes her. When she makes her mind up on something, she "nails" it.

And, how about the Saturday morning when our Priest from Sacramento visited Marysville to perform the liturgy at the Ahepa Hall? Gaye dressed all our daughters in their finest as she always did for church, and off we went to the hall. After the service, I went directly to the golf course, and Gaye, to the grocery store in our neighborhood with all the daughters packed in the "infamous" station wagon. She told the girls to stay in the car, as she would be right out after getting a loaf of bread. Having purchased the bread, she got back into the wagon and headed home. When she got there she ordered all the girls to take off their Sunday best and get into their play clothes. This they did.

A half an hour later, Jamie came into the kitchen still wearing her church outfit. Gaye admonished her, saying, "You're still in your church dress? Get into your play clothes right now!" To Gaye's surprise, Jamie started to cry and responded, "You left me at the grocery store, and I had to walk all the way home!"

I vividly recall this last traumatic experience with the station wagon. It's transmission malfunctioning, I parked it on 18th street, between the Marysville High School campus and the old Yuba Junior college campus; left the key in the ignition slot and placed a large self drafted 'FOR STEAL" sign on the front window, secured by the wind shield wipers. Two hours later there is a knock on the front door of our home, it was sergeant Nicholau, my cousin, of the Marysville Police Department.

"George" he said "go now to the high school and drive your car home before you become an accessory to the theft of your own car!" I laughingly barked, "Hell, Nick, no one would want that jalopy in the first place, and secondly, the transmission failed me, so I coasted it to a stop there. I put the 'for steal' sign on out of frustration, and walked home."

"George if it is still there a couple of hours from now, I will have to ticket it. In any event, get the 'for steal' sign off the car window." I promised him I would and he just shook his head in disbelief as he headed back to his patrol car. And within the hour I made a deal with Dave Wheeler, the owner of the Cadillac dealership in Yuba City, towards a new Cadillac and the old car became his responsibility to tow away.

The Nicholau Clan 1982

Discipline Is Never Easy

Lest I have given you the impression that discipline was an extinct species in our home, let me assure you, that was the furthest from the truth. Gaye's and my discipline philosophy was simple: that we be on the same page; consistent, fair, and articulate in the presence of our children. And that love, love, and more love, be the basis of our discipline stratagems. On that note, unlike most parents, I hit upon a formula, although a bit radical, that best suited my persona. My wife went along with it – albeit reluctantly. However, our daughters never suspected a hint of a chasm between us. That is important. The genesis of the formula follows.

As an impetuous young boy, many were the times where my wants were abruptly settled with an emphatic NO. And that was that! A single mother during the heart of the depression beset with the challenge of rearing three boisterous sons and an angelic daughter left little room for debate. Under those circumstances dialogue was a luxury she could not afford. The outcome of her children proved her methods to be warranted. The underlying reason of success being the undeniable love behind her discipline.

A culture change was inevitable during my parenting years. Thus my parental discipline methodology evolved. On a permissive note, for whatever reason, each of our daughters had the right of a rebuttal if denied a request. During the dialogue, if I was backed into a corner with a parental last-ditch retort- "because I said so" – I would lose the debate and my daughter would be permitted to pursue her request.

Under that self-imposed format I confess I would occasionally succumb to a daughter's request and she would gain permission to pursue it. Let me be clear on one point. When I say my permission, I am speaking equally on behalf of Gaye's authority. And vice versa. That is where being on the same page kicks into the plethora of do's and don'ts we both embrace. When I did give in, it would be because my daughters logically dispelled all concerns I perceived not to be in their best interest.

I recall an example when my oldest daughter, Dessi, asked for permission to go to a school weeknight basketball game. I was somewhat taken aback that she would even make such a request.

"Go to a basketball game on a school night?!!!' I said "Sorry, Dessi. You know the rules you have your home work to do tonight."

She countered "Dad, I already completed my assignments for tomorrow. Let me show you."

"No Dessi, that's not necessary. I believe you. Yet I don't want you to go because you have school tomorrow and you will be tired."

"No I won't dad. I don't go to bed before ten pm on school nights as it is, and the game will be over by 9 pm. So you see there is no reason for me to be more tired."

"Ahh, Ehh, If I am hearing you correctly you have finished all your homework. You are caught up on all your classes, and you will be home before 9:30 p.m. Is that so?"

"Yes dad."

At this point the "because I said so" response was a no- no.
I said, "Then you have my permission to go."

"Your mother will pick you up from school around 9pm. OK?"

"Thanks dad. Don't worry about my school work - I am getting good grades"

It is an added blessing when your children know you have their best interest at heart and they respond accordingly.

Another incident worth discussing, an errant one on my part, is the time I disciplined Dorre, with 'capital punishment' – a spanking- because of an infraction she allegedly committed. I confronted her in our kitchen, in the presence of my other daughters. Two very important things ensued that influenced my discipline approach from that day forward.

First off, Dorre, four and a half years old, was innocent of the act I confronted her with, but she did not "tell" on her guilty five and a half year old sister, Dessi. She absorbed her punishment without a whimper. Dessi, in the vicinity, belatedly stepped forward, her guilty conscience overbearing, and volunteered that she was the culprit. Startled, I immediately gathered both girls and apologized to Dorre in front of her sister. And I humbly explained to her that there are times that parents can be wrong. The important thing is that the parent admits it and makes amends.

Then the oddest thing happened. Especially now as I look back upon it. Instinctively I turned to Dessi and instead of severely punishing her I found myself commending her in Dorre's presence for stepping forth to tell the truth. I told both children that I would never discipline one of my daughters for being truthful even if they committed an infraction I did not approve of, and complimented Dorre on her loyalty to her sister by remaining silent. (The infraction in this incidence was throwing their mother's red lipstick into the dryer after smearing it all over a toilet seat. Gaye turned on the dryer and some of the clothes came out bright red!) After reprimanding Dessi for her prank, I told both girls their honor was more important than any infraction. By being truthful, corrective measures can be taken. The alternative untruthful behavior compounds the severity of an infraction. As it turned out, the rearing of our six daughters by being consistent, fair and articulate, and of course with God's blessings, proved to be a pretty sound basis from which to work.

A few years later, during a confrontation- I experienced an epiphany. The importance of communication verses intimidation. I still vividly recall looking down on my three-year-old daughter Jamie over an infraction, waving a formidable index finger in her face shouting "Don't you ever do that again!!" "Do you hear me? I don't want to tell you again".

I do not know what possessed me. That very moment I noticed a look of alarming fright in my daughter's eyes, as she trembled. I spontaneously fell on my knees placing my eyes at her eye level, and as this took place in our kitchen, I looked up towards our sink. There, at what seemed a story height, was the sink faucet hovering overhead. On the left of the sink, still a "story" higher was a light switch attached to the kitchen wall. The tabletop of our kitchen island seemed to be insurmountable-yet when I stood up only tummy high for me!! That experience was indelible in my mind, and to this day I credit it as the tipping point in my communication skill not only with my children, but with whomever I am carrying on a meaningful conversation. Eye contact with whom you are carrying on a dialogue is paramount! An overbearing approach is counter-productive. After all you are trying to communicate, not intimidate.

   Lesson learned. How does that saying go? "From the mouths of babes"? Or, in this instance, "from the eyes of babes". Of course all efforts of communicating with your children, eye contact not withstanding, is for naught, if not done with love, love, and more love!! Children have an insatiable appetite for heart felt parental love and respond accordingly. Setting that example is paramount, for it won't be long, Good Lord willing, before they too will be parents and someday be in your very shoes. Did I just say *shoes?*

■ ■

   The foregone appears to be a natural introduction into my parental relationship with my six grown daughters. Looking back, upon the preschool, grammar school, high school, and university parenting years, I count my blessings on how heartedly all six daughters bought into their mother's and my parental guidance. All parents want, and hope, for the best for their children, and in their own way dedicate themselves in both time, and self sacrifice, on behalf of the welfare of their children. It is the nature of parenthood to do so. I emphasize this point, for I feel full credit for a happy God fearing child, goes to the child for opting to obey the good intentions of their parents, more so than the parent's admonition to their child.

   My prioritized time is their time. For an example of that commitment, I will share with you its' genealogy.

   On a particularly busy afternoon at the pharmacy with my red phone ringing often – the doctors direct phone to the pharmacy- and a detail pharmaceutical representative standing nearby waiting for me to give him a moment of my time, the outside phone line rings and it is one of my daughters needing my attention. The moment I heard "Dad", I cut her off saying "not now Dorre, I'm too busy to chat with you" and hung up the phone. The red phone silent, I turned to the detail rep, and before I could invite him to present his message, he volunteered, "George, that was one of your children you just hung up on, and you made a grave mistake." He didn't have to say another word. I immediately realized without thinking, I had just put my career ahead of my child. A career pursued at the expense of your family's welfare is a disaster waiting to happen. Without further hesitation, I thanked him and excused myself to the representative, dialed my home number and apologized to Dorre for cutting her off on the phone, and encouraged her to feel free to call me at any time for anything. She then proceeded to share a concern with me with regards to something that was upsetting her at school. We talked it through and the result was that my daughter felt better, and so did I. Never again would I put work before family. That mentality in my persona exists to this day. My family, and now my extended and to ever be extended family, will forever have the priority of my time, love and energy.

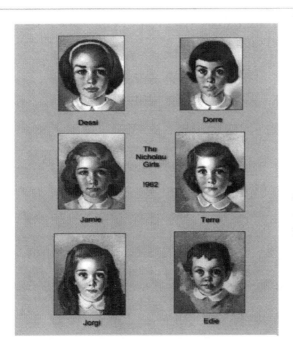

SafeSave Pharmacy is Born
(and Edie too)

In February of 1961, two landmark happenings ventured into my life- or better put- into our lives, Gaye's and mine. One, a heavenly gift from God. The other, a business enterprise.

It was on this day of our Lord, that we were blessed with a nine and a half pound bundle of effeminate joy, the one and only Edie Nicholau who was privileged to be the baby girl of the six Nicholau daughters.

The other event was the signing of a lease on 737 Colusa Avenue Yuba City, California, in a mini shopping center project under construction. With the huge success of the Marysville Clinic Pharmacy, I was looking forward to expanding my pharmaceutical enterprise by joining in partnership with Steve Wisner, a fellow pharmacist in the area. Pharmacists were in grave shortage during the post war years, and throughout the ensuing years into my retirement in 1987 and beyond! By shortage, I mean to such an extent, the registered pharmacy employee dictated to the employer the terms of agreement, with one exception, of which I will address later. The pharmacist shortage obligated the employed pharmacist to work ten to twelve hour days to be on duty during open hours of the pharmacy. No exceptions!! To comply with the reality of the "on duty law", I worked for thirty years at the Marysville Clinic Pharmacy, before I could arrange to hire a part time pharmacists for a two week vacation! Fortunately, mine was a professional-only dispensing pharmacy, and I would close on weekdays at 5:30 and on Saturday at 12:30. Coaching football and playing golf were my outlets.

The new "retail" pharmacy, would be open seven days a week from 9 am to 10 pm on weekdays, and on Sunday from noon until 5 pm. Having formed a partnership and procured a lease, I now had to come up with a name for the pharmacy. This I did after several days of brain storming hundreds of possibilities. Finally, I hit upon a name that would meet my high professional standard, and still resonate a competitive message to potential customers.

SAFESAVE Pharmacy. The motto I came up with was "Service is not our motto, it is our business."

Our weekly ads in the local Appeal Democrat newspaper featured very competitive sundry prices, our logo, and a highlighted statement "We pledge prompt courteous service and 24 hour emergency deliveries" "We may not be the cheapest, but we are the best bargain for your pharmaceutical needs!" My home phone number would be included in the ad for emergency situations.

SafeSave Pharmacy proved to be an instant success, both in the sundry department and in the prescription dispensing department. The store represented an innovative approach to the pharmaceutical industry. The success was so apparent that Steve and I ventured into a second SafeSave pharmacy in the Linda area of our community, but it did not flourish. So we closed the store.

Gaye and I at Safesave Pharmancy

Because of the shortage of pharmacists, I pledged to my clinic doctor partners that I would not compromise my commitment to the Clinic Pharmacy, even if it meant closing SafeSave Pharmacy, because of the shortage of a registered pharmacist. I gave them my word to that effect, and they agreed to allow me to expand on my own. Push came to shove several times as the SafeSave Pharmacy was on the brink of having to be closed because of a pharmacist shortage, but I never entertained the thought of letting my doctor partners down to bail out the store, even though I could have doubled my net income if I left the Clinic Pharmacy to manage my SafeSave Pharmacy venture. My honor to the Clinic Doctors was not negotiable.

My partner, Steve Wisner, had an opportunity to better himself associating with another pharmacy in the area, and we mutually agreed upon a buyout settlement between us, making me the sole owner of SafeSave Pharmacy. The most fortunate thing that could possibly happen to me with regards to my SafeSave Pharmacy venture, was the employment of Ernie Low, a registered pharmacist. Since Ernie's employment, several pharmacists were hired, worked for a few years and left. Only Ernie throughout the years stayed loyal to me. Now get this – even though he had far better offers proposed to him from the escalating number of chain store pharmacies coming into the fast growing Yuba City area, he turned them all down. Pharmacies, such as Long's, Payless, Walgreens, and several of the local established pharmacies were all competing for registered pharmacists to work for them. The chain stores offered fringe benefits including health care, guaranteed vacation, and retirement programs. Ernie, knowing my predicament, stayed with me, without any of the perks and fringe benefits.

All our transactions were sealed with a handshake. Not one paper trail exists between us throughout our association. There were times Ernie worked ten hour days, weeks on end, between the quitting and hiring of pharmacists. Remember, I gave my word to my Clinic partners that I would not compromise my association with them. As difficult as it was to do, I kept my word. And how much more difficult it must have been for Ernie, to turn down opportunities of far greater impact, at that time, on his future. Any time Ernie wanted to discuss business with me, he would show up and present his request or concerns, and I would listen. His requests were seldom, and always very fair. I would agree to his terms with a handshake, with very rare exception, and the terms would be negotiated on the spot. What a treat it was to do business transactions with a handshake. That type of trust and honor seems to be extinct in today's society.

Ernie's reward for his loyalty, with the term "reward" a gross understatement, materialized in 1987, the year I retired from the Marysville Clinic Pharmacy, when the pharmacy in the doctor's complex, due to limited doctor's office space, was converted into a pediatric ward at the clinic. When I closed the doors of the Clinic Pharmacy, I transferred all my prescription records to SafeSave, for refill and follow-up services to my customers. Because of SafeSave's success, it's value on the open market was appreciable. I requested a meeting with Ernie in December of 1987 to discuss our future SafeSave Pharmacy relationship. My meeting with Ernie follows.

"Ernie, you've been with me for over twenty years and all of our agreements were sealed with a handshake. Now, please listen to the propositions I am about to offer you, and choose the one that best suits you. Number one, pick your own salary figure and operate as you are now. Number two, accept a 49% partnership as of the first of the year, 1988, and operate as you are now. Number three, SafeSave Pharmacy is 100% yours, less current inventory. Pay off the inventory over three years – if needed take more time. The first two options were presented to Ernie in case he did not want the full responsibility and risk of ownership.

Ernie's reaction, "you mean I will be the owner of SafeSave, January first if I choose number three?"

"Yes, Ernie you earned this right several times over. At crucial times, if you had quit on me, there wouldn't be a SafeSave pharmacy to inherit. Think it over Ernie, and talk it over with your wife, Cinda, who also is a registered pharmacist, and let me know which of the three offers best suits you. Before you decide, there is one request I make, if you choose number three; as long as I, Gaye, or one of our daughters need something from SafeSave, you will, if feasible, supply it at no charge. If you sell the Pharmacy, the buyer would agree to honor our pharmaceutical needs as it is with you." (This latter request was renegotiated upon Ernie's retirement, in all fairness to the new buyer of Safe Save Pharmacy. The new owners agreed to supply only Gaye's and my needs at cost. Ernie discussed this issue with me and I thought it was a fair request and released him from the sell clause of our agreement.)

Ernie extended his hand, like he had done time and again and said, "I choose offer number three."

I shook his hand and that was that. No hassle, no last minute discussion. Period!

Inventory was taken of the stock, and Ernie was the owner of SafeSave Pharmacy. To this day, April 7, 2006, as I am recording this history, 19 plus years later during Ernie's ownership of SafeSave Pharmacy, I have never had occasion to put my hand in my pocket for any item I got from SafeSave Pharmacy. Ernie's honor precedes his many other attributes as a man of singular character.

A bunny just hopped into my mind, with it's tail waggling among my cerebral cells. Here's why. In the late 50's and early 60's, during Easter vacation from High school and the University, my girls all helped out, either at our Safesave Pharmacy or the Marysville Clinic Pharmacy, earning some spending money. Safesave Pharmacy, being a general retail layout, featured among its multi faceted inventory, a sundry of Easter specials. When customers came into the store for prescriptions or sundry items, we invited them to look over our Easter specials and if they spotted something they wanted for their kids, we had them sign an Easter day delivery sheet, stating their address and the specific time of day, they wanted their purchase delivered to their home to surprise their child with a real live Easter "bunny" greeting them with a gift. We had two professionally sewn Easter Bunny costumes made with an Easter Bunny paper mache head which our daughters would put over their heads to go with the rest of the plush, believable bunny outfit. At the specific time, our daughters, in costume, would ring the doorbell where the parent was waiting for the delivery. Upon opening the door, the family was greeted with a hopping bunny, tail wagging, and excitedly presenting the child with the ordered Easter basket. In all instances the child would go bananas; some scared, some elated. The promotion went over big in our community and our Easter orders ballooned year after year until our daughters retired as Easter Bunnies. Gad, but it was thrilling to see the reaction of the little kids when being greeted by an Easter bunny on Easter Day. I'm not sure who enjoyed it more, the children or the "bunny".

      One of the many blessings that enriched our daughter's lives is their overall academic achievement in their pursuit to live a happy useful Christian life. An edict I consistently allude to, if you are to enjoy the fruits of your labor. From the day my daughters would enter kindergarten, it was my wife's and my fondest hope that their formal education would lead to University diplomas.

      With this goal in mind, we encouraged and monitored their study at home. TV was limited during weekdays to two hours after their homework was completed. I emphasized this point earlier in my memoirs, when Dessi asked for permission to go to a basketball game in the middle of the week. But more than that, I wanted to create a desire from within to want to go to college upon graduation from high school. I started creating this desire by periodically sharing my college experiences in such a way that it wetted their appetite for the college culture. My wife Gaye, a graduate of San Jose State, also had interesting tales of college life to share with our daughters.

Together, Gaye and I would take our daughters to Saturday afternoon football games played at Cal's Memorial Stadium. I, having earned my letter in football, gave my daughters added interest in the game itself. At the pre-game celebration, the Cal Band would march up to the stadium from the Campanile, with the cheerleaders, and at intervals stopping the procession to lead all the following students and visiting fans in songs and cheers. One game a year, at half time, all past varsity football players would trot out to the middle of the field as their names and class year were announced over the stadium loud speaker system. The daughters got a kick when my turn came to trot on the field during the halftime celebration. All this heightened their appetite for wanting to go to college – the University of California, in particular. The proof of "our indoctrinating pudding," is that all six daughters graduated from a University as boasted elsewhere in my memoirs. And five went to CAL! The sixth went to usc. Ouch!

All six girls, once settled in their adopted sorority, and having adjusted to the increased speed of the University learning cycle, graded their University experiences as an unforgettable accomplishment in their life's pursuit. Mission accomplished!

CHRISTOS ANESTI!

Tempus Flute~ I hope I have that right. Latin for "time flies". For today, as I write my memoirs, is April 5th, 2006, the fourth week of Easter Great Lent. My daughter Jamie asked me what I gave up for Lent this year, and giving it some thought, I came up with the following answer.

Nothing and everything. Nothing, not because I couldn't find anything to forego. Quite the opposite, in fact. So many flaws are apparent in my persona that I could not justifiably prioritize one over the other. Instead I have decided to take a broad-brush approach; encompassing everything. I am pledging to mentally concentrate on living a more pious life overall, each day of Lent, hoping this behavior will factor into a permanent lifestyle.

Accordingly, my game plan during Lent is to take valued time from each day to critique my mannerisms of that day. I plan to cull out an overt transgression each day, which I am certain will exist, and focus upon correcting that transgression the following day. In this way, I will be able to address several of my inequities without the responsibility of having to prioritize one over the other.

Flashback to Easter time when I was a young tot. Easter was the most sacred celebrated feast day of the year. The whole Greek community of Marysville and Yuba City would gather at the home of a designated host for that year's celebration to pay homage to Christ's Resurrection. One or two lambs would be prepared on a spit, to be barbequed over a dug-out pit filled with hot ember glowing coals, in the host's backyard.

I recall an Easter celebration at the Antone home, when I was just seven years old. At the party, I maneuvered myself under a table where the men drinking their retsina wine sat, while reminiscing over the good old days of celebrating Easter in the "old country". Periodically they would all get up from the table to dance the Tsambico, a Greek dance mainly for men whose gyrations and dexterous movements would be vociferously encouraged by all in attendance motivating the dancers into the execution of somersaults, and leaps and bounds, all at a frenetic pace. Each time they would get up to dance, I would sneak out from my 'den' and drink what wine was left behind in their glasses. The last thing I remember was my father shaking his head with all sorts of sounds coming from his mouth! Thank God is was not a preview of coming attractions of my life.

As I write my memoirs, today is Easter Sunday, April 23rd, 2006. Christos Anesti!
(Christ is Risen!) Today we celebrate Christ's giving of His life through the torments of crucifixion on the cross. He arose from His tomb to conquer death, by death, and all people under Hades torment were freed, forgiven of their sins, and welcomed into Heaven. A day worthy of celebration, indeed!
One such celebration stands out in my mind. When the kids were growing up, Gaye and I were usually the designated hosts for the Easter festivities where we would have our home and back yard filled with family and friends to celebrate the day. My brother, Nick was the annually appointed barbeque specialist, and rightfully so, as no one could barbeque like Nick. He had his own signature marinade that was anxiously anticipated throughout the whole year awaiting the sacrificial Easter lamb. At this particular Easter celebration I sauntered over to my chef brother as he was turning the lamb slowly over the smoldering coals deep in the dug out pit. It was around 3:00 p.m. and I had worked up a good appetite. Up to that point I had harassed my brother throughout the day with a steady stream of "when will the lamb be ready?" To which he would tactfully ignore me. However, upon this last inquiry he said, with his hand that held his retsina wine glass moving toward his lips, "George, when I'M done, the LAMB will be done!!" While expressing himself, he thrust his hand-held wine toward the lamb, causing him to lose his balance toward the smoldering pit. I caught him just as he was falling toward the hot coals. Without hesitating he calmly said, "Let's take the lamb off the spit. I'M done!" And so they were, both brother and lamb…done to perfection.

My dear brother, Nick.
"When I'M done, the LAMB'S done!!"
He was a class act.

Brotherly LOVE at it's best

While still in an Easter reflective mood, I must share with you the reaction to the Nicholau's young family Sunday church attendance episodes. Because the nearest Greek Orthodox Church was in Sacramento, we would venture there once a month, packing our six daughters into our station wagon to worship a Sunday liturgy. I can still hear my daughters harmonizing to the popular songs of the era as we would drive along. This is just one of the thousands of priceless memories that we have shared throughout our lives.

Important Greek culture information is warranted for one to adequately appreciate the gravity of what is to follow. The adopted ethnic procedure of the first generation Greek family is to promote the marriage of the daughters, preferably in the order of their seniority. To exacerbate this custom, it is the responsibility, and the expectation of the father of a daughter, not only to solely foot the bill of the marriage celebration, but also for the respective parents to negotiate a meaningful dowry, as a gift to the groom. Please keep this ethnic ideology uppermost in your mind as I move forward on this church attendance novelette.

Before going to Sacramento to church, Gaye always insisted that all six daughters be neatly groomed and dressed to the hilt, with hat and gloves, no less! After each of us lit a candle, did our cross, and placed the candle in it's proper place in the narthex of the church, we would then proceed single file towards the front pews of the church, so the youngest daughters would have a clear view of the service during the liturgy.

During this 'procession' consisting of a mother and a father and six daughters filing down the isle of the church, many of the parishioners would look towards the fair sexed family, and in unison, do their cross out of empathy for the father (assuming the impact on the father's obligations to his daughters in their forthcoming marriage "contracts.") Their genuine concern complimented me, for little did they realize what a blessing the Lord honored me with, in choosing me to be the paternal steward of six, no make that seven earthly angels. Each day of my life I include in my prayers the many blessings God has bestowed upon me through my unprecedented wonderful family.

However, leaving the pious atmosphere of church, and for a bit of levity, the truth be known I, too, had a price to pay. Proper etiquette in our home stated that toilet seats should be left in the down position. With four bathrooms serving seven females, I finally contracted CTES – acronym for Chronic Tennis Elbow Syndrome – Cause? You do the math!

Misadventures in Golf

I recall when I first ventured into the tumultuous – there must be a much more emphatic word I could use- hobby of golf. An embarrassing incident worth mentioning, involving shoes, took place on the first Tee of the Plumas Lake Golf Course in the Marysville area.

I was thirty-one years old, a post WW II naval officer, by military standards considered a gentleman, and totally absorbed in my pharmaceutical profession. Being an athletic enthusiast all my life, I felt it would be therapeutic to become involved with an outdoor hobby that would reward me with a needed break from the all-encompassing professional pharmaceutical responsibilities. I chose golf. Little did I imagine at the time that choosing golf as a relaxing hobby would catapult me from the frying pan into the fire. Especially when I viewed it as a pressure release safety valve from my professional responsibilities. What I am implying is that the competitive addictiveness of golf was insidiously flip-flopping my livelihood priority with my hobby aspirations! It is feudal to explain the logic of that statement when the former finances the latter. Only those who embrace the *hobby* of golf can relate to the dilemma I voluntarily created in my lifestyle. In retrospect it proved to be a wise choice. I challenge any golfer to make a positive swing thought during a competitive match with his mind focused on anything other than a helpless golf ball. At that point in time, success is measured in the outcome of the shot.

  With regards to my shoe vs. golf story, a friend of mine, Elton McDaniel, a general contractor, also joined me as a neophyte in the adventure of golf. We opted to play our first round at the Plumas Lake Golf and Country Club. Not being privy to the proper dress code, and etiquette of the sport, I met Elton on the first Tee casually dressed in my tattered yard tennis shoes, waiting our turn to Tee off. Just as we were about to Tee off, a popular threesome, consisting of pillars of the community, I might add, sauntered up to Elton and myself, asking if they could joined us. Of course, we agreed, assuming that a five-some was allowed, or else they would not have asked. Now picture this setting. I am on the first Tee wearing tattered tennies, while all the other golfers, Elton included, were wearing Golf cleated shoes. The pillars of the community consisted of Mr. Ray Manwell, a famous attorney, and Mr. Buck Manford, a retired rancher, aka Scrooge, a hell of a competitor who could hear the ashes from a cigarette hitting the turf when in his putting stance. He was a super guy, nonetheless, who wore his emotions on his sleeve from the first Tee through the 18th green. Lastly, there was Glenn Potter, not only a past champion of Plumas Lake, but of more significance in my case, my high school football coach!

  Now picture me, a professional pharmacist with a reputation as a future pillar of our community, focusing not on the stature of the golfers in our group, but on their golf shoes!!! Black and white were Mr Manwell's footwear, while stylish winged tipped brown golf shoes shod coach Potter's feet, and militant spit-polished plain toe, black shoes, that matched his competitive persona, were worn by Buck Manford. Instinctively, I found myself, consciously placing my borrowed canvas golf bag conspicuously laid across my feet covering my rag tag tennies, while exchanging pleasantries among the group, before my turn to Tee it up.

I noticed it took a bit of time and concentration by each golfer before going into their swing at the ball. Well, needless to say, when it was my turn, to camouflage my shoe faux pas, it took me less time to address the ball and swing at it than it took each of them to just pick a club out of their bag.

Thank God for coach Potter, who aware of my dilemma, tactfully alleviated my embarrassment after a couple of holes by volunteering, "This must be your first go at this game, George."

I sheepishly responded, "You've got that right", and facetiously commented "How did you guess?"

"Well," he said, "Not by your golf swing. You seem to have a natural talent for the game. But, I suggest you try spiked golf shoes in place of tennis shoes, if you are serious about the game."

That broke the ice, and we all had a hearty laugh over my tennis shoes. And you know what? I think I still have those tennies, or a replica, in my closet. Heaven forbid! In any event, for certain I do have in my closet, having bought them from the Pro shop that very day after my first round of golf, a genuine pair of lizard leather, black and white. wing tipped Foot Joy, top of the line golf shoes. You guessed it. You can see them in their original box, sitting comfortably in the closet. I wore them several times before I had a chance to show them off inconspicuously, ha ha, in the company of Glen, Ray and Buck. While I have worn out many pair of golf shoes, the original lizard skin black and white shoes still await my next novel experience with them. Why so- I don't really know. Hopefully, somewhere between the lines of my writings, and suspect psyche, with your intervention, daughters, we will solve the mystery behind my shoe fetish.   HELP!

More on golf. Let me share some comical experiences I encountered through my golf fellowship.

Frank Colt, now deceased, a perennial champion of the Yuba Sutter area, became my golfing buddy, and mentor. A diminutive person of 5'7", 135 lb stature, Frank could really move a golf ball. His distance, as spectacular as it was, played second fiddle to his accuracy and touch around the greens. Enough about Frank's talent, this story is about me. Suffice it to say, Frank taught me good fundamentals of the golf swing that eventually earned me a single digit 6 handicap. He was noted for his one liner quips. A particular Sunday morning I recall telephoning Frank, saying, "Frank what a great day for golf. I will be heading to the golf course at 10 am."- Before I could utter another word, he quipped, "George, I can't stop you." Talk about a timely squelch!

A sequel to Frank's teaching ability: he did such a good job on me, that I qualified twice to meet him in the finals of the Peach Tree Golf and CC gross score championship tournament. Both times it turned into an effort of futility on my part. The closest I came was two down with one hole to play on our 36 hole tournament. This, after I shot a 35 in the afternoon round on the front 9 of the match. That 35 earned me a half with Frank for the nine holes! At least I was losing to a statewide respected champion golfer.

In another situation, in a handicap tournament at Peach Tree, my opponent was Matt Little. After 7 holes of play, I was three up on Matt, and I felt sorry for him as he was having an off day pushing his shots to the right. On the 8th Tee box, I remarked, "Matt, would you be receptive to a tip that may help you?"

"George" he replied, "the way I am playing today, any suggestion would be welcome."

I offered my tip. He not only took it, but also won holes 8 and 9!!

Teeing off on #10, a relatively short 4 par hole, he reverted to his old swing and pushed his Tee shot into the right rough, a few yards short of the fairway trap. I exclaimed "Oh no Matt!"

I followed with my Tee shot down the middle of the fairway. His second shot was topped, and slithered into the fairway sand trap.

Again "Oh no Matt!"

I hit my fairway shot onto the green, 12 feet from the pin. Matt hurried his third attempt, and sculled the ball out of the trap, with a vicious swing that set the ball careening 3 feet above the fairway like a misguided missile to land in front of the green, rolling 20 feet off the elevated back of it.

Still again, I said, "Oh no Matt!"

He irritably went to his ball, set up and struck it towards the green. The ball gathered speed up over the back of the green and started rolling towards the hole. It hit the pin, doing a pirouette, before settling at the bottom of the hole!

I blustered out, "Oh shit, what does that give you, Matt?"

He smiled, as he picked up his ball from the bottom of the cup, and casually said "For your edification, George, that is three Oh no's and one Oh shit!!"

The match was even through the 11th hole. I three putted the 10th hole, while absorbing a valuable lesson on the back lash effects of verbalizing deceptive, self serving comments, feigning empathy towards an opponent. Fortunately, at day's end, I did survive.

Lesson learned: "It isn't over until it's over" and do not lose sight of good sincere sportsmanship during a golf match. Matt, to his credit, for years to follow would needle me with an "Oh no George", followed by a hearty laugh.

The Nassau bets I was exposed to, within our prestige group at Peach Tree Golf and CC in the early 60's, were 50 cents to a dollar denominations. Including team bets, individual side bets, and the inevitable presses that occur during a round of golf, one's financial obligation on a bad outing would be in the neighborhood of ten to fifteen dollars, tops. That was big within our group in the 60's.

With that background, I will fast forward to a visit I had with my close friend Jim Kourafas, AKA the "Golden Boy" around the Fresno links. Jim, a 2 handicapper, was the club champion at Sunnyside Golf and Country Club in Fresno. His golfing buddies included the "high-roller" cronies who enjoyed the competitive camaraderie and ribbing among themselves, more than the monetary exposure they were playing for.

On occasions when I would visit Fresno, Jim saw to it that I would be included in his group for that day's golf match. Knowing I was a late comer to the game, flirting with a 15 handicap at that time, he would, for my sake, volunteer to take me for a partner on a side bet of the usual five-five and ten dollar no press best ball game. His individual customary bets with his cronies came with automatic press bets whenever one was two holes down during the 18 hole match. At my exposure I was comfortable because the most I could lose was 20 dollars. My ball striking talent was never a cause for alarm among our opponents. If Jim played well, we'd do okay. If not, I enjoyed a maximum of 20 dollars worth of great fellowship on the golf course. Also, I would more than compensate for our loss during our 19th hole exposure, as it was the custom for the winning team to host the post golf libations.

It was customary for me to call Jim, beforehand, when I intended to head to Fresno for a golf venture. He would arrange for a game. I would do likewise when he would visit Marysville, Well, this particular day I dropped in on Jim without forewarning, as I was on my way to LA for a pharmaceutical convention. To this day, I can remember Jim, being ticked off, as he had a hot, high stake, get-even match with his usual group. Yet he didn't feel comfortable leaving me waiting for him at the Clubhouse, so he arranged with the pro and his buddies to have this unsuspected intruder join them as a five-some. While gathered on the first Tee, his twosome opponents, knowing Jim was pissed off, asked him, in a poorly camouflaged conciliatory tone, if he wanted a side bet with me as his partner, thinking it would distract his focus on the foursome big match. Jim, never one to back down from a challenge, especially when provoked by the tone of the challenge, looked towards me and, asked if I was interested.

My retort: "No problem".

Being aware of my Marysville frugal background golf stakes, the twosome inquired if I would want a game with their ongoing bets. Jim looked my way and said

"Do you want to take them on?"

"Sure." Of course, I felt they were just trying to accommodate me on a side bet with the usual 5 –5-$10 denomination. Again, I surmised the most I could lose would be 20 dollars knowing they were already playing for big money on their own game. The format of their game called for automatic presses as previously alluded to, and the bundle press on the backside if one team was down on any units. Jim was always the official scorer among the group.

On the first Tee, on this particular day, I was experiencing a phenomenon I was not accustomed to among this group. A reserved, quiet, serious approach to the game. The usual levity was missing among the foursome. It soon dawned on me why; the exposure was substantial. The serious atmosphere, along with unusual attention to good golf etiquette prevailed throughout the first 17 holes.

Getting ready to Tee it up on the 18th Tee Jim was distracted by Leo Michaelides, an opponent, asking Jim "How about a get-even bet with you and George?"

Jim looked startled and annoyed remarking, "No way. You get out the same way you got in. You have a unit press coming in George, and my match, period!" I looked at Jim a bit confused and volunteered, "Hell Jim, it's among friends, and it's only money, let's do it." Thinking of our customary Fresno bets, I figured by winning the press we would win 40 dollars, by halving the press we'd win 20 dollars, by losing the press we'd break even for the day. Big deal. WRONG! A lesson learned, and never forgotten: Do not question Jim's authority unless you are willing to pay the consequences. Jim looked at me and countered, "George, you want to play this hole for the bundle? You realize we are 6 units up on the original bet? He is entitled to a unit press if he wants it."

"No problem Jim. It's only money." I was so out of character it stunned him and more so the rest of the group, although I must admit I was confused over his 6 unit up statement. Again, knowing me to be a spend thrift golfer he bewilderedly reiterated in a staccato pace, *"You - are - willing - to - play - this - hole – double- or -nothing - for THREE HUNDRED DOLLARS?!!"*

My state of shock had to have been registered to all those about me, as I tried my best to camouflage it with an emphatic "sure" – which I believe came out like a parched high-pitched "yeah". In the first place, I had no idea where we stood, only that we were not losing. In Fresno, all bets once made, are tallied in units as the match progresses, not in dollars, and we were 6 units up, which with automatic presses, factored into $300!! We were playing for 50-dollar units! Not the 5-10-20 dollar match I assumed we were playing for. My faux pas aside, Jim accepted the get-even bet.

On the par 4- 18th hole, Jim, I am sure, not from pressure, hell, he thrived on pressure, but from my intervention, was irritable. As a result, he grossly missed his only drive of the day, pulling it out of bounds left of the fairway!! If you have never witnessed a white knuckled Greek squeeze the grip of a golf club with a life and death hold, you have really missed an entertaining sight. The load, for the first time in our match, rested SOLEY on my shoulders, although I did come through earlier in the match on 2 of the 17 holes played. As painful as it is, even at this writing, to document the fiasco of the 18th hole, I've got to do it. Here goes.

Fraught with emotion and heart thumping pressure, the best I could do after two shots from the Tee, is still be 10 yards from the four par18th green. Fortunately, neither of our opponents was on in regulation. One was over the green, and other to the right of the green. I still had complete control for the successful outcome of our bet. Don't I wish? To state the pressure took its toll would be a gross understatement. It took me two strokes to negotiate the last ten yards to the green. I might add, this day was the genesis for the YIPS with my putter that now and again, at the least opportune time will show it's ugly face. Our opponents faired just slightly better; for 2 puts later, I picked up my ball from the bottom of the cup for a horrendous six, realizing a par 4 would have won 600 dollars, or a bogie saved 300 dollars only to lose with a double bogie. Breaking even for the day. Now this comment is important. Jim, the renowned sportsman, never flinched or admonished me from interfering on the bet format, or for my choking performance. The match was history, we all shook hands and headed for the 19th hole where the usual camaraderie and socializing excelled.

A by your leave comment- Jim's stature on the golf course was tantamount to Rhett Butler's character in "Gone With the Wind". He commanded a great presence. His group worshipped the "Golden Boy" and arranged many of their matches around his presence. The good Lord destroyed the mold after Jim's demise. (Or did He? Jim's son Tom, in a golf venue, is a chip off the old block). Jim projected an outstanding persona for other's to embrace. I know the forgone hyperbole sounds a bit much, but I assure you it is not so. To know Jim, as I knew him, you would find it very difficult to embellish his endearing character.

**Me, Alex Spanos, and my close friend Jim Kourafas
In front of Alex's jet**

Now for a sequel to "the high stakes story". Months later I phoned Jim. I was again heading through Fresno on my way to LA for a pharmaceutical meeting. I was one of the trustees for the California State Pharmaceutical Association. I asked if he would arrange for us to play a round of golf on a stop over. He informed me he was committed to a tournament at the San Joaquin Golf and CC, but he would be happy to set me up with his Sunnyside group. I thanked him and told him the approximate time I would arrive in Fresno. Upon arriving at Sunnyside Golf and Country Club, his buddies, all single digit players, greeted me warmly. We had lunch before heading to the first Tee. The foursome consisted of, Mike Mathieson, Monte Shevelut, Bill Van Dyke, and myself.

Through Jim, I was familiar with Mike Mathieson, and he introduced me to the others saying, "George, you and I will take on Monte and Bill. Is our usual Nassau format satisfactory with you?"

Being officially Jim's guest, there was no way I would embarrass him, so I lied, "Great. Let's do it".

To this day I do not remember- other than the aforementioned 18th hole described earlier - playing with more pressure on each shot from the beginning until the end of the match. Incidentally, I shot within my 15 handicap. I had no choice. Though I was quiet throughout the match, the other players were loose, with much levity shared among themselves.

After the match we retired to the clubhouse for some refreshments and Mike said, "George, sorry we didn't do well, we are down three units."

"Hey, no problem" I faked. "I loved the chance to play with all of you."

While we were having our lunch, I motioned for the bartender to come over to our table. Bill Van Dyke spoke up, "George. You are our guest. You don't put your hand in your pocket."

When the Bartender sauntered over, Bill ordered another round of drinks. But before the bartender got away, I asked him if he would bring me a blank check. Mike Mathieson, startled, looked at the bartender, and bellowed, "Forget it." Then looking at me, with a duplicitous smile he offered "What the hell is this? George, you mean you don't have a dollar and fifty cents to cover your loss?"

"Hell", I countered, "I thought we were playing for ..." That's as far as I got when Van Dyke sympathetically remarked, "Forget it George, we'll collect from Jim."

Immediately thereafter, seeing the bewildered look on my face, there was an explosion of laughter by all three hosts. Jim had shared my previous 50 dollar experience and had me set up for a perfect Friar's victim, even to the extent of Mike strategically three-putting two holes, to assure the loss.

Although I was the butt of the joke, it had a perfect ending. I must add, it couldn't have happened to a more gullible candidate, perpetuated by a more congenial group of super guys. I often wondered how boring it must have been that day for Jim's buddies to play for 50-cent units. Hopefully, their sacrifice was compensated with interest, by my reaction to their Oscar winning performance.

While I am thinking about my true friend and cohort Jim , I suppose this is a great time to relate a golf story about Tom Kourafas, Jim's oldest son. It occurred at my home course - Peach Tree Golf and Country Club. Tom, a scratch handicapper, who lettered in golf at the University of Southern California, was my guest invitational partner in our annual member-guest tournament. One of the special challenges in the format of the tournament was a long ball drive contest on the 10th Tee of the course. A local, highly touted golfer, Jim Troncatty, stepson of the local pro for Peach Tree, was noted for his prodigious long drives, and thus a shoe-in favorite for the prize. He was in the foursome ahead of us. There was a back up delay on the tenth Tee and Tom and I witnessed Jim's effort while waiting our turn to follow them on the Tee.

Jim Troncatty hit a beautiful, powerful, skyward launched drive down the fairway just 10 yards off center. All who witnessed the drive, and Troncatty in particular, assumed that was it. The ball ended up 20 yards past the longest drive to that point and was exceptionally accurate---well past the 250-yard fairway marker. Troncatty, rightfully so, had a look of invincibility on his face.

When it came our turn to tee off, Tommy turned to me and said " do you mind if I shoot first and give it a go?"

"Hey, be my guest" I quipped. I was hoping he would accept the challenge, for I believed if anyone was going to pass Troncatty, it would be Tommy.

You see, at Peach Tree our second hole is a 505 yard par 5, and on that 2nd hole during a practice round, Tommy hit a supper drive 50 yards past the 225plus yard fairway traps.

When we reached his ball, he asked his father Jim, in our foursome, what club he thought he should use.

"Tom" I jumped in "this is a 5 Par – hit all you got."

"Son," his father advised, "you are a good 230 yards from the green."

On that information, he pulled out a 3 iron and hit the ball through the green!!

Now to prepare for the long ball effort, he just took three iron clubs from his bag and swung them several times for the warm up. He put the clubs back in his bag, pulled out his driver, and the explosion of the club face smashing the golf ball was a preview of coming attractions. That ball launched off the tee like a rocket missile screaming into the sky. It literally looked like a jet in high gear when it reached 200 yards out, sailing a good 20 airborne yards past Troncatty's ball. And likewise, just yards off center.

Troncatty, witnessing that drive, put his driver back into his bag with no fanfare. He acknowledged Tom's monstrous drive with an unbelieving frown. Still in wonderment, he took off down the 10th fairway with his foursome. When he reached Tom's ball he looked back and with a salute acknowledged Tom's drive.

I don't know who enjoyed that spectacle more; me, Jim, or Tommy, but one thing I do know, it was a day I will never forget.

My Best Friends

With Harry Pappas

With the "Golden Boy"

Leo Michaelides & Jim Kourafas

With Jim Kourafas in front of Alex Spanos's jet

With Elie and Koula Skofis

Sam Menzelos, Elie Skofis, and Ted Efstratis

**With my close friend, Harry Pappas
A friendship that began at Cal**

**With my close friend Paul Christopulos
Also, a friendship that began at Cal**

Moving on, I just have to relate to you a household golf misadventure when Gaye and I lived with our young daughters, Dessi, Dorre, and Jamie, in our first dwelling; a one bedroom apartment over a saloon. I use the word misadventure advisedly. Picture, if you will, a one-bedroom apartment, built over a two-car garage, which called for a twenty-step stairway from the street entrance to the apartment. A security gate was locked from the inside to prevent strangers from the railroad tracks to enter the premises. The structure of the apartment was physically joined to Yiayia's home, which in turn, was situated on a second story over a bar- the Columbia Bar on E Street- not to be confused with the "D" Street Columbia Restaurant. The building was in the lower commercial area of town. To go from mother's house to the apartment you negotiated three steps down from her porch to the front door of the apartment leading into the kitchen. Oh yes, I forgot, in our apartment there was always the presence of the proverbial playpen in the living room area, to accommodate not one, not two, but three toddlers.

This abode was our home for the first four years of our marriage! It blessed us with daughters, Dessi, Dorre, and Jamie. Imagine mom, pop, two toddlers and an infant crammed into a twelve by ten foot bedroom, furnished with two cribs and a basinet!! and you get a fair idea of the most flexible, resilient and angelic wife's introduction into the real world of motherhood. Meanwhile, I capitalized on the Greek ethnic role of being the man of the house. "Mar Mar", my endearing acronym for my wife, not only tended the youngsters during the night hours, but did all the cooking for the family. Not to mention the unexpected guests that I would, on the spur of the moment, invite over for breakfast before a round of golf, or for dinner after golf, or doctors from the clinic for lunch, into our compact 7 foot by 10 foot kitchen. Gaye would also convert the large sink in the kitchen, several times a day, into a "bath tub" to bathe our children. We have home movies documenting this fact for perpetuity.

Now I will get on with the in-house golf incident I started eons ago. Peggy Steel, a very close friend of Gaye's, had just that day delivered one of her children at Rideout Hospital, located 4 blocks from our apartment. Gaye asked me to babysit our only daughter at that time, Dessi, while she went to visit Peggy. Of course I "characteristically" volunteered to do so. And in doing so, I planned to use my babysitting time to monitor my golf swing.

At this point in time, I was really getting hooked on golf. In fact, I was becoming a compulsive victim of the game of golf. I admit to fanaticism in my pursuit of excellence. On that note, I had read a million articles on the importance of a quiet head movement during a golf swing.

Being a consummate innovator, I conjured up the following drill to monitor my head movement during a full golf swing. This I did by taking a bar of soap to make a perpendicular and horizontal T mark on the mirror that hung above the couch on the wall of the living room of the apartment. I would address an imaginary ball with my driver, while looking into the mirror, positioning my head just under the horizontal mark and next to the perpendicular mark of the T. I would then swing my driver while monitoring my head movement from the fixed point of the T in the mirror. Repeating the swing time and again, I got to the point where I was satisfied that I remained within the accepted tolerance of head movement for a good golf swing.

I hit on a great idea. That evening Dessi was entertaining herself in the playpen in front of the couch when was abruptly removed from the playpen and placed on the couch below the mirror. I tipped the playpen up on its long end side. Then I confiscated a heavy winter blanket placing it over the open end of the playpen facing me. I put several heavy books on top of the blanket to hold it in place. Next I substituted one of her two-inch square rubber alphabet building blocks for a golf ball placing it five feet in front of the blanketed playpen.

With this set up, I addressed the rubber alphabet block "golf ball", and swung the club while monitoring my starting head position movement with a 'T' marked in soap on the mirror above the couch. The smack of the club meeting the rubber block was ecstasy only to be rivaled by the smacking sound of a rubber block when it crashed into the suspended blanket. I repeated this exercise several times gaining more confidence and unbelievable excitement after each shot. My head movement, I'm happy to report, was golf neutral!

This experiment proved to be so successful, I just had to try it with a real golf ball for the ultimate thrill! I retrieved the ball from my golf bag. I placed it on a paper modified golf tee, about 5 feet from the blanket over the crib opening, and proceeded to address it. I slowly wound up into the top of my back swing. Wow~ it suddenly occurred to me that even from 5 feet to the blanket, I still could possibly miss the narrow "range" – then what? I moved a foot closer to the draped blanket and repeated the back swing. Again I stopped. I still wasn't sure of myself. Yet, just four feet from the "range", how could I miss? The third time was a go. I wound up to a full powerful back swing position, keeping my head fixed, and uncoiled with full force down towards the innocent golf ball. Don't ask me why. But something didn't feel right, and I attempted to abort the swing. But, to no avail. The force of the down swing was like a free running locomotive heading right at the ball. The aborted attempt pulled the club head off track so that when the club head smashed into the ball it shot with bullet-like force to the left of the "range".

What followed was pure panic personified. The first recollection I have of the errant projectile was a crashing explosion as it flew into the hutch beyond the dining room table. The hutch displayed beautiful expensive wedding gifts. If that wasn't enough damage, there was a succession of explosions coming from so many directions simultaneously; I thought that I was in a no-man's war zone!

My physical reflex reaction to the explosion was to sling my body over baby Dessi, sprawled on the couch where I had placed her. After what seemed an eternity of BANGS – followed by a still louder Silence!! I immediately looked about the room to assess the damage. It was extensive. A broken clock, shattered glasses, a broken silver picture frame and an heirloom plate that was a wedding gift from one of my college acquaintances, Georgia Katsanos, whose specialty was ceramic art. (Fortunately the plate, after professional repair by Georgia survived the fiasco. It now hangs on the wall of our dining room.) To exacerbate the calamity,

I spotted a hole in the ceiling from the ricochet golf ball, and a broken plastered ball mark over the wall facing the bay window.

Days later I found a ball mark indentation over the couch below the bottom edge of the hanging mirror. Thank God it did not hit the mirror for I am sure it would have exploded into many jagged fragments. I did my cross and thanked God for the saying – "all's well that ends well." Albeit I was stretching the euphemism of "all's well", but at least Dessi was not scathed. The ball had innocently settled under the coffee table in front of the couch. I drowned it the following Sunday on the third hole at Plumas Lake Golf and country club. I can truthfully say that is the only golf ball, of the many I drowned throughout the years, where I experienced no regrets.

There are more hilarious golfing adventures I encountered throughout the years that would qualify for entertainment to write about. However, enough for now.

O Hell, overruled by the anointed golf enthusiast.

Practicing my golf swing, slow motion, with Jorgi riding her tricycle nearby. Don't worry. There was no golf ball involved in this practice session…and I resisted the great temptation to swing full speed.

How about the time I crashed a golf ball into my brand new Oldsmobile convertible windshield, parked just outside my garage. You see, I had moved my golf range from the upstairs apartment into the garage. Again, after much success in the garage set up with a real golf ball, I missed the 'range' and the ball struck the cement wall behind it, and ricocheted with bullet speed, smack into the car windshield that I had just backed out of the garage to make room for my practice session. Joe Duraque, my insurance agent, shook his head in disbelief when I reported the details on the "accident".

Or, the incident where my two 'angelic' grandsons Nick Adams and George Chuchas, crashed my private electric golf cart into the tennis court fence at Peach Tree G&CC while trying to emulated their Papou's eccentric golf cart parking maneuver.

This happened as Nick jumped from the cart using the steering wheel for leverage, thus veering the cart into the tennis court fence. The damage to the cart and fence was a bit extensive, yet I accepted full responsibility for the fiasco. For had I not braggingly shown off my specialty maneuver of getting off the golf cart while it was still moving, they never would have attempted to copy their "Papou". (Grandfather) The whole maneuver had to be evacuated at precisely the right speed, about 15 to 20 yards from it's final destination (a throwback from my Navy "no bell docking" experience) allowing the cart to settle unmanned at just the spot I wanted it to, for the convenience of the pro shop employees. I had perfected my signature move.

As for the accident, Hell, I think I would have been disappointed if they had not tried to outdo Papou. They are the greatest. Right off they assumed full responsibility, and offered to pay for all the damage. Now, that is the sign of responsible manhood. Of course, I denied them that privilege. It was worth the incident to bring out the responsible virtue of my grandchildren.

For the record; though having started golf in my thirties, I did become proficient enough to support a 6 handicap. Also a rarity in the golfing world, I have shot my age four times. To date I accomplished it first when I was 77 years old, again at 79, again at 82, and just last year, two days after my 87th birthday, I shot an 85 witnessed by Dave Arnes and Bob Eckardt, two of my golfing cronies. Again, during this proof reading, I must update you on a braggadocios bet I made with myself. Not having shot my age during my 88th year, I bet I would not get my hair cut during my 89th year until I shot my age or better. At this writing 5/29/2008, my shoulder length hair bares witness to my failure to date. Reason, two cataract surgeries which have put a damper on my golf exposure. Now that I started to play, post surgeries, I do believe I will be getting a haircut soon.

There exists an unmistakable adage in the realm of golf instruction. The higher one's handicap, the more willingly he volunteers the unsolicited secrets of the golf swing among his peers. And to my discredit, I am no exception.

A lesson with my grandson, Nick Terzakis, went like this. The first mistake I made, as you will soon agree, was to let him use my driver, but it was more suited for him than his beginning club. During the lesson, Nick would make a very good smooth swing and hit some great shots with my driver, but I wasn't satisfied with his distance and kept encouraging him to swing smooth but faster. This he did, and the ball went further.

I kept insisting, "Faster, faster, through the ball, Nick." He would meekly comply.

Finally I yelled, still faster, "Damn it, attack the ball, let it all hang out".

(Mr. Daly, a tour professional golfer, noted for his prodigious long drives, has coined this phrase when asked what his secret was: GRIP it and RIPP it.)

Nick gave me a frowning look, said not a word, addressed the ball, and as Daly advised, "gripped it and ripped it" with all his might. What followed was a loud thud sound with the club head of my driver, and my knees, hitting the turf at the same time. My knees were next to the still teed up ball while the driver head was thirty yards up field.

My "OH NO" was heard a couple of fairways away. The look on Nick's face was indescribable, unless you can imagine a faithful Christian encountering the devil for the first time. He was so genuinely apologetic that I felt more sorry for him than I did for myself. After all, he was just following his coach's directions. His dad joined Nick in insisting they buy me a new driver. That, of course, was not an option. My rebound reaction was to face reality, and we all had a good laugh over the incident.

The good news, the fine Samaritan that I am, was that I found out the driver, when sent to the manufacturer for repair, had a lifetime guarantee. Not only was it replaced with a new shaft, but upgraded to their latest model at no charge! I can't wait until an even better model is produced by the company, so that I can arrange for another driving lesson with my powerful "A" student. I know I can't swing fast and hard enough to break the shaft of a club even if it was made of glass. But with Nick, steel seems vulnerable.

March 26th, 2007, I just learned today the two drivers I lent to Nick to try, now that he is on the Rio Americano High School golf team, have both been sent to the respective manufacturers for replacement of broken shafts. Daly, I'm giving you fair warning: enjoy your long drive reputation for now. But look in your rear view mirror for one Nicholas Terzakis as your successor.

From Golf Shoes to Loafers

On Christmas morning of 1992, I opened a present from my most pragmatic, thoughtful, and loving wife, Gaye. Surprise! It turned out to be a pair of exceptionally comfortable soft leather loafers. You see, she noticed that I was over-extending the life expectancy of my present loafers to the point of no return. Indeed they had holes in the soles, were taped, and even strong-thread sown to keep them "alive" for just one more year of evening blissful comfort. (Always for just one more year.) But alas, even I admitted they really were too well-done for further abuse. But damn it, that was not the end of it.

I found myself in a quandary faced with a real dilemma. After all the years of faithful service, I could not bring myself to renege on my shoe fetish by heartlessly discarding a pair of depressed, tearful, loafers in the trash can. No way! It just didn't set well with me to reward years of obsequious loyal service to its master by so denigrating their favorable service. Besides, the loafers were far too wasted for the goodwill bin. So I did the alternative. I stashed them along with my other still serviceable old timers as a paradigm for them to follow. As a rewarding quipster, I buried them in the 1992 shoebox casket, from whence Gaye's loafer present came, before placing them beside the aforementioned old timers. I just know the retired loafers love the honorable gesture bestowed upon them. They literally earned their rest in pieces – I mean in peace!

Should any of you be privileged to visit my "mausoleum" closet before Mar Mar exercises her housecleaning chores in a pragmatic vein by renovating my shoe crypt, you will, I am sure, likewise be excitedly impressed by those tried and true generic, antique, non-concord loafers, resting side by side among their classic priceless connoisseurs.

Eminent Domain

Please allow me to switch gears, yet again, while I reminisce about my Mother's later years. In 1957, Mother used capital from her state eminent domain project to purchase a home in east Marysville; approximately one and 1/2 blocks from my present home address. The irony is that she had the home fully paid for, and was reluctantly preparing to move into it when she experienced a severe heart attack. I mentioned reluctantly because of her fond memories, and her sad memories, in her downtown Marysville home, where she lived all but one year of her 43 years in America. Before going to Greece, Mother was advised to take out a life insurance policy for herself and her children. This she did. Thus, from her daughter Athena, and son Alexander's insurance policy settlement, she had the capital to purchase the building that was our home, and the bar below it. Without a monthly rent payment and a lease arrangement with the Columbia Bar, she was able to support herself and her two surviving children.

     Her memories of her beloved children and husband were fixed within the walls of 132 E Street, Marysville, California, with a telephone number 889. Forced to move, due to the eminent domain settlement, her priceless "boxe" (yard) was gone. Her approximate location to her downtown jaunts, gone. Her convenient distance to the two movie houses of the era, the National, then located at First and D Street, and the Lyric theatre, located between Second and Third on D Street, gone. Her many impromptu visitations by her good-hearted friends would be slashed due to lack of transportation to the East Marysville location. All this weighed heavy on her mind as she was struggling with her heart condition.

     I remember countless times when stopping by on my way home from work, I would find her rocking and crying in a dark room in her home. Memories of her deceased husband, and the agonizing pain of burying her son and daughter in Greece never left her. As much as she tried to subdue her depressive state she just couldn't defeat it. Earlier, her three sons and daughter did help her conquer the loss of her most beloved husband, because she knew she was their sole hope for salvation. She focused solely on her children's welfare. That mindset helped Mother to cope with the loss of her sweetheart companion, our dad. You see as long as her children were happy, vibrant and doing well in school, and admired in the community, she was totally preoccupied with what the future would be for her children. She was a God loving, single, proud mother of four!

The trip to Greece changed her forevermore, as it would any mother, and overwhelmed her with complete guilt in being the key player in the demise of her only daughter and her second son, where an academic scholarship awaited his enrollment at the University of California upon our return from Greece to America. Under that state of affairs you will find it hard to fault her depressive state. I know she tried extremely hard to live on for the sake of my older brother Nick, and me. Mother's depression took a gradual turn for the worse a few years after my brother married his sweetheart, Marian Karnegas, and I married my sweetheart, Gaye Bravos. Her recidivism was not due to the marriage of her two surviving sons. She was ecstatic in both instances. Her elation was rewarded during her twilight years with seven grand children, three blessings from Nick and Marian and four from Gaye and me. Our daughters Jorgi and Edie were yet to be born. She loved her grandchildren and they adored her. How could they not? She showered them with tender love and care as only a loving grandmother can. Our six children were likewise loved by my mother in law Lula Bravos. In my daughter's eyes, grandmothers are the greatest, and a much needed relief from Mom and Pop. And that's the way it should be.

I guess seeing her two sons happily married and blessed with beautiful families, it rebounded on her psyche that it could not be so with Alexander and Athena. "What have I done?!" She always blamed herself for the loss of her two children. This mood would be cyclical, but at times deeply crippling. Still, for the sake of her extended family she would recover from her melancholy state, especially when surrounded with her new found love, her grandchildren.

But when that bulldozer hit her "homestead", it seemed to be the straw that broke the camel's back. From the E street home she was directly admitted into the Rideout Hospital for treatment of her acute heart attack. She never did move into her East Marysville home. She never left Rideout Hospital. I do believe the thought of starting all over again in a new home environment, plus the ongoing grieving over her deceased children, overwhelmed her. She knew her two surviving sons were healthy and happily married with beautiful children, and it was time for her to rejoin her family in heaven. She knew from her heavenly abode she could once again reunite with her mother, father, husband, son and daughter, while still looking after her two earthbound families.

     Mother never lost faith in God. Morning, mid afternoon, and evenings she would get on her knees facing east by her 22 by 26 inch icon in her bedroom depicting Christ's crucifixion, and pray, thanking Him for the many blessings she enjoyed. She prayed for the good health of her two remaining sons and their families. She prayed for the blessings of all the departed souls that had touched her life. She would thank God for her many blessings and ask forgiveness for her sins and transgressions. This she shared with me time and again-- that the importance of a loved one not be forsaken when he or she is departed from life on earth. Through example she had instilled into my brother and me, the true value of faith. It may appear contradictory to laud mother's faith, while documenting her periodic depressive states. I assure you it is not so. In the end it was her faith that pulled her through her depression, and likewise gave her the strength, when as a young 35year old single mother, needed it to raise a family of three sons and a daughter, during the Great Depression. Yes, Mother lived a righteous Christian life.

     My personal epitaph, which gave me the strength to accept her passing on into Heaven reads *"Eulogy to mother: Her greatness as a lady was attributed to her faith, compassion and sincerity! Her greatness as a mother- was attributed to her insatiable love and devotion to her children. When you have been blessed with a mother that great, you do not spend your time grieving over her Heavenly gain!"* This thought is ingrained in my mind with my daily prayer to God. *"Mother I will never forsake you"* no more than I would my father, brothers Nick, Al, and sister Athena, my son Edison, and my daughter Jorgi. May God continually bless them in their Heavenly eternal life".

The Realities of Parenting

Recall the first of the two happenings on February 1st, 1961,was Edie's grand entrance into this world? Having read about the hardships and anxiety caused by the shortage of pharmacists in the SafeSave enterprise, I have got to tell you, by comparison. the rearing of daughter number six- Edie- the pharmacy shortage dilemma was but a speed bump on the road of business, while the rearing of Edie proved to be a mountain barrier on the road of life! It is amazing how quickly the baby daughter of a family of six daughters mentally approaches adulthood. It appears Edie, the sweet bundle of joy, was stealthily scouting her elder sisters on the pros and cons of the Nicholau discipline offense, and cleverly countered with a camouflaged defensive plan of her own.

I must admit her game plan merited high marks, for how else would her mother be called by the MUHS principle Mr. Ron Ward, requesting a conference. Gaye, due to the accolades from teachers and administrators showered on our other five daughters during their high school experiences, showed up for her appointment expecting like adulation on Edie's decorum and class room performance. WRONG!

As Gaye relates the conference with Mr. Ward, the principle of the high school, it went like this.

"Nice to see you again, Mrs. Nicholau."

"Thankyou."

The administrator, as tactful as possible, when in reality there is no tactful approach, said,

"Mrs. Nicholau, are you aware your daughter Edie is cutting classes?"

"Not *my* daughter." Shockingly retorted Gaye.

"I'm sorry to have to tell you, but it is true. This week she missed several classes leaving early," countered Mr. Ward.

"This is hard to believe. None of my *other* daughters cut classes."

"That is true, and that is why I'm calling it to your attention, before I take more serious measures. I just thought you should know."

"Thank you, I needed to know. I appreciate you're telling me, and I promise you my husband and I will discuss her behavior and take what ever measures are necessary to solve the problem."

"Again, I am sorry I had to tell you," offered Mr. Ward, "especially after the exemplary track record set by your other daughters. May I ask, how are they doing in college? They were a pleasant treat here."

"Don't be sorry, Mr. Ward, you are doing George and me a favor and Edie a salvation. Again I thank you. As for our daughters in college, they are doing well and we are exceedingly proud of them."

Edie was disciplined, and her sisters all chipped in to straighten her out. For whatever reason, Edie was rebellious in high school, and to this day she feels guilty about her behaviors. Perhaps being the sixth, with her older five siblings being exemplary in disciplinary matters, she wanted to distinguish herself…and distinguish herself she did! She got our attention alright, and in the process Gaye and I learned something about standing firm in our values and moral expectations for our daughters. When it came to our child's well being and happy future, we would not bend on the big issues. Shortly after the fireworks of realizing her rebellion, it was brought to our attention that Edie was graced with native operatic talent and acting ability. This I believe also played a key role in Edie's rehabilitation. She took a deep interest in her school assignments from that point on, and upon graduating from Marysville High School she enrolled at Yuba College. Under the encouragement of Joaquina Calvo Johnson, the Yuba College music instructor, Edie grew in stature as an excellent student and developed an exemplary character. Upon graduating from Yuba College she was accepted at the University of Southern California's nationally renowned music conservatory. She successfully auditioned for the limited quota of students accepted at the University. Edie won awards for her talent, and starred in several USC sponsored operas. Upon graduating she performed as principle soprano in other operas in the Los Angeles area and in the state of Washington. Currently she has a private voice studio, from which several of her students have auditioned and been accepted into top vocal conservatories and opera houses in the country. Her reputation as a salient voice teacher precedes her. She has a waiting list of potential students who must pass a strict disciplined audition before Edie places them on her waiting list.

Chris Delegans, Enter Stage Right

Edie went on to graduate from USC and later to earn her Masters degree in music from USC. During her sophomore year at USC she met her heart's desire, a super guy, Chris Delegans, a graduate of the University of Puget Sound in Washington, with a double major in finance and economics. Their chance meeting that lead to their engagement merits elaboration, if no other reason than for its novel like unfolding.

Their paths first crossed at a Greek Orthodox Young Adult Conference in Oakland California, where Edie's eyes caught, and focused on, the eyes of Chris Delegans. When their eyes met they froze, forming an electric conduit between them! The rest of their courting is history that can best be explained by the two of them. (These are *my* memoirs!)

They did not see each other again for five months, but kept AT&T solvent. As Oliver North would say, "Now here is a story worth telling." The Saturday before the Thanksgiving Holidays, (five months after they met) the University of Washington football team was scheduled to play Washington State. Washington State was Chris's Dad's alma mater. The game was to be played in Seattle at UW. Chris had arranged to meet his Dad in Seattle after the game and borrow the family car, in order to drive to California to meet the parents of the girl of his dreams. (He had incessantly talked about Edie to his mother and father since the Orthodox conference in Oakland).

Washington State won the hard fought game, so before the car exchange, Chris and several of his buddies went to a party at a University of Washington fraternity after the game. Chris was offended by a University of Washington student's demonizing remarks directed at Washington State's football team. He responded with demonized remarks of his own with regards to the Washington team. This was not the smartest move to make in the enemy trenches. The verbal altercation escalated into a physical battle. Chris wrongly assumed his buddies at the party would join him in the fracas. They in turn, correctly assumed the number odds were overwhelmingly against them and fled while they were ahead. Chris was a big, handsome, homespun farm kid. And to this day, Chris swears he gave more than he received, and what he received was telling. From the looks of Chris's black eye, I hate to think how bad off one or two of his assailants looked.

Anyway, the black eye plight escalated ten fold. Chris knew if his mother spotted him with a black eye, there would be no way he would be allowed to meet his future fiancé's parents in that condition. So for the first and only time in his life, Chris's Dad, George Delegans, withheld information from his wife, and after the game reluctantly gave the car to his son. His father promised not to tell his mother about the horrible black eye, knowing how much it meant to his son to pursue his dream, and was certain his wife, Alexandra, would not allow her son to meet a promising Greek girl with a "shiner".

On his way to Marysville, California, a good normal 12 hour drive, Chris missed a cut off and ended up in San Francisco, from which he had to back track another 2 and one half hours to Marysville. Ah, but for the invincible perseverance of youth in love. Except for an occasional pit stop for gas, Chris drove straight on into the wee hours of the morning, and all day before reaching his destination, our home in Marysville at 1:00 A.M., when he rang our front doorbell.

Our initial meeting was one for the books. I opened the door and there standing before me was this tall handsome man wearing a cowboy hat and sun glasses in the dark. Removing his sunglasses and exposing an alarmingly brutal black eye, he extended his right hand towards me saying "I'm Chris Delegans from Washington. Your daughter invited me to come to California to meet you and Mrs. Nicholau".

I, of course, in a state of shock focused on his right eye, swollen, red where it should be white, and black and blue everywhere else. This, I thought in my mind, was the guy my daughter was boasting about for weeks?

Consciously, I said, "Pleased to meet you, Chris, come in. What the hell happened to your right eye?"

"I'm sorry to meet you this way. Last night was the Apple Cup; the University of Washington- Washington State football game, and I got into a fight with a guy denigrating my father's alma mater, Washington State. If it's any consolation, the other guy is a bit worse off."

"Put 'er there, kid" I said as I extended my right hand inviting a firm handshake. "Anyone who'll stick up for his father's alma mater, is a real man in my eyes. I'm pleased to meet you. Gaye, let me introduce you to an all American kid. Chris, meet my wife Gaye".

In hindsight, I cannot envision a more bonding meeting than what I experienced at the front door of my home during that Thanksgiving break. However, in truthfulness, the introduction to each of my prospective future "sons" features a novelette approach of it's own.

But wait. There is an interesting sequel to the Edie, Chris plot. I suggested that Chris, at once, call his parents and let them know he arrived without incident, and to put me on the phone, so I could speak with them. This he did, and after assuring them he was safe, he put me on the phone to talk to his parents. I took the phone and Alexandra Delegans, his mother, was on the line. Our warm greetings having been exchanged, I began to praise her son via a Greek colloquial utterance, "immaste apo ena pani" translated "Chris and I are cut from the same cloth" for I was singularly impressed with his broadcasted honorable swollen black eye! I expounded how proud I was to meet a boy with fire in his heart to defend that in which he believed to be sacred.

Chris was standing close by, as I was conversing with his mother. He was violently motioning with his hands signaling no!, no!, while shaking his head in a negative way -- but I had no idea what he was driving at. His mother, quite shocked, politely inquired, "Is Chris's eye black?" During her inquisition, Chris was, by now, on his knees begging for the phone.

Silence on my part.

"May I please talk to my son?" she asked.

I handed the phone to Chris, and the lecture he received must still be embedded in his mind. With an untimely enthusiastic compliment, I compromised the peace and tranquility of Chris and his Dad for days on end, before the happening was filed in the history cells of Alexandra's memory bank. The proud mother of two daughters and an adventurous son, she had everything to be proud of, and nothing to apologize for in the rearing of her beautiful family. Gaye and I have hit it off great with the Delegans family, which includes my adopted sister Rose Hanches, Alexandra's mother. Referring to Rose as my adopted sister is the highest compliment I can pay her. Rose passed on into Heaven on March 2, 2012; a few months before her 100th birthday.

One thing I wish to emphasize at this time. Without exception, how fortunate and proud Gaye and I are with our daughters' choice of the men they chose to love, respect, and honor "until death do them part". Daily, Gaye and I thank God for His grace bestowed upon the Nicholau family. In my writings I have had the occasion, several times, to brag about the extent of love for my eleven "children" , my daughters and sons; Jim, Griff, Art, Denny and Chris. At the time of this writing, our loving daughter Jorgi Boom, Denny's true love, has passed over to eternal life in His kingdom. The "son" Gaye and I have come to know, Denny, is, if at all possible, more concerned over our welfare since his eternal loss, than ever before. Such is the good character of all our blessed 'sons". As Gaye and I sense it, they love their spouse and adore their second parents. I quote "sons" out of respect for their biological parents.

Joe Namath?

Dessi and her husband to be, Jim Chuchas, first met at the baptism of my brother-in-law's adopted child, Kristen. The baptism was celebrated at Gaye's brother Ted's house. Dessi and Jim seemed to enjoy each other's company. Dessi was a junior at Cal, and Jim, a senior at Davis. Dessi came home from the event and said, "I met the man I'm going to marry and I don't know if I like him!" She had another year at Cal and marriage was the last thing on her mind. Jim, likewise, returned to Davis, and told his roommate almost the very same thing! He said, "Well, I met my future wife, and I'm just not ready to get married!" Talk about a match made in heaven.

After a while Jim acquiesced and asked Dessi on a date, and came to our house to pick her up. Dessi, being the oldest of the six sisters, was peppered with endless questions from her younger siblings. When Jim entered our home, he was offered a soft drink and was served in our extensive family room, surrounded by all five sisters. Privacy in the Nicholau family was nonexistent when it came to boy meets sisters. After formal greetings, everyone was involved in conversation about everything and nothing, when Jim, God bless him, felt so comfortable and welcome, that he slipped off his loafers, stretched out in his swivel chair, and nonchalantly placed his stocking feet on the coffee table. It seemed so natural, as a warm honest gesture emitted from a casual low-key collegial guy, that the incident for all present, was inconsequential. That is, until after Dessi and Jim departed on their date. After which Dessi's younger siblings stated their infatuation with how much Jim looked like Joe Namath. And then, in chorus. the five daughters harmonized "Here comes the bride!" Clairvoyance at its highest.

**A picture of me at Dessi and Jim's wedding.
An aside: We never put a swimming pool in our backyard.
Planning ahead, that's where the band would go for our
daughter's wedding receptions.**

It is not uncommon for a father to question the character of his daughter's fiancé. In all truthfulness during courtship, rarely does one meet the stringent qualification for a coveted son in law to be. It becomes a matter of hope, for the best eligible bachelor, to be the choice of your daughter. Biased, you say? To the nth degree, I answer. Does daughter know best? Thank God, if our daughters' choices are the rule, the answer is an emphatic Yes!

What's In A Name?

  I first met Biff – no, I mean Griff- in a Lyons restaurant adjoining Macy's department store in Sacramento. Why in Sacramento? Because Biff, I mean Griff, is an impressive negotiator. He agreed to meet me half way from Piedmont, so we could better get acquainted. You see, for all practical purposes, my spirited Jamie, and Griff – I got it right this time – had already promised to one another their heartfelt love. From then on it was a matter of working out their game plan. And, this they successfully did, to the blessings of both the Adams family and the Nicholau clan. The problem was,Gaye and I had never met him before learning he and Jamie were "engaged".

  I'm moving along a bit fast. You see, I think by looking for perfection in my innocent daughters' choice of a husband, it is impossible for me not to be critical, matter not the immaculate character of their "victim". In Biff's – there I go again – Griff's case, sensing my invalidate posture, he tactfully, but emphatically, stood his ground on his intentions towards my daughter, based on their consummate love for each other.

  Please do not read disrespect for Griff when I mispronounce his name – Griff or Biff. It is not uncharacteristic for me to do so, time and again, with people I consider to be more than acquaintances. I chalk it up to dyslexia, and poor memory retention, when it comes to names. To cover up, many is the time I will greet a close acquaintance with "Hi there", because at that moment I cannot recall their name. Shame on me, but it is what it is. My daughters are no exceptions. It is amazing how many times I'll address one of my daughters with the name of one of her sisters. They have come to expect it. They consider the source, a loving, doting, hair-brained father. Griff, as do my other "sons", overlooks my faux pas.

  Daily, I have come to appreciate more and more, Jamie's good fortune in choosing Griff to be her one and only love. He too, like his brother in-laws, is a winner, a great father and a super husband to Jamie. Their parental skills are exceptional. Both of their children, Nicholau and Elizabeth, are graduates from the University of California. Elizabeth, at this writing, is very, very happily married to Farquhar Forbes. Nicholau is very happily married to Lydia Hoffman. The Forbes, Elizabeth and Farquhar, are the proud parents of Alexander and William, our great grandsons. Their home is in Inverness, Scotland. And our grandson Nicholau is enrolled at Golden Gate University studying to become an attorney. Joan and Bill Adams, Griff's parents, are the most friendly, hospitable couple. As is the case with Gaye's and my other in-laws, we hit it off great. Griff's sister, Jennifer, the beautiful mother of three children, is married to Joe Kapp, a Cal football star quarterback, who played in the Rose Bowl and the Canadian football League, before quarterbacking for the Minnesota Vikings in the national Football League.

Speaking of in-laws, how fortunate can parents be when their new found in-laws are harbingers of good tidings in our extended family growth. Without exception, Anna Chuchas and George, her husband, having passed over into Heaven; Bill and Joan Adams; Nicholas and Sophia Terzakis, Nicholas now in Heaven, Arlene and Dan Boom and Rich and Karen Brooks, Denny's parents; and George and Alexandra Delegans, have been an added blessing to Gaye and me. We feel very comfortable in a friendly, happy way when we have an occasion to be together. Love and respect are mutually enjoyed without protocol barriers of any kind.

Only Because You're Jewish

Terre's by chance meeting with her haberdasher's "daily dressed for meetings" husband to be, Art Terzakis, needs to be told. At that time Terre, noted for her outstanding accouterment skill, was employed by I Magnins. A socialite client of hers was hosting a surprise birthday party for a mutual friend in the political arena, who knew Art through Art's position at the State Capital. Art was invited through the wife of a friend of the hostess to attend the party, as was Terre, by the hostess. When I inquired how they came to meet for the first time they shared the fact each had no intention of attending the party, yet for the unknown "fateful" reason, both did. At that time in her life, Terre had disappointing experiences with her various Greek boy relationships, and swore to herself she was not going to date a Greek boy AGAIN!

At the party, Terre met this well dressed debonair young man who approached her with a caviar appetizer. Her first impression was that this nice man was Jewish. She politely thanked him but turned down the appetizer saying " I'm sorry but I only like the Greek caviar appetizers." "Oh, you mean tarama?" was his quick reply. Uh-oh…then and there Terre realized he was GREEK; but more than that, a very polite, well-mannered and thoughtful person. She immediately reconsidered her biased opinion of the Greek culture.

That evening passed in a mutual congenial way. Days after the party, Art would "inconveniently" be passing through I Magnin's on his way to his office in the Capital from his lunch reprieve. Time and again, there was mutual meeting of eyes and the rest is history that can best be recorded by the Terzakis'!

Our blessed grandson, Terre and Art's only child, Nicholas, is at this writing a freshman in High School. He is a six-foot plus handsome GREEK boy with excellent intellectual credentials and outstanding athletic endowments. He has a dry wit that challenges that of his father and mother's persona. When Nicholas is not studying or participating in sports, he is tinkling the keys composing a new piano score. Latest news alert: 4-21-2009, just learned grandson Nick has committed to UCB to further his education. Just another chip off the old block.

Our 'sons'
Jim, Art, Griff, Chris, and Denny

A By-Your-Leave

    This bright sunny morning in La Quinta, Tuesday April 18, 2006, on the patio of our condo, I am in an ecstatic mood. Why? I don't expect you to understand, because a fetish does not encourage normal behavior over one's moods. Now, here is why. Moving from the patio into the kitchen, my feet are comfortably nestled in all genuine leather, Italian Georgio Brutini, premier black 8 and 1/2 medium loafers, tapping on the marbled floor beneath my kitchen office desk, as I am writing my memoir. Thanks to the generosity and compassion of my angel, Gaye, they now represent the latest in the ongoing collection of my shoe compulsion. The extemporaneous rhythm created by the solid leathered soles echoing on the marble floor is a welcome background to my itching mind, constantly searching for the ideal expression in my suspect scribbling. Having exposed the secret crutch to my literary "competence", I will now move on to a more sober boy-meets-girl topic.

Denny Boom

After a disappointing espousal experience, daughter Jorgi sought and was awarded both a civil and an Orthodox approved divorce. She then moved from Scottsdale Arizona, where she was teaching biology at the local high school, back to Marysville to resume her life. The timing of her move was during the school year at Marysville High School, and all the teachers were in place. Jorgi was substitute teaching when she was hired in a secretarial capacity by Angelo Tsacopoulos, a super philanthropist and mega realtor in the greater Sacramento area. This she pursued until she ventured on her own to become a Public Relations entrepreneur. Her Public Relations firm took off on a high note, and Jorgi ended up successfully lobbying notable issues through the legislative process. Of particular importance was Jorgi's influence on the Rumsey Band of Wintun Indians. Because of her background in education, she worked tirelessly to successfully promote a state of the art elementary school building on the Rumsey tribe reservation. An impressive official opening ceremonial celebration, consisting of top state educators, along with key Rumsey Tribe personnel, was held in her honor. A bronze plaque honoring her contribution is prominently displayed in the school recognizing her total dedication on behalf of the Rumsey Band Wintun Indian children. Jorgi leaves a legacy of truly 'no Rumsey child left behind'. All the above was made possible through the blessing, enthusiastic encouragement, and significant support of Jorgi's loving compassionate husband Denny Boom.

Denny and Jorgi were classmates at Marysville High School and had dated during their high school days. Denny readily admits Jorgi was the "apple of his eye". However, upon graduating from Marysville High, Denny matriculated at the University of Oregon, where he was an outstanding athlete. He participated and starred on Oregon's baseball team.

Jorgi matriculated at UC Berkeley; thus their paths were moving in opposite directions. Upon graduating from Cal, Jorgi met and married Chris Katsenes. As mentioned earlier, their relationship ended in a divorce.

Allow me to back track to her new single commuting days from Marysville to Sacramento, where she had her office. This one particular hot summer day she was driving my '77 Cadillac Seville with a perfectly good air conditioner. Jorgi hated air conditioning, which caused her to put the windows down, and drive at a high speed to combat the heat. Denny Boom was also returning to Marysville from his job in Sacramento in a pick up truck, as Jorgi "flew" by. He recognized the car and Jorgi as she passed him. He immediately sped up to catch her, but to no avail. When he came into Marysville he called the house and asked Gaye if he could speak
to "Parnelli"? "Who?" Gaye asked, "Jorgi" Denny laughingly said. Gaye told Denny, Jorgi was taking a shower to cool off, could he call later. This he did, and razzed Jorgi about her speeding.

The "speedy' reintroduction of Jorgi and Denny led to Jorgi still reluctant to make a serious commitment. Denny's persistence, embellished with true fathomless love, won her over. Jorgi's reciprocal love and devotion towards Denny made them a winning married couple.

Both Jorgi and Denny embraced a deep sincere faith in God. They made their vows in the Greek Orthodox Church, after Denny had volunteered and completed his Orthodox indoctrination. To this day, despite the most tragic event in his life, the passing over into heaven of his one love, Denny seeks God's blessing in his every day pursuits to live a useful, Christian life. He has not forsaken his one true love. Daily he prays for her eternal life to be blessed in heavenly peace. Denny, at this reading, 4-31-2009, is serving on the Sacramento Diocese Parish Counsel Board of Directors.

During their thirteen years of marriage, they were the most enthused, happy couple one could ever wish for. They complimented each other to the point where they amalgamated into one. Jorgi's signature laugh was once again free and vibrant. Many thanks to Denny's impact on Jorgi's revitalized person, she elevated the tone of happiness among those around her.

Jorgi and Denny during their annual visit to their condo on Maui

We Lose Our Jorgi

On July 31, 2004 Jorgi peacefully and knowingly passed into heaven. Out of God's respect and deep love she fought gallantly until her last breath to express her appreciation for the gift of life. She wanted Christ to know how much she appreciated His many blessings throughout her earthly existence. I recall my last long walk with my darling Jorgi. Her body was wrought with chemotherapy treatment, yet she would not give in to its devastating discomfort and infirmity. She would limit her pain relieving medicine schedule, opting instead to be aware of her struggle to overcome her illness.

On that last long walk with Jorgi, I kept asking her if we should turn back for home. I could see she was suffering, but she emphatically insisted on continuing forward as she wanted to build up her strength and not give in to apathy. Her self-imposed mantra was "to Christ my God, I will put up an earthly fight, and willingly abide by Thy will."

I mentioned above "she peacefully and knowingly" passed on. That phraseology is by choice. After Father Dogias, the residing Priest at the Church of the Annunciation in Sacramento, had given Jorgi Holy Unction, she insisted on limiting her pain therapy schedule so that she would remain mentally alert to all happenings about her.

Jamie, Gaye and I, after being by her side all day, left Jorgi's bedside in Sacramento and headed for our respective homes with the intent to come back early the following day. Gaye and I opened the back door to our home to the ringing of our phone. It was our daughter Dorre, suggesting we come back, as Jorgi's demise was imminent. We immediately headed back to Jorgi's home in Sacramento.

Later that evening, witnessing her immense struggle with excruciating pain, I was standing at the foot of her bed, holding a large heavy icon. Denny was standing next to her on the right side of the bed, and Gaye and our daughters, except Jamie, who had returned to the Bay Area with the intent of coming back in the morning, crowded near the head of the bed on the left side. From my position at the foot of the bed, I heard myself saying, "It's OK to let go Jorgi, you've proved to God your respect for His gift of life. It's OK to go. He is waiting for you in Heaven."

Immediately after my remarks, she picked up the heavy golden icon lying on her bed and kissed it. The strength for her to do so had to come from above. She then reached for Denny's hand, kissed his hand and turned toward Gaye and whispered "Mom" and rose from a pillowed position, extended her arms about Gaye and hugged her, then whispered to Dorre and hugged her. She then hugged Dessi, Terre and Edie. Then she hugged me, and lastly fell into Denny's arms. She then laid back, seemingly pain free, and passed over, invited into Heaven, for life eternal, among the angels of God, where there is no suffering or pain. The date, July 31, 2004. Jorgi, your memory will never be forsaken on earth.

Thank you God for allowing me to express my lasting memory of my darling Jorgi, while alone in my kitchen in Marysville. My tearful grief was expressed in private and heard only by Jorgi as an act of love, not sorrow.

Daughter Edie expressed it most effectively for all of us when she said, "The night Jorgi passed over was the most beautiful, and yet most horrific day of my life. Most beautiful, second only to the miracle of the birth of my son, because I witnessed the miracle of her leaving this earth, and most assuredly entering into heaven. The most horrible because of the agonizing pain she was in; made ever so much worse with the thought of never seeing her again, or hearing her patented laughter.

**Jorgi, with her Godparents
Hal and Stell Athon**

**Our last Easter with our Jorgi
Jorgi is standing, far left**

Education

Through impulsive recall and circuitous route, I have, up to this point, written what I perceive to be interesting (whether they be impetuous, exhilarating, or unbelievably tragic) happenings in my life. In so doing, I am certain I have overlooked some engaging events, just as I have no doubt, overindulged in others. So what do you expect from a novice biographer – perfection? I have written about my single digit years, grammar school, high school, college and World War II. I have also written about my entrepreneur experiences in pharmacy, my love of family, my love of football, as well as golf, my great losses, and my great victories to date. There is one area I have saved until now. Education.

My standard of living and the success in rearing my family was made possible through my parents consummate love, tempered with firm justifiable discipline, leading me to believe in the value of true faith, and the absolute necessity of an outstanding education.

As first generation immigrants, my mother and father felt blessed to be in America. They made it a high priority to adopt the American way of life, in spirit, as well as in necessity. I recall as a youngster, my father preaching the merits of freedom as exemplified in the American democratic system. He set the example by mastering the English language, and speaking it every chance he had. My mother, as mentioned earlier, studied and passed her citizenship exam to become an American citizen. She was so proud of that fact. My parents embracing of the American life style in no way minimized their love for their country of origin. As I have mentioned before, and it bears repeating, my father emphatically preached to us to be proud Americans and to do nothing to embarrass our American nationality, while acknowledging and respecting our Greek heritage.

On that theme, he emphasized the importance of a good education. A privilege he did not experience in his native country. The essence of his axiom on education included the following message for his children. "The more educated you are, the more opportunities you will have for success. The more successful you become, the more respect you will receive from your peers". A non-debatable truism.

    I have previously written how through my innate athletic skills, I earned a scholarship that enabled me to earn my pharmaceutical degree. It was through my father's edict that I was able to stay the course over the inevitable academic speed bumps I encountered along the way. By highlighting my father's influence, I do not slight my mother's support in both the monetary and physical sacrifice that she endured during my college years. Her proud realization of her two surviving children being successful, each in his own way, happily married with wonderful children of their own, and her priceless grandchildren, produced a glow in her persona that said it all. (Mother, while in heaven, know that your son Nicholas and I reaped the fruits of your immeasurable love, Herculean strength of will, and incalculable faith, during our life's journey, just as while earthbound, did your daughter Athena and son Alexander.)

    Now it's pay back time for my educational scholarship-enabling factor. Experiencing the doors it opened for me, I felt obligated to pass on my good fortune to other potential financially disadvantaged students who otherwise would be deprived of a higher education. I began to repay my debt through motivating athletes with whom I was in close contact in high school and at Yuba College, as a volunteer football coach. I hit upon a technique which served me well in selling them the absolute importance of **"learning to like that which you have to do, for then you will always be doing what you like"** in the pursuit of leading a successful life. I brought this lesson home to the athletes during scrimmages and other isolated drills. When preparing for an opponent during practice, one weeknight we would have a live scrimmage. One could sense the desire to excel in each player's heart as he tried to convince the coach he deserved to be on the "first team'. As the scrimmage would escalate in tempo, an outstanding play would ensue whether on offense or defense. I would then shrill my whistle and all the players would stand pat in their tracks.

I would compliment the key players involved and comment "I see where your preparation drills are paying off. I hope you now see the value of hard work in fundamentals to enable you to do a job well. There is no short cut to success. The more you practice, the better you get and the better you get the more you like what you are doing." (Now here is the gist of the interruption.) "**Remember that lesson in your school work. Do your homework, be prepared, and you will, believe it, get hooked on the academic challenges in the classroom**." This whole stint would take about a minute from contact to say, and it had a positive academic effect on many of the athletes. Of course their parents, who were observing practice, also relished it. The theme was repeated several times during drills and scrimmages, to continue to impress upon the athletes the importance of an education.

A sequel to the message was further exploited during the school's Big Game week, both at the high school and junior college level. During Big Game practice I could sense the ultra high intensity and desire to do what ever it takes to win the game. During the season's last Big Game scrimmage, at some point during the skirmish, I would blow my whistle, get the whole squad together and ask them point blank, in a bark "**How bad do you want to win this game**?" Their reaction to the question was an unrehearsed lion's roar of wanting. Emotional outbursts would erupt from individual players with a common denominator, "Coach, tell us what you want us to do to win and we'll do it. We will not be denied."

I expected no less of a reaction, as there was madness in the tone of my question to them. "Boys" after the roar, I enthusiastically replied, "**Remember your desire to win and take that same intensity to excel in the class room and you'll not be denied in your pursuit to live a winning life. That is what justifies sports in the academic environment of high school and college. You have learned, in order to succeed in sports, you must be willing to pay the price, and you welcome the challenge. Embrace that philosophy in the real world, and you won't be denied a rewarding livelihood.**"

As a volunteer coach, none of the above would have been possible if I did not have the respect of the hired teacher coaches at Yuba City and Maysville high schools and at Yuba College. For their support and confidence in me, I am forever grateful as it enabled me to make the first down payment on my appreciating compound interest on my outstanding education balance.

From the athletic field I became singularly focused in the all-encompassing academic classroom environment. I owe so much of my well being to my formal "charitable" education, that I knew I had to get more involved with needy financially stricken students, if I was serious about balancing my education account. With this background incentive, I volunteered, giving motivational talks at the elementary and high school level on the value of being a participating student, versus a sedentary spectator in the classroom. Preaching that they take advantage of the opportunity to learn during their school days, and attend each day with the goal of becoming eligible to attend a University of their choosing upon graduating from high school. Reminding them to not let financial matters deter them from pursuing a higher education. There are grants sponsored by philanthropic, corporate and government entities begging to be awarded to qualified students. Note this, the irrefutable fact is, the higher your formal education, the more financially endowed you will be, and the higher the standard of living you will enjoy.

And now, let me share with you the best kept secret in the higher education arena. It is the Community College system! It is so, for all students who wish to continue their education, but especially for financially strapped students, and late bloomers who need remedial studies to bring them up to standards for enrolling into a University or State College. Community colleges are also great for re- entry students, regardless of age, who wish to continue on in their education from whence they left off, or wish to change their vocation in order to pursue their livelihood.

My reputation for giving these talks preceded me at our local community college, Yuba College. A trustee for the college, at that point in time, was transferred out of the area, and a committee composed of an administrator, faculty and classified personnel approached me at my pharmacy, and asked me if I would be interested in running for the open seat. I said I would on one condition. That is, that the committee set up a meeting so we could review from whence I came in the field of education on the community college level. After that session, if they still wanted me to run for trusteeship I would. This was done. They endorsed my predication as a trustee for Yuba College and I was successful at the election poles in 1979, for my first term as a Yuba College trustee.

    Now I felt I was really in position to make meaningful payments towards the balance due on my "education" account. I enthusiastically and heartedly committed myself to the stewardship responsibilities of a trustee to Yuba College. I familiarized myself with the machinations involved in the honored position by attending a CCA Statewide sponsored seminar on the do's and don'ts of a successful community college trustee. I found it to be very informative, and helpful in preparing me to get off on the right foot in advocating my agenda on behalf of the welfare of our students. I had the basics ingrained in my mind through past experience; through a formal education where I earned my pharmacy degree, and where I later founded the Marysville Clinic Pharmacy and Yuba City SafeSave Pharmacy. The universal basics in essence, are 1) be a good listener to words spoken 2) observe body language 3) maintain good eye contact 4) keep an open mind on controversial issues under discussion 5) be goal oriented 6) do your homework 7) be resilient 8) do not be swayed by political pressure and lastly, 9) willingly and righteously give in to logic, not to rationalization. Giving into logic on controversial matters shows strength in leadership, not weakness.

    After twenty plus years as a trustee, I now find myself more in debt to my education account than when I started! How can that be? Simple. I find the pursuit of making a positive difference in "my" student's welfare so gratifying, that I'm getting further in debt for the privilege of serving as one of their trustees. I am proud and fortunate to be of sound health during my tenure. To date in my

20+ years as a trustee I have missed only one stated meeting!! It was during the summer months and I was vacationing in Greece. Since retiring from my pharmacy livelihood in 1987, I spend 5 to 6 months of the year on the golf course in the Palm Springs area, and commute by plane and auto during those months to meet my trustee commitment to my students.

Putting it into perspective: it is 1,120 mile round trip from Palm Springs to Marysville, x 5 trips = 5,600 miles x 20 years 112,000 miles and still growing. I do this at my own expense and feel privileged for the opportunity. As long as I am an asset to the college I will continue to accept the challenge in a heartbeat.

I do not write in detail the time and expense I endure to meet my commitment to the college for self-gratification. I do so to impress upon my grandchildren the importance of finding a worthy cause that will give them the opportunity and the privilege to repay society for any benefits they may be reaping during their life's journey. If they can do that, they will be enriching their life's journey while being rewarded in "liking what they have to do."

To say all the years on the Board have been serene would be misleading. There were tumultuous times, during deep financial adversities, that precipitated unrest among and between the board, faculty, and classified personnel. The ups and downs of overseeing the management of a Community College District go with the territory of being a trustee. The district is financially driven and in money restraint budget years, tough decisions have to be made in favor of the welfare of our students. My fiduciary modus operandi, depending on the circumstance, is to "think students first" then act. (This philosophical approach I adopted from the former Vice President of Yuba College, Al Brill). When doing so, I try not to favor one group of the college family over another.

As an aside, I have been credited with the christening of the "Family" phrase in referring to employees of the College, be they administrators, faculty, classified, or custodial employees. I emphasize the "family" theme, as that denotes equality of respect and worth of each individual and employee of the College district. A dictum adhered to in my professional entrepreneurship. Of course, the degree of responsibility with each classification may differ significantly, but that does not deter from the importance and necessity of each employee's contribution to the whole. The welfare of our students in their pursuit of higher learning is the primary and only reason for the existence of the college. I am singularly pleased to see the employees, to the person, have endorsed, and adopted the "family" logo. It is not uncommon to hear the "family" phase battered around in discussing information and action items in the agenda of our monthly meetings. In my mind the phrase symbolizes a positive cultural lineage among all employees of the college.

As a multi-term president of the board of trustees, throughout my tenure, I have had the opportunity to meet many dedicated, qualified, individual trustees seated at the table, governing with like zeal. And for that, I am grateful and our students are the benefactors.

Oh! For what just popped into my mind. I wouldn't wish the predicament I am about to reveal to you, where shoes again become the focal point, to happen to any one of you, or to any one else. I have no choice but to share my embarrassment with you, for as President Clinton once said "what is, is". Although I do not necessarily approve of the idiom as an appropriate comment in his embroiled state of affairs, I must admit it best describes my dilemma. To paraphrase the President's locution, in my reference "this is what was, that is"!

On April 20, 2006, the Woodland Chamber of Commerce, along with the Woodland Community College Foundation, hosted a celebratory occasion to recognize the thirteenth anniversary of the Woodland Community College. State legislators, Woodland CC President, District Chancellor of Yuba College, and lastly, I, as President of the board of trustees for the District, were on the speaker's schedule. The total program lasted less than 15 minutes, as each speaker delivered succinct, interestingly factual, and at times humorous remarks. For once, I too was surprisingly brief.

So far, so good, but here is where "it hit the fan". On preparing for the occasion, I wore my Brioni suit, Ralph Lauren red striped dress shirt, and a complimentary tie. My dress code was further complimented with my Gucci shoes. I must admit I was "dressed to the hilt", as the saying goes.

When the time came to depart from Marysville for Woodland, I got into my 430 Lexus coupe convertible only to notice it hadn't been washed for over a month. No way do I dress in my Hollywood best, and drive this class of the Lexus line for the occasion, in an unwashed dirt-crusted car. So, out of the car I get. I slip off my Gucci's, and wear an old pair of dilapidated, yard-designated loafers that I keep in the garage for just such emergent situations. Not having time to change my clothes, I very carefully washed the car without compromising my suit. I then quickly get into the car, and off to Woodland I go. Time was of the essence, but I was certain I would get there with minutes to spare – if I didn't get ticketed for speeding!

Just as I believed to be in the clear, it hit me like a bolt of lightening. I left my Gucci's in the breezeway at home, and was wearing my scarred, worn out, deformed, sloppy shaped, water-drowned loafers! Too late to turn back, or to stop in Woodland for a pair of shoes! Sometimes one paints oneself into a corner and must make the best out of a sad situation. Such was the case I inadvertently inherited with my impaired memory bank.

Now, what to do plagued my mind, and after hopeless mental resolutions were entertained and discarded, I decided to grin and bear the impending plight. The bear part came naturally. The grin, a consummate fake! Given a chance, I would share my predicament in a jocular mode and be done with it. Not having been afforded that opportunity, I mingled with the crowd as I would if I was wearing my Gucci's. I give due credit to the multitude at the gathering, as I experienced no outward shirk from the anyone there, with one noticeable exception. It is amazing how good manners can camouflage a fellow's faux pas. I sensed they knew that I knew I goofed, and they let it be.

There was that one exception, and who could blame her? A California State Assemblywoman, representing the Woodland area, caught politicking with an eccentric, when there were so many dignitaries she could be visiting with. This is my take, not hers. The truth be told, she was very congenial and responsive to my politicking on behalf of Yuba College. However, I must add, I could not help but witness a startling state of shock when she happened to lower her head, and got the first glimpse of my counterfeit Gucci's. A sentence later she politely excused herself to greet the Woodland Mayor, who happened to be passing by. I have great respect for Assemblywoman, Lois Walk, on her tactful departure. I can just sense her inward self-disciplined thought - "who am I to judge?"

A Trustee's Valediction

My farewell message.

"The legacy I endeavor to accomplish during my tenure is the importance of a family concept to be embraced by all Yuba College personnel from janitors to staff members, to teachers, to administrators, to trustees. All working together, creating a climate that best enables our students to reach our goals.

In this vein, I have grown with abandon at Yuba College. What a rich and fertile environment it has been for me- bursting with pride to be physically and emotionally engaged within the Yuba College family. On occasions, while roaming the campus, I would engage a student and inquire about his or her studies, dreams, and well being, while stealthily, through osmosis, revisit my experiences during my collegiate years- the anxieties, the highs, the lows, and most of all, the panic uncertainty of academic success.

Thanks to the interaction I experienced with our students, I have put my aging process on stand-by. Through my retirement from the board, I will gradually transfer into a glorified Papou (Grandfather) status to our students, and will always be there in spirit.

It pleases me no end, in knowing the continued success of our students under the family concept, will be my ongoing legacy at Yuba College.

I wish to acknowledge and thank my constituents for their loyalty and the trust they put in me as their representative on the board. On that note, I pray daily to be a worthy trustee on their behalf, and a consummate steward of our students.

A truism: I could not have accomplished my mission without the benevolence, support, and occasional critique from all members of the college family. To all past and present Board Members, the camaraderie that I encountered during my tenure will be everlasting with me.

Gaye, my wife, and mother of six daughters, and loving partner for more than 61 years, has been at my side throughout this venture, a criterion who kept me in perspective when I was in err of judgment.

I wish the very best for the new members of the Board, and may their stewardship embrace the family concept of Yuba College to the ongoing benefit of our students.

May God continually bless Yuba College, and the students which she serves."

A Weak Moment of Braggadocio

It is amazing how each of our daughters have excelled in their chosen profession. I must have mentioned it before, but it's worth repeating. Five of them are graduates from the University of California with degrees ranging from MD, PhD, Ed.D, Masters, and Bachelor's degrees. Edie, our youngest daughter is a graduate from USC, where she earned her Masters Degree in Vocal/Opera Performance. She opted to attend USC (not my beloved CAL) because of its outstanding reputation in the performing arts. (Darn it, as if I didn't know better. I forgot to take my visor cap off and now while reminiscing, I am experiencing a proverbial swell-head headache from it's restriction.) When will I learn?... thanks a lot daughters – hat off – headache relieved.

PGA WEST, a.k.a. Paradise

I had mentioned spending five to six months out of the year since my retirement in 1987 in the Palm Springs area. Here is how that came about. While in my seventies
(years of 'youth', that is, not a golf score, sadly) I was invited to be the guest of my college classmate, Harry Pappas, who has a home in Rancho Mirage. Gaye and I enjoyed the experience so much I made up my mind that upon my retirement, I would seek a place in the Palm Springs area for a second home. It so happened in 1986, Landmark, a renowned corporate golf course builder, started the PGA West Golf Course complex in La Quinta, California, twenty miles east of Palm Springs. It was the talk of the dessert. The complex was started with three championship rated golf courses; one designed by Pete Dyes, one by Arnold Palmer, and one by Jack Nicklaus. To inaugurate the complex, Landmark negotiated a contract with the annual Bob Hope Classic to host their tournament at PGA West. (The PGA West complex is now the home of six championship designed golf courses).

In 1986, I took a one-month vacation, and rented a condo at Sunrise in Rancho Mirage. Besides playing golf during that time, Gaye and I looked over several country club condos and houses in the area in preparation for buying a place upon my retirement. It so happened, a year later, I did retire and we headed for Palm Springs and stayed at a motel while we cased the PGA West complex.

My "son" Chris, and daughter, Edie were living in Los Angeles at that time, where Chris worked for Security Pacific Bank, and Edie was finishing her master's degree at USC. Together we would daily visit the PGA complex, and one day I inquired about the price of a membership. I was hooked. After my inquiry, I was told "had you been here last week you could have purchased a membership for $40,000. Today it is $50,000 and that will go up again in the near future." (Membership today, 2008, is $120,000).

This was on a Monday. I immediately inquired who was in charge of the membership sales, and was referred to Katie Gardner. I went directly to Katie's office, introduced myself, and explained my interest in joining PGA West. I also, in all honesty, told her that I was financially strapped, having put six daughters through the university system. Could she in any way help me purchase my membership at last week's price? It would make the difference of whether I could afford to become a member of PGA West. Katie (talk about irony) took a liking to me because of my commitment to my six daughters, four of which were, like Katie, members of the Delta Gamma Sorority. She said for me to come back an hour later, and she would know if it could be done. I returned in an hour, and she said I would be eligible for the $40,000 membership fee if it could be finalized that day, Monday. I thanked her profusely, and wrote the check there and then. The advantage of a membership at that time was, it covered all expenses, from cart fee, range fee, and golf privileges on any of the three courses. There also was no minimum fee that had to be spent quarterly, as expected in other clubs.

    I must tell you, in 1987, La Quinta, the city of the PGA West complex, was a small city of a Latino population situated in the barren south area of the dessert. The 111-highway leading from Palm Springs to La Quinta was a two-lane sparsely traveled highway with very few stop signs. Today it is a multi lane (4 to 6 lanes) highway, with a myriad of stop signs and bumper to bumper traffic most any time of day. At the site of the PGA West golf course in 1987, the main off ramp from Highway 10 was Jefferson Avenue, then a graveled two-lane road, and now, a four lane highway. Where there were acres and acres of agriculture land, there now exist acres and acres of condos, houses, and over 120 golf courses in the Palm Springs Coachella Valley area!

    Having acquired a PGA West membership, Gaye and I gave serious thought to purchasing a home, rather than having to rent each year. We looked at several homes within two to three miles of the complex, and almost purchased one on Washington Street about 2 miles from the golf course.

Everyday, I would visit the PGA complex and watch condos being built and gave a lot of thought to purchasing one on site if the price was affordable. One day, Gaye and I were impressed with the Champion 4 model condo at PGA West, as it fit our budget. Golf, being the incentive for my wanting to spend time in La Quinta, I rationalized my best bet would be to live within the golf complex of which I was a member.

With that conclusion, daily I started to plot the sun and the scenery within the complex where the Champion 4's were being built. Having arrived at the truism, that a condo facing south was the ideal location in the dessert because of the trajectory of the summer sun, I next started plotting the scenery of the available Champion 4 condos that faced south. This I did at the main sales office where there were three large architectural displays showing the location of all the condos surrounding the three golf courses.

The problem was, condos facing south with a scenic view were not the best kept secret, for all of those spots were flagged in the miniature display fixtures with a "sold" pin sign. Yet every day, for three days straight, I would visit the sales center hoping to see something I could settle on. I did spot a champion 4 that had a good view, but it faced west where the afternoon sun would beat right into the condo; unless all the curtains were pulled shut until the sun set below the Santa Ana Mountains. As I was about to make a commitment for that condo, a salesperson walked over to the display fixture where I was standing and removed one of the sold pins on a champion condo that was facing south, with a picture scenic view on the Palmer Course, located above the sixth green. The view took in the 6th green, 7th tee box, and featured the beautiful lake running down the west side of the 7th fairway. No condos, present or future, to block the view then, or ever! Also, it had an outstanding view of the Santa Rosa Mountains that bordered the south-west side of the Palmer Golf Course.

As I was about to OK the original condo, I immediately reneged and put my gold pin in the now vacated southern view condo. The sales person challenged me, and said "that sight was being put on hold". I countered, "not any longer, that condo is bought as of right now." Luckily, "Megalos" Peter Allison, an attorney cousin of my "son" Chris, was with me and rebuked the sales person, asking him to show us the statement that denies a buyer the right to put a pin in an open available spot. He backed off and I purchased the condo that moment. I paid an extra $10,000 on the deposit for the location. Today, my location in itself, generates a value of 25 to 30 thousand dollars! As they say in real estate: location, location, location.

**Our second home in La Quinta, California
PGA West**

The more I think about my timing in becoming a member, and in the purchasing of my beautifully located condo, the more my ethnic Greek background challenges the "maxim" of the 'luck of the Irish".

Gaye and I have enjoyed our Palm Spring's winter site home going on twenty plus years. The real satisfaction in our investment is the pleasure we experience when family members find time to join us at our resort home. I cannot over emphasize the joy Gaye and I glean from our God fearing, beautiful extended family sharing with us our blessed twilight years in the desert.

A slice of paradise

On co-mingling family occasions, whether in Palm Springs, Sacramento, the Bay Area, or in Marysville, the fellowship exponentially increases our blessed lives a thousand fold. Time and again, I find myself sitting back in my family's company, counting my blessings, just for the privilege of being a part of such a fun loving family, totally at ease with each other, thoroughly enjoying the moment. That may sound braggadocio, but it's true! Such is the chemistry within the extended Nicholau family. And for that loving chemistry, I thank Dorre and daughters' spouses Jim, Griff, Art, Denny, and Chris. And most of all, my tireless angelic Gaye, who's sumptuous repast at the various family gatherings makes for a perfect setting.

Gaye and I on our 50th Wedding Anniversary

Epilogue

There are colloquial sayings that survive time due to their undisputed logic. The one that comes to mind, and seems appropriate in this instance, is the colloquy "what goes around, comes around." I started my memoirs with my relationship with my shoe fetish. Now it is proper, and advisable, that I revisit the statement regarding the hording of 39 pairs of soles- "why haven't I discarded or worn them during the past decades?" I hinted that by the end of my memoir I would, or you would, find the answer to that riddle. Well, I haven't, and if you have, surprise me with your conclusion.

Wait! I think I've got it. By Jove, I know I've got it! Symbolically, it is set at 39 pairs to match my stable, youthful, internal clock set at 39 years of age!! By God that's it! Riddle solved. Or, it could be that my blessed 90 plus earth years, to date, are as ageless as the 39 pairs of shoes?

Make that 40. Gaye just went shopping and brought home *another* pair of Nike slip on tennies. I like them. I think I'll keep them. And I am sure I will get around to wearing them....someday....when I can bear to part with the old faithful's I am sporting right now.

I cannot over emphasize the pleasurable high I have experienced while writing my life's adventures. I strongly recommend to each of my daughters and their spouses, individually or conjointly, to put pen to paper, highlighting their life's happenings. In doing so, if enriched with true faith, you will be, as l am, youthfully re-energized. The chuckles you will recall will far out weigh the mishaps that untimely punctuate our lives. If you doubt this axiom, I challenge you to sit down the next time you have a free moment and dash off a pleasurable life's experience, and judge for yourself the euphoria you will become heir to!

Hopefully, those who will take the time to read my memoirs will be fractionally entertained to the extent I was, in my adventurous pursuit of writing it.

Warning, please stay tuned, as I am having a difficult time throwing in the towel. If something special comes forth during my earthly time, I will appendage my memoirs, if for no other reason than its' therapeutic effect on my persona. Not to mention a package I just received from my daughter Edie in the mail today. The package contained three erasers, one for pencil, one for ink, and an all-purpose pontoon shaped eraser. What is she trying to tell me?

Now go forth – Loving what you have to do to live a happy useful Christian Life, and you will always be doing what you love. Nothing is more rewarding than to hold onto Love as your guiding angel!

An aside, for what it is worth, I share with you *Papou's* Profound Discourse Recipe. Daughters, sons, grandchildren, great grandchildren, and those Good Lord willing, to follow:

When chitchatting in person, or electronically with your parents, or grandparents, enrich their twilight years with well-mannered love-based talks. Among and between yourselves, a laid back vernacular will do. With your children, parental loving care is vital. With your spouse, endearing warmth is the requisite. With a friend, go with the flow. In your livelihood endeavors, silence, fortified with intelligent hearing skills will prove to be your best communication tool.

Corinthians I Chapter 13:13 "Now abide faith, hope, love. These three, but the greatest of these is love."

Epigraph

A Tale of Two Hearts
The Car Story

    Family, hold fast please. I beg your indulgence for a heart-rendered epic. One that I must reveal for my own peace of mind. Throughout my memoir, as you have noticed, I put due emphasis on the essentiality of love, love, and more love. Just the other day, 8/24/2009, I experienced an epiphany that caused a euphoric high far above the norm. So much so that I am compelled to add "the car story" to the final draft of my memoir. I do this to illustrate to you how love never fades away. Rather it enriches itself when one is privileged to share it with a lifetime partner. Such a deep love proved to be a tipping point on my making a critical decision. A decision that led me to a true understanding of the generic meaning of the most powerful four-letter word in the English language: a word that will stand the crucible test in any tongue. LOVE!

    It was August the 24th 2009, Monday morning, when I knew that I had to right a wrong. And I had to do it in a stealth way. You see, the preceding Friday, I promised Gaye that I would not commit to a new car before getting an appraisal on how much it would cost to bring her 1998 (Jorgi"s gifted Lexus) 400GS sedan into certified condition. Under that pledge she agreed to go car shopping with me. If the repairs on the '98 Lexus were prohibitive, we would then pursue the latter. Why the need for such a condition?

    The Lexus was Jorgi's personal car that she babied with loving care. As addressed earlier, Jorgi fought a relentless battle with cancer that she lost in July of 2004. Six months later, the time being during the Christmas Holidays, just before New Years Day, Denny surprised Gaye with Jorgi's keys to the Lexus, along with a signed pink slip making her the owner of the car. Before it was presented to Gaye, Denny took it to the Lexus dealership where the car was routinely serviced and gave them the order to go through it thoroughly and take care of anything it may need, including a new set of tires. He felt that Jorgi would approve of him doing so.

That being the case, Gaye felt from day one, that Jorgi's spirit was always with her when she drove her car. This was unbeknownst to me at the time. But it really hit me hard when I realized the depth of her attachment to Jorgi's Lexus. An emotional attachment she experienced whenever driving Jorgi's car.

With that background let's move on into the machinations of negotiating for a new car. Unless the reader of this novelette has personally experience negotiating with a seasoned car salesperson, she or he cannot grasp the severity of the emotional "throb" the perspective buyer must overcome to best negotiate his/her case. You are not only bargaining with the salesperson; you're dealing with the Toyota Company's dealerships Operation Manager, quarterbacked by the all American dealership owner! The "game plan" follows.

I, the customer and the persevering salesperson, hassle over a price. The sales person gives in, but not to the extent to make the deal. He senses that and says "I'll talk to the manager and see if I can make you a better offer." Moments later he returns with a counter, dramatizing what a good deal it is- yada,yada,yada. I am still not satisfied and tell him so. "I think we are still far apart, but thank you for your help" and started to leave. "Wait" he said "Let me try one more time. I'd like to put you into that car". Off he goes. Now the manager comes back with him, and says, "George" greeting me by my first name because he knew me from Peach Tree Golf and country Club, "What will it take to make the deal?"

"Dennis" I counter, likewise using his first name, and continued with a bottom line proposal, that I thought was most unlikely to even be considered – $1,500 under the best offer on the table. "George, give me a moment and I'll see if I can make it work." Back he goes to his office, I assume to confer with the owner of the dealership. A few minutes pass, he returns and says, "You've got a deal. The new models are due and we will go the extra mile to accommodate you. I hope you appreciate the fire-sale bargain you are getting."

Unbelievable!! But, believe it. I just bought a new car!!!

Gaye was in a state of shock. I reneged on my agreement that emphasized I'd only negotiate, and not commit, until I got a bid on the cost to bring the Lexus GS400 into certified warranty condition.

She tried her best to part with Jorgi's car, but to no avail. Her crest fallen tears were relentless. Knowing the Lexus qualified for the 2009 stimulus government "clunker car" program, which guaranteed the dealer $4,500 for the Lexus that equaled the amount that was allowed towards the trade, exponentially exacerbated her despondent mood. The thought of the car being crushed into a flat metal piece of junk, which was mandated under the clunker program, was the tipping point in her emotional frame of mind. The ill attempt to suppress her tears was to no avail. Her tears were relentless. The secretary who was recording the paperwork for us to sign was empathetic to Gaye, and she asked, "Why are you so sad?" When I explained to her the reason for her sadness, she too, had tears in her eyes, crying while completing the paperwork.

I mentioned earlier that I had to correct a wrong. This I did. The very next morning, without Gaye's knowledge, I called the general manager, Dennis, who was sympathetic to my plight, and arranged it so that I could buy the Lexus back for the $4,500 he allowed for it, without having to add the cost of license and sales tax. He said, "If you can get me a check immediately, today - before it is registered in the clunker program this afternoon, I can make it happen." Wishing to surprise Gaye, rather than using our joint checking account, I called my daughter Dorre in San Francisco, and asked her to make a check out to the Yuba City Toyota dealership, and to call the manager Dennis Taylor apprising him that the check was in the mail. This she did, and the rest is history. I reimbursed Dorre for her involvement, and Jorgi's 400 GS Lexus was once again part of the Nicholau family.

But not so fast. To surprise Gaye I still had to get the car into our garage without her knowing anything about my ongoing buffoonism. I was determined to surprise her, and mentally record for prosperity the breathless wonder response that I would witness!

My daughters no longer believed in the true existence of Santa Claus, but I still did! And I still had one more "bike on the roof surprise" left in me, only this time for my angel Gaye. Plus, the roof would have to forego this particular 'gift', as the garage would have to suffice.

Unfortunately my well intended stealth plan went astray. It just so happened as I was putting the Lexus into the garage, Gaye came out of the house with scraps she intended to put in our disposal bin.

"What's going on George!? What's happening?!! Why is the Lexus in our garage?" was the extemporaneous confused surprised outburst. My knee jerk reaction was "What are you doing out here? Get back in the house!!"

"Why, what are you doing?" was her response.

"Just please go back into the house." Oh hell, I give up. My intentions were admirable. My stealth result was disastrous. Nevertheless, that being so, I must admit, I've been sleeping well since a wrong has been righted.

Finally, I post script this allegory to my memoirs that you, too, will have the courage to right a wrong, if for no other reason than to experience the high that comes with making amends. I am still on cloud nine, and the best of it is Gaye is there with me. The reincarnation of Jorgi's gifted 400GS Lexus is the cause, not for it's worth, but for it's intrinsic emotional value. So there you have it. I might not be perfect, but I do take responsibility for my imperfection. I strongly advocate you do likewise if you experience imperfection in your tribulations. I'll let you in on my best-kept secret. I am constantly searching for a "harmless wrong" that I can correct just so I can, for a moment, revisit that elusive high I have alluded to in this parable.

A reminder – Corinthians Chapter 13:13 says it all.

A parting thought~ In my geriatric years the younger I think the wiser I become.

Out of this life I shall never take things of silver and gold
that I own,
All that I cherish and hoard away
After I leave, on this earth, must stay.

Thought I have toiled for a painting rare
To hang on the wall,
I must leave it there.

Though I call it mine and boast it's worth,
I must give it up when I leave this earth.

All that I gather and all that I keep
I must give up when I fall asleep.

And I often wonder what I shall own
In that other life when I pass alone.

What shall they find, and what shall they see
In that soul that answers the call for me.

Will the Great Judge learn when my task is through
That my spirit had gained some riches too?

Or, at last, shall it be mine to find
That all I worked for, I left behind.

Author, unknown

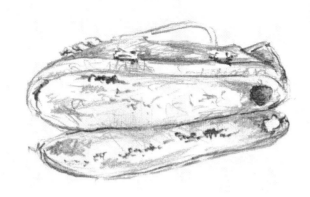

Throughout my memoirs, readers surely noticed an underscored theme of my Christian Faith. It is my open-hearted belief that my positive life's accomplishments, of which there are some, are of His influence, while my noticeable negative demeanors, of which there are many, are the product of my delinquency, for which I daily seek His forgiveness.

THE END

…..Of the beginning….
Stay tuned